War In Peace

Volume 11

War In Peace

The Marshall Cavendish Illustrated Encyclopedia of Postwar Conflict

Editors-in-Chief
Ashley Brown
Dr. John Pimlott

Editorial Board
Brig-Gen. James Collins Jr (USA Retd.)
Vice-Admiral Sir Louis Le Bailly KBE CB
Ian V Hogg; David Floyd
Professor Laurence Martin
Air-Vice Marshal SWB Menaul CB CBE DFC AFC

MARSHALL CAVENDISH
NEW YORK, LONDON, TORONTO

Reference Edition Published 1985

Published by Marshall Cavendish Corporation
147 West Merrick Road
Freeport, Long Island
N.Y. 11520

Printed and Bound in Italy by L.E.G.O. S.p.a. Vicenza.

British Library Cataloguing in Publication Data

Brown, Ashley
    War in peace : the Marshall Cavendish
    illustrated encyclopaedia of post-war conflict.
    1. History, Modern—1945-   2. War—History
    —20th century
    I. Title   II. Dartford, Mark
    909.82   D842

    ISBN 0-86307-293-3
        0 86307 304 2   vol. 11

Library of Congress Cataloging in Publication Data

Main entry under title:

War in peace.

    Includes bibliographies and index.
    1. Military history, Modern—20th century.   2. Military
art and science—History—20th century.   3. World politics—1945-
I. Marshall Cavendish Corporation.
U42.W373 1984   355'.009'04   84-19386
ISBN 0-86307-293-3
        0 86307 304 2   vol. 11

Editorial Staff

Editor	Ashley Brown
Editorial Director	Brian Innes
Editorial Manager	Clare Byatt
Editorial Editors	Sam Elder
	Adrian Gilbert
Sub Editors	Sue Leonard
	Simon Innes
Artwork Editor	Jonathan Reed
Artwork Buyer	Jean Morley
Picture Editor	Carina Dvorak
Picture Consultant	Robert Hunt
Design	EDC

Reference Edition Staff

Editor	Mark Dartford
Designer	Graham Beehag
Consultant	Robert Paulley
Indexers	F & K Gill
Creation	DPM Services

Editorial Board

Contributors

David Blue served with the CIA in various countries of Southeast Asia, including Laos, and is a writer on and a student of small wars.

Gordon Brook-Shepherd spent 15 years in Vienna, first as lieutenant-colonel on the staff of the British High Commission and then as a foreign correspondent for the *Daily Telegraph*. A graduate in history from Cambridge, he is currently Chief Assistant Editor of the *Sunday Telegraph*.

Jeffrey J. Clarke is an expert on recent military history, particularly the Vietnam War, and has written for the American Center of Military History.

Major-General Richard Clutterbuck OBE has been Senior Lecturer in politics at Exeter University since his retirement from the army in 1972. His works include *Protest and the Urban Guerrilla, Guerrillas and Terrorists* and *Kidnap and Ransom*.

Alexander S. Cochran Jr is a historian whose area of research is modern Indochinese affairs with particular reference to the war in Vietnam since 1945. He is at present working in the Southeast Asia Branch of the Center of Military History, Department of the Army.

Colonel Peter M. Dunn is a serving officer in the USAF. His doctoral thesis is on the history of Indochina during the mid-1940s.

John B. Dwyer served both with the infantry and with armoured units in Vietnam. He was editor and publisher of the Vietnam veteran's newsletter *Perimeter* and has been a writer and correspondent for *National Vietnam Veteran's Review* for the past few years. His particular interest are Special Forces and Special Operations.

Brenda Ralph Lewis has specialised in political and military history since 1964. She s a regular contributor to military and historical magazines in both Britain and the United States.

Hugh Lunghi served in Moscow in the British Military Mission and the British Embassy for six years during and after World War II. He was interpreter for the British Chiefs of Staff at the Teheran, Yalta and Potsdam conferences, and also interpreted for Churchill and Anthony Eden. He subsequently worked in the BBC External Services and is a former editor of *Index on Censorship*.

Charles Messenger retired from the army in 1980 to become a fulltime military writer after 21 years service in the Royal Tank Regiment. Over the past 10 years he has written several books on 20th century warfare, as well as contributing articles to a number of defence and historical journals. He is currently a Research Associate at the Royal United Services Institute for Defence Studies in London.

Billy C. Mossman is a well-known American writer and historian. He is currently working on a volume on the Korean War for the US Army Center of Military History.

Bryan Perrett served in the Royal Armoured Corps from 1952 to 1971. He contributes regularly to a number of established military journals and acted as Defence Correspondent to the *Liverpool Echo* during the Falklands War. His recent books include *Weapons of the Falklands Conflict* and *A History of Blitzkrieg*.

Chapman Pincher is one of England's leading authorities on international espionage and counter-intelligence. He is the author of political novels and books on spying, the most recent of which is *Their Trade is Treachery*, which deals with the penetration of Britain's secret services by the Russian secret police.

Yehoshua Porath is a noted scholar at the Hebrew University in Jerusalem. He has made a special study of the Palestinian problem and is the author of two books on the subject, the most recent of which is *The Palestinian Arab National Movement 1929–39*, which was published in Britain in 1977.

Contributors

Antony Preston is Naval Editor of the military magazine *Defence* and author of numerous publications including *Battleships, Aircraft Carriers* and *Submarines.*

Brigadier-General Edwin H. Simmons, US Marine Corps, Retired, is the Director of Marine Corps History and Museums. At the time of the Inchon operation and the Chosin Reservoir campaign, he, as a major, commanded Weapons Company, 3rd Battalion, 1st Marines. Widely published, he is the author of *The United States Marines.*

Ronald Spector is an expert on Vietnam and has recently completed a book on that subject for the Center of Military History in the United States.

Andres Suarez served in the Cuban ministry of education from 1948—1951, took part in the Cuban revolution, and served in the ministry of housing from 1959 From 1965, he has been Professor of Latin American Studies at the University of Florida. Other publications include *Cuba and the Sino—Soviet Rift.*

Sir Robert Thompson KBE, CMG, DSO, MC is a world authority on guerrilla warfare, on which he has written extensively. He was directly involved in the Emergency in Malaya in the 1950s and rose to become permanent Secretary for Defence. From 1961 to 1965 he headed the British Advisory Mission to Vietnam and since then he has advised several governments, including the United States, on counter-insurgency operations Sir Robert Thompson is a Council member of the Institute for the Study of Conflict, London. His books include *Defeating Communist Insurgency and Revolutionary War in World Strategy, 1945—69.*

Patrick Turnbull commanded 'D' Force, Burma during World War II. His 29 published works include a history of the Foreign Legion.

Contents of Volume

Bad neighbours

The origins of the Iran-Iraq conflict

The origins of the Gulf War between Iran and Iraq which broke out in 1980 lay deep in the history of the region, and though the trigger for the conflict was a territorial dispute, religious and ethnic rivalries played an important role. The Iraq-Iran border marked the boundary between the Arab and Persian cultures, dominated respectively by the two major sects of Islam – the Sunni and the Shi'ia.

The historic split in the Islamic world resulted from a dispute during the 7th century over the control of the empire which had been created by the wave of Arab conquest after the death of Mohammed. The Shi'ites wished to see the political power of the Caliph in the hands of Islamic leaders who were direct descendents of the Prophet. During the civil war which resulted, the Shi'ites were defeated, and the Sunnis became the majority sect in Islam, controlling the Arab empire and its Turkish successor. Only in Persia (as Iran was then known) did Shi'ism become dominant, reinforcing the traditional conflict between Arabs and Persians.

Although Iran was the only country where Shi'ia Muslims were the politically dominant group, Shi'ites formed the numerical majority of the population in nearby Bahrain, in the eastern oil-producing area of Saudi Arabia, and in Iraq. These three states were all ruled by Sunnis, however. As long as the Iranian government was essentially secular and opposed to Shi'ite fundamentalism, as under Shah Reza Pahlavi, this religious division in the area had little significance for international relations, but if a militant Shi'ite regime came to power in Tehran, as happened in 1979, it was bound to turn these Shi'ite majorities into potential agents of Iranian influence.

Territorial disputes between the Turkish empire and Persia, inherited by Iraq and Iran, centred on control of the Shatt al Arab waterway at the head of the Persian Gulf. An international commission in 1913 fixed the frontier from Mount Ararat in the north to the Gulf in the south, giving control of the Shatt al Arab to Turkey and establishing the eastern, Iranian bank as the boundary. After the foundation of Iraq at the end

of World War I, however, Iran refused to recognise the 1913 agreement and claimed the centre of the river channel as its new border. Bilateral negotiations failed to achieve a solution, and in 1934 Iraq appealed to the League of Nations, which in 1937 proposed a compromise settlement which was accepted by both sides. The new agreement recognised the 1913 treaty, except that the border from Abadan to the Gulf was fixed as the centre of the Shatt al Arab channel.

The overthrow of the conservative pro-Western Hashemite monarchy in Iraq in 1958 brought to power a militantly Arab-nationalist regime. This coincided with the rapid expansion of Iranian power under the Shah and Iranian efforts to become the dominant regional power after the decline of British influence in the Gulf. Iran reopened the border dispute in 1959 by contesting the 1937 agreement and establishing a naval base in the Shatt al Arab. The Iranian move posed a direct and serious threat to Iraq, which depended upon access to the Gulf for its vital oil exports.

The dispute escalated in April 1969, when Iraq demanded that Iran observe the 1937 treaty. Baghdad insisted that it had the right to collect tolls from Iranian

Previous page: Iraqi commandos (above), fresh from the front, and (below) Iranian paratroopers. Iran's armed forces were greatly weakened by the Islamic revolution, and their superiority in equipment was reduced by a severe shortage of spares and skilled maintenance personnel.

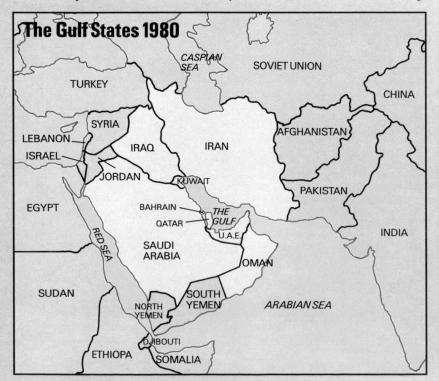

The Gulf States 1980

TURKEY
CASPIAN SEA
SOVIET UNION
CHINA
SYRIA
LEBANON
ISRAEL
IRAQ
IRAN
AFGHANISTAN
JORDAN
KUWAIT
PAKISTAN
EGYPT
BAHRAIN
QATAR
THE GULF
U.A.E.
INDIA
SAUDI ARABIA
OMAN
RED SEA
SUDAN
SOUTH YEMEN
NORTH YEMEN
ARABIAN SEA
DJIBOUTI
ETHIOPA
SOMALIA

with a rapid increase in American military support for Iran, and the declaration by Washington in 1972 of a 'twin-pillar' policy in the Gulf, by which the US would exercise local influence through building up its main regional allies, Iran and Saudi Arabia. Finding herself isolated among the conservative pro-American regimes which predominated in the region, Iraq felt the need to consolidate its own internal stability, which was threatened by a number of divergent pressures. As well as the Iraqi Communist Party, which though periodically a coalition partner of the ruling Ba'ath Party was seen as a serious security threat and rival for power, Iraq contained a number of ethnic and religious-based opposition groups.

The most important of these during the early 1970s was the Kurds. Concentrated largely in the north of Iraq, the Kurds constituted some 20 per cent of the country's total population. Their demands for an increased share in the nation's economic resources and greater regional autonomy brought them into conflict with the unitary Arab nationalism of the Ba'ath Party. The Ba'athist government attempted to integrate the Kurds more closely into the nation on several occasions and in 1970 agreed to the establishment of a Kurdish Autonomous Region in the north, following this in 1971 by a National Action Charter which granted limited rights to opposition groups, including the Kurds.

Many Kurds wanted more than autonomy, however, and favoured a totally independent Kurdish state, which would unite the Kurds found in most countries of the region, including Iran. In 1972 fighting broke out between Kurdish guerrillas and government forces. The Kurds, who at one stage fielded an estimated 50,000 to 60,000 guerrillas,

Above left: Pride before the fall: the Shah's generals at the height of their power. Above: Iranian mullahs, armed with East German MPiKM assault rifles, represented the new Iran. Centre left: Iraq's President Saddam Hussein, who mistakenly believed he could take advantage of the chaos of the Iranian revolution. Below left: The face of Ayatollah Khomeini dominates a rally addressed by Prime Minister Bani Sadr. Tension between these two men would affect the course of the war.

ships in the Shatt al Arab, that the Iranian flag should be lowered by ships using it, and that no Iranian naval personnel could be stationed there without Iraqi permission. Tehran's response was to abrogate the treaty and to despatch gunboats into the waterway.

Control of a central sector of the Iran-Iraq land border was also a contested issue – both sides claimed control of a strip some 210km (130 miles) long running from Khanaqin and Qasr-e-Shirin in the north to Badra and Mehran in the south – but it was control of the Shatt al Arab which was central to the Shah's whole strategy for establishing Iran as the dominant regional power. Only Iraq, which in July 1970 sought arms from Moscow and in April 1972 signed a 15-year Treaty of Friendship with the Soviet Union, posed a significant challenge to Iranian ambitions.

The move by Iraq towards the USSR coincided

The rival forces

The armed forces with which Iran's Islamic Republic entered the Gulf War were predominantly a product of the previous Iranian regime. The Shah had used the country's oil revenues to finance a rapid expansion and modernisation of Iranian military strength, although an acute shortage of skilled maintenance personnel had left the Imperial Iranian forces heavily dependent upon their main source of training and supplies, the United States.

Under an agreement concluded between the Shah and President Richard Nixon in May 1972, the United States had promised to supply Iran with whatever conventional weapons she requested, including advanced F-14 and F-15 aircraft. By the end of 1976 Iran had acquired some $11·8 billion-worth of aircraft, becoming the fourth largest air-power in the world. By the time of the Shah's fall in January 1979, the Iranian Air Force possessed 445 combat aircraft, including 188 F-4D/Es, 166 F-5E/Fs and 77 F-14As. Iran also had seven squadrons of transport and tanker aircraft.

The Iranian Navy was by far the largest of any Gulf state. Vessels included six destroyers, three of which were armed with surface-to-surface missiles (SSMs); four frigates, also armed with SSMs and with Seacat SAMs; and a number of smaller vessels, including four corvettes, five minesweepers and 14 hovercraft.

The Iranian Army was equally lavishly equipped. The armoured backbone of the Shah's army contained 875 Chieftain tanks, 400 M47/48s, 460 M60A medium tanks and 250 Scorpion light tanks. Helicopter units were equipped with 205 AH-1Js, 295 Bell-214As, 50 AB-205As, 20 AB-206s and 90 CH-47C helicopters. With a strength of some 150,000 men, the Iranian Army represented a formidable military force. A 1976 US Congressional report came to the conclusion, however, that Iran would remain unable to conduct

a major campaign without a large-scale American resupply operation for at least the next five to 10 years.

The dependence upon US support was highlighted by the events which followed the January 1979 revolution. The total break in relations between Tehran and Washington which resulted from the Iranian seizure of the US embassy hostages in November 1979 led to a rapid decline in the condition of many of Iran's high-technology American weapons, such as the F-14 fighter. Many senior Iranian officers had been purged, and the combat-readiness of the Iranian armed forces was severely weakened. The new regime distrusted the armed forces, which had been closely identified with the Shah, and hence much of the responsibility for the fighting in the Gulf War was to fall to the newly-created Revolutionary Guards, composed of fanatically loyal supporters of the Ayatollah Khomeini, and other militia units.

Since the early 1970s, the main source of Iraqi arms supplies had been the Soviet Union, but during the late 1970s the Baghdad government made efforts to diversify its sources of military equipment, and placed large orders with, among others, French arms manufacturers. The Iraqi Army, which numbered 200,000 men, was equipped with large numbers of Soviet and French armoured vehicles, including 2500 T54/55 and T62 tanks, and 100 AMX30 medium tanks.

The Iraqi Navy was a small force, mainly composed of Soviet-built patrol vessels, but the air force was equipped with a large number of Soviet and French aircraft, and had 150 MiG fighters and 60 Mirage F1C/1Bs on order. As well as 12 Tu-22 and 10 Il-28 bombers, Iraq possessed 115 MiG-21s, 80 MiG-23Bs, 60 Su-20s and 40 Su-7Bs. The 11 Iraqi Air Force helicopter squadrons were equipped with 41 Mi-24 Hinds, 47 Alouette IIIs, 35 Mi-4s and 78 Mi-8s. Iraq also boasted a large number of SSMs and SAMs.

occupied a strong position in the mountains of northern Iraq, and received large amounts of financial and military support from Iran. The Shah supported the Kurds with the sole aim of forcing Iraq to accept a negotiated settlement to the border dispute on Iranian terms. Between 1972 and 1975 Iranian support allowed the Kurds to resist a number of large-scale government offensives, and when the Kurds began to be pressed by heavy Iraqi air attacks, an estimated 1200 Iranian troops were sent into Iraq to man the Kurds' air defences.

By 1975, the war seemed to be turning slowly in favour of the Iraqi Army, whose tactics and performance had gradually improved. Iraq and Iran therefore began secret negotiations, which resulted in the Algiers Declaration of 6 March 1975, and in the signing of an Iran-Iraq Treaty of International Boundaries and Good Neighbourliness on 13 June. The treaty settled the border dispute, with a recognition of the *thalweg*, or mid-channel, as the dividing line in the Shatt al Arab, and contained an agreement not to interfere in each other's internal affairs. In accordance with this latter provision, the Shah cut off aid to the Kurds and within two weeks Iraqi forces had entered the heartland of the Kurdish resistance almost unopposed.

The 1975 rapprochement between Iran and Iraq depended upon the strict observance of the principle of non-interference in one another's affairs, and the stability of the border agreement required the maintenance of mutual confidence between the two governments. Iraq therefore began to clamp down on the activities of Iranian exiles who opposed the Shah's regime, and a number were forced to flee the country or find refuge in friendly embassies in Baghdad.

Mullahs in exile

Many of the Shah's opponents among the Iranian Shi'ite clergy had established themselves in Iraq, around the country's holy shrines and most important mosques. The Ayatollah Khomeini, for example, who was the most prominent of the Iranian mullahs to be exiled by the Shah, had lived since 1964 in the city of al-Najaf, near the mosque of Imam Ali. During the pre-1975 confrontation with Iran, Khomeini had been requested by the Iraqi government to broadcast propaganda attacks against the Shah, his arch-enemy. The Ayatollah had consistently refused, however, supporting neither the border claims of the Baghdad government, nor its radical Arab nationalism, which he saw as disrupting the unity of the Islamic world.

The growing opposition to the Shah within Iran during 1977-78 was reflected among the Shi'ite opponents of the Iranian regime exiled in Iraq. The Ayatollah Khomeini, in particular, exercised an enormous influence over events in Iran by means of illegally distributed cassette recordings of his speeches and sermons, which called for the overthrow of the Shah. In response to this threat to the increasingly close relations between Iran and Iraq which had developed since the 1975 agreement, the Iraqi authorities imposed house arrest upon Khomeini in September 1978, and later expelled him from Iraq when his attacks on the Shah continued. Waiting in his French exile for the fall of the Shah, which he grimly prophesied as imminent, Khomeini listed his enemies as: 'First, the Shah, then the American Satan, then Saddam Hussein and his infidel Ba'ath Party'. As the iron grip of the Shah turned into a desperate clutching

at power, it became increasingly clear that the 1975 border agreement would not be accepted by the regime that would succeed him, and that the strict Iraqi observance of the treaty's non-interference clause would be interpreted as outright hostility to the Iranian revolution and open support for the Shah by the fundamentalists whose protests were undermining the stability of Iran.

It was therefore unsurprising that the overthrow of the Shah in January 1979 soon led to the wrath of the Ayatollah Khomeini being directed against 'Saddam Hussein and his infidel Ba'ath Party' in Iraq. Though on 5 April the Iraqi government congratulated Khomeini on the establishment of an Islamic Republic, relations between the two countries rapidly deteriorated. During June and July there were a series of anti-Iraqi demonstrations in Tehran and along the Iran-Iraq border, and Tehran Radio began to broadcast attacks against President Saddam Hussein, accusing him of having cooperated with the Shah against the Islamic revolution, and calling upon Iraqi Shi'ites to rise up and overthrow his Ba'athist regime. Iraq reacted by expelling a number of dissident Shi'ite mullahs, who found refuge in the holy city of Qom in Iran.

The threatened Iranian export of its Islamic revolution to its Gulf neighbours was linked to a number of territorial disputes, including the old conflict with Iraq over the Shatt al Arab. While Iran began to talk of the annexation of Bahrain, and called that state's predominantly Shi'ite population to rise in revolt, Iraq countered with a call for Iranian recognition for what it termed 'Arab rights' in the Shatt al Arab and for Iranian withdrawal from three islands in the Straits of Hormuz which had been occupied by the Shah in 1971.

Pro-Iranian Shi'ite opposition groups such as the al-Dawa Party became increasingly active in Iraq during 1980, carrying out a number of sabotage attacks and assassination attempts. Saddam Hussein

Top: An Iranian BH-7 hovercraft, one of a fleet bought by the Shah for rapid intervention across the Gulf. In the war of attrition with Iraq, hovercraft had little role to play. Above: Ecstatic Iraqi airmen greet a Soviet-made Tu-22 bomber on its return from a raid against an Iranian airfield during the opening days of the war.

Top right: An Iranian F-4E Phantom. Though the more advanced aircraft of the Iranian Air Force, such as the F-14, soon ceased to be operational without US technical support, the older Phantoms were kept in the air by cannibalising equipment from other aircraft. Above right: The main burden of the Iranian military effort fell on poorly trained and equipped Baseej volunteer militiamen such as these. Used in brave but ill-conceived human-wave assaults, their casualties were enormous.

reacted with typical ruthlessness, and in April 1980 Mohammed Baquir al-Sadr, Iraq's most prominent Shi'ite leader, was executed for treason. In Iran, the Ayatollah Khomeini proclaimed a three-day period of mourning, elevating al-Sadr to the status of an Islamic martyr. In an echo of his successful tactics against the Shah, Khomeini called on Iraqi soldiers to desert.

The increasing interference of Iran in Iraqi internal affairs rapidly brought the key 1975 treaty into question, and on 10 September 1980 Iraq claimed that, contrary to that treaty, Iranian troops had failed to withdraw from territory around Zain al-Qais and Saif Sa'd. Iraq warned that if they did not withdraw they would be expelled by force. On 14 September, General Fallahi, the chief of staff of the Iranian Army, claimed that the 1975 treaty had been forced upon Iran by 'foreign powers', and that it would no longer be observed. The Iraqi response was formally to abrogate the treaty on 17 September. Border clashes and artillery duels had already begun several months

previously, and on 22 September Iraqi units entered Iranian territory.

As in most modern wars, it was not immediately obvious who had been the aggressor. Although Iraq had taken the first step of launching an outright invasion, it was clear that Iran had posed an increasingly serious threat to Iraqi security. It was less clear whether Saddam Hussein merely aimed at trading conquered Iranian territory for an Iranian recognition of the 1975 Shatt al Arab boundary, or whether his aim was to trigger the overthrow of the Khomeini regime, which itself proclaimed coexistence to be impossible. It soon did become clear, however, that the Iraqi invasion, which had been based on the calculation that the fundamentalist government was weak and isolated, and that the Iranian armed forces were disaffected and ready to revolt, had only strengthened the grip of Khomeini, and that the long war ahead would be one of attrition, in which Iran would hold many advantages.

Robin Corbett

The gamble that failed

The opening phases of the Gulf War, 1980-82

After months of border conflicts, on 22 September 1980 Iraqi forces crossed the border into Iran and simultaneously launched artillery and air attacks on Iranian towns and military installations. The unreliability of the military communiques and the absence of independent reporting make it difficult to give an accurate and detailed account of the fighting but it seems that Iraq committed eight or nine divisions in three areas. The southern front was the longest, stretching down from an area around Musian almost to the Karkheh River, southward to the east of Susangerd and Ahvaz, and along the Ahvaz-Khorramshahr highway to Khorramshahr. An armoured division was apparently used against Khorramshahr and two more to the north against Ahvaz and Susangerd. In the central sector, a further division, possibly mountain infantry, was used against Mehran. In the north, Iraq drove across the border in divisional strength, taking an area including Qasr-e-Shirin, Pol-e-Zeharb and Naft-e-Shah by the 25th.

The land war was complemented by air attacks. On 23 September Iraq launched air strikes deep into Iran, bombing Mehrebad airport outside Tehran and, according to some reports, damaging Iran's early-warning system; Ahvaz, Dezful, Bushehr and Ker-

manshah were also hit. Iran bombed airfields at Basra and declared Iran's coastal waters 'war zones', prohibiting ships carrying Iraqi cargo. In the ensuing two days both states bombed oil installations in attempts to cripple the other's war capacity. Iraqi attacks closed the Iranian refinery at Abadan but attempts to bomb the terminals at Kharg Island, Iran's major oil export centre, met with little success. Iraq's Fao terminal was hit, however, and Iraq was unable to export any further oil through the Gulf. According to military communiques, 100 planes were destroyed in the first three days of the war.

Iraq had the advantage of surprise but only proceeded slowly across the flat desert of Khuzistan, capturing large swathes of territory but remaining outside the population centres. Iraqi forces pressed close to Susangerd, Dezful and Ahvaz, capital of Khuzistan, making no attempt to capture or encircle them but putting them under artillery bombardment. With a population of 14 million, Iraq was loathe to take high casualties in combat with Iran which had a population of 40 million.

As the northern fronts stabilised Iraq shifted some forces to the south. Iraq had crossed the Shatt al Arab in divisional strength near Khorramshahr on 22

Above left: While a Soviet-made BMP-1 APC is refuelled from a tanker, an Iraqi T55 presses forward. Iraq failed to exploit its initial advantage of surprise, and the invasion soon slowed to a halt.

The Iraqi Offensive September 1980

main axes of Iraqi advance

Iraqi airstrikes and artillery bombardments

main axes of Iranian counter-offensives

Main picture: A column of Iraqi Czech-manufactured OT-64 APCs speeds through the desert during the invasion of Iran. By October 1980, the initial mobile stage of the war was already over, and the battle for Abadan marked the beginning of a war of attrition, with each yard of ground bitterly contested. Above: Iraqi troops celebrate their early successes. Unwilling to accept high casualties, Iraq was soon forced onto the defensive.

September but the city proved a tough nut to crack. Although Iraqi military communiques claimed the capture of Khorramshahr early in the war, by the end of September there were still reports of street battles and sniper fire in the southern suburbs of this refining centre. The Iranian resistance in the city came from the Pasdaran (Revolutionary Guards) and the Baseej (Mobilisation Organisation of Militia), the headquarters of which were in the central mosque. These pockets of resistance, plus Iranian control of a key bridge over the Karun River, delayed the Iraqi advance on Abadan, Iran's major refining city about 13km (8 miles) to the south, built on an island bounded by the Shatt al Arab, the Karun and the Bahmashir Rivers. On 11 October, however, the Iraqi forces put down a pontoon bridge across the Karun and moved down to the Bahmashir. On 13 October, Khorramshahr finally fell and although Abadan was encircled by land, the Iranian defenders were reinforced by sea and air. Iranian forces dug in at the northern tip of Abadan Island.

By the middle of October 1980, the Iraq-Iran frontline had become fixed and the war settled into

one of attrition, with Iraq regularly attacking Dezful – a provincial town, military centre and airbase – with Frog-7 surface-to-surface missiles and launching heavy artillery bombardments of Ahvaz and Abadan. Iraqi strategy was to avoid fighting close battles and rely on artillery bombardments to soften up Iranian positions in the hope that resistance would crumble. Since Ahvaz, Susangerd and Dezful were easily resupplied this was unlikely. It was not to happen in Abadan either. The sole further Iraqi advance came in December when an Iraqi mountain division crossed the border in the far north near Penjwin.

The Iranian side launched airstrikes against oil and military installations, but not against civilian targets. Regular shelling of Fao prevented any repair to oil terminals, and refinery complexes at Baiji and Kirkuk were hit. Iraq's oil exports were reduced to a fifth of pre-war levels. Iran did attempt a series of small counter-offensives in the Qasr-e-Shirin area but these came to a halt each time they confronted concentrated formations of Iraqi troops. On the ground this stalemate was to last 18 months until March 1982.

For Iraq, the 10,000 square km (4000 square miles)

of Iranian territory captured were a bargaining counter for an Iranian recognition of Iraqi territorial rights over all the Shatt al Arab estuary. The Ba'athist government in Iraq also calculated that military defeat would be the straw to break the back of the Iranian Islamic Republic. However, the invasion backfired in that it only helped to consolidate the more fundamentalist wing of the Iranian regime, which formulated terms for ending the fighting unacceptable in Baghdad: the overthrow of Saddam Hussein, the Iraqi president; complete Iraqi withdrawal from Iranian territory; full war compensation (in 1983 this was put at $150 billion); and the return to Iraq of 100,000 Shi'ites expelled from the country by Hussein.

Digging in

Since a political solution was not possible, and since Iraq was unwilling to take the cities of Susangerd, Dezful and Ahvaz and unable to take Abadan, there was little for the Iraqi forces to do but sit in comfortable dug-outs, provided with television and videos, launching occasional artillery barrages on the Iranian towns. While the Iraqi forces could do no more, lacking any particular strategic objective that was attainable without heavy casualties, the Iranian Army was also unable to mount a sustained counter-offensive in any sector. Political divisions at home, purges of the army and air force after the fall of the Shah, problems of coordination between the regular army, the Revolutionary Guards and the Baseej, and international isolation making the purchase of spare parts almost impossible, were factors producing the impasse on the Iranian side. Of Iran's 800 Chieftain tanks possibly only half were operational. Under the Islamic Republic, it has been estimated that around 250 generals had been purged and although some military analysts have argued that they were no great loss, such a shake-up would require time to reorganise the army.

Yet, at the beginning of 1981, Bani Sadr, the Iranian president, announced a counter-offensive. The timing of the offensive was determined by the political in-fighting in Tehran between the Islamic Republican Party, the political organisation of the fundamentalist clergy, and President Bani Sadr. The January 1981 offensive was an attempt to enhance the latter's waning prestige. Attacks were made on the front near Gilan Garb and from Susangerd, where the major fighting took place. The Iranian forces were repulsed with heavy losses of men and equipment,

Above: An Iraqi prepares to fire his RPG-7 during the battle for Khorramshahr. The town was stubbornly defended by Revolutionary Guards and militiamen. Right: Iranian women pick their way through the rubble of their homes.

particularly of M60 and Chieftain tanks. It was reliably reported that Iraq captured about 100 Chieftains, many of them undamaged. The failure of the offensive only served to discredit Bani Sadr and throughout 1981 a prolonged and bloody power-struggle in Tehran paralysed government decision-making. By the end of the year, the fundamentalists had won and the stage was set for a massive Iranian mobilisation on the basis of an Islamic crusade against a 'godless Iraq'. It also gave General Qassem Ali Zahirnezhad, Iranian Army chief of staff, the pause in the fighting that he had demanded so that the new young conscripts could be trained and spare parts secured.

By late 1981, there were indications that the initiative was passing to Iran. In September, a mixed force of Revolutionary Guards, Baseej and regular army pushed the Iraqi forces over the Karun River. Then, on 22 March 1982, Iran's major offensive, codenamed Fatah (victory), began.

The offensive involved a six-pronged attack. It began in the central sector, west of Dezful, where the First Infantry Brigade, under the command of Colonel Hussein Saadi, broke through the first line of defence west of the Karkheh River and within five hours took an 80km (50-mile) system of linked trenches and dug-outs. According to Colonel Saadi, Islamic 'martyrs' were used to clear the minefields in a pattern of mass-wave attacks and bloody carnage which were to be the hallmarks of the Iranian advances through 1982 and 1983. Unconfirmed reports stated that 80 per cent of the casualties were Revolutionary Guards. After a week, according to Colonel Saadi, Iran had retaken 3000 square metres (3600 square yards) in this sector, killed 6000 Iraqis and captured 15,000.

The greater willingness to take casualties by the Iranians was not the only factor in changing the balance. The stabilisation of power in Iran had also brought about greater coordination of the Iranian forces. Colonel Sayyid Shirazi, the overall field commander, 34 years old and only a captain at the time of

Right: Iraqi troops dug-in on the outskirts of Khorramshahr watch for an Iranian counter-attack. The town finally fell to Iraq on 13 October. Bottom: Iraqi troops, prepared to face surprise attack in the recently conquered town, leap from their truck, guns at the ready.

the Islamic Revolution, had welded together a combined force of three-and-a-half army divisions, 40,000 Revolutionary Guards and 30,000 Baseej.

On 30 April, the Iranian government announced its 'Jerusalem offensive' with a two-pronged attack on Iraqi positions in Khuzistan. Regular army units and Revolutionary Guards crossed the Karun River on pontoon bridges, again relying heavily on manpower – according to Iraqi communiques 24,000 Iranians were killed in the first four days. They established a narrow bridgehead, securing control of a substantial middle section of the Khorramshahr-Ahvaz road. Iranian forces also pushed southwards from Susangerd dropping airborne commandos behind Iraqi lines southwest of Ahvaz.

After exaggerated claims of success on both sides, it became clear that the Iraqi forces had initially been taken by surprise but were able to hold the Iranian advance and follow a pre-arranged plan of withdrawal in the second stage of the Iranian offensive. On 10

Opposite top: Iranian General Zahir Najad explains the March 1982 offensive which pushed back the Iraqis in several sectors. Opposite bottom: Iraqi dead being buried in a mass grave. Both sides suffered heavy casualties, but Iran was more prepared to pay the price of victory. Below: Iranian Revolutionary Guards advance under fire during street-fighting in a village near the strategic Shatt al Arab waterway. Below right: A group of Revolutionary Guards, fanatical supporters of the Ayatollah Khomeini.

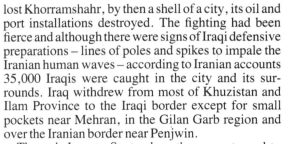

May, independent observers reported an orderly withdrawal of fresh Iraqi troops and undamaged equipment. It would seem that the 6th and 12th Brigades of the Iraqi 3rd Division took the brunt of the fighting in the Khorramshahr area and the Iranians captured its commander, Brigadier Yunis Rashid. The Iraqis withdrew one of the two divisions around Khorramshahr and all its forces from the desert south-west of Ahvaz to the Iraqi border. The Iraqi government claimed a strategic withdrawal with the aim of 'inflicting heavy losses on men and equipment, thereby exhausting Iran and forcing it to recognise Iraq's territorial and maritime rights'. The earlier Iraqi rationale of holding territory to secure its rights had been forcibly changed.

The Iranian Army retook Hoveyzeh and Hamid, the latter 24km (15 miles) south of Ahvaz and Iraq's most forward position. By the end of May Iraq had lost Khorramshahr, by then a shell of a city, its oil and port installations destroyed. The fighting had been fierce and although there were signs of Iraqi defensive preparations – lines of poles and spikes to impale the Iranian human waves – according to Iranian accounts 35,000 Iraqis were caught in the city and its surrounds. Iraq withdrew from most of Khuzistan and Ilam Province to the Iraqi border except for small pockets near Mehran, in the Gilan Garb region and over the Iranian border near Penjwin.

Through June to September, the war returned to one of long-range artillery duels and sporadic pushes. The Iraq Air Force bombed Kharg Island in June without preventing the shipment of oil and, with more bravado than effect, went through the sound barrier over Tehran. The Iraqi Army during this period was able to establish strong ground defences to protect Basra where there was limited depth. Successive lines of minefields, barbed wire, trenches, tank positions and reserves and supplies in the Basra palm groves forestalled a big Iranian push in July when Iranian forces attempted to dislodge troops to the north of Basra and drive to the Baghdad-Basra highway. According to an unnamed Iraqi colonel, six Iranian divisions took part, although US intelligence sources mentioned only five. Between 60,000 and 70,000 combined Revolutionary Guards and regular army were confronted by seven Iraqi divisions.

Iran's failure to make an impression at the Basra front brought a shift in the fighting further north as the Iranians attempted to retake Qasr-e-Shirin and Naft-e-Shah. At the beginning of November Iraq moved heavy artillery and a tank brigade to the vicinity of Mandali, a town 8km (5 miles) from the Iranian border midway between Baghdad and Kermanshah. On 3 November Revolutionary Guards stormed Iraqi positions and after fierce fighting involving an estimated 50,000 Iranian troops, Iraq admitted that Iranian troops had crossed 5km (3 miles) deep into Iraqi territory. Although the Iranians recaptured most of the territory taken by Iraq in 1980 in this sector they were unable, or perhaps unwilling, to make any further advances. This last offensive of 1982 formed the pattern for the ensuing two years of the war: heavy casualties, with Iranian forces suffering three for each Iraqi one, and very limited territorial gains for either side. **David Pool**

Airborne artillery
Close air support since World War II

The pattern of warfare below the nuclear threshold for which the great powers prepare is one of large-scale mechanised combat, in which the forces on the ground are closely supported by fighter-bombers armed with a variety of devastating ground-attack weapons: a pattern derived from the German successes of 1939-41. What is most interesting to note about warfare since these early German victories, however, is how difficult it has often been to translate the power of the ground-attack aircraft into effective close support for ground troops. The development of close-support tactics in a variety of settings has been one of the most difficult problems in warfare since 1945.

The ability of the Allied air forces to intervene directly in the land battle during the latter part of World War II was considerable. However, ground-attack aircraft generally were not controlled with sufficient precision to permit them to respond quickly and accurately to army requests for air strikes, in the manner of artillery. They were rather used to carry out pre-planned attacks on previously located enemy forces, or on armed reconnaissance missions seeking and attacking targets of opportunity.

An exception to the general practice was the 'cab rank' system first instituted in Italy in 1944 to provide a quick response to army requests for support. This involved relays of ground-attack aircraft, in radio contact with an observation post on the ground, flying holding patterns over the front line. When the ground observer had spotted a target, he passed its position on to the fighter-bombers using an aerial photographic mosaic with coordinates superimposed on a grid. Although this system allowed the aircraft to carry out an attack within minutes of the target being spotted, it was very wasteful, as it required ground-attack

machines to be continuously, and expensively, airborne on the off-chance of being directed to a worthwhile target. It also presupposed that the situation on the ground was static rather than fluid and that the air force using these tactics had undisputed air superiority over the front line. In fact, during 1944-45 Axis opposition to the Allied air forces was at best sporadic and there were numerous fighter-bomber aircraft available. For example, a force of 3000 aircraft was available to support the breakout of Patton's Third Army from the Normandy beach-head in 1944. Moreover, the Allied rocket- and bomb-armed fighter-bombers (the RAF's Hawker Typhoon and the USAAF's Republic P-47 Thunderbolt) were excellent ground-attack aircraft.

In 1945, therefore, the problems of providing direct air support for ground forces were largely those of command, control and communication, rather than of effective aircraft and weaponry – a situation that

Top: An F-100D of the US Air Force fires rockets at a target in South Vietnam; this type of aeroplane carried out more close air support missions than any other in Vietnam. Above: This US Army officer is summoning an airstrike in support of his men. It is extremely important to have good ground-to-air coordination for a successful close support strike.

was to be reversed in the next major conflict, the Korean War (1950-53). The early months of this war revealed serious shortcomings in the first-generation jet, the Lockheed F-80 Shooting Star, when used for close support. Operating from bases in Japan, the F-80s had only sufficient endurance to remain over targets in South Korea for 15 minutes. Even when the initial North Korean attack had been pushed back and airfields in South Korea became available, Shooting Stars required extensive engineering work before they could be made suitable for close-support operations. For weaponry, too, was a problem: the F-80s were not then fitted with bomb racks and had to rely on their built-in armament of six 0·5in machine guns, plus four 5in HVARs (high velocity aircraft rockets) carried underwing.

To compensate for this, the F-80, lacking the propeller torque of piston-engined fighter-bombers, was an exceptionally steady gun platform and the 5in HVAR was capable of killing a Soviet tank. The range problem was tackled in the short term by improvising an increased capacity auxiliary fuel tank for the F-80s, allowing them 45 minutes over the battleline, and piston-engined F-51 Mustangs, well able to operate from rough airstrips, were withdrawn from Air National Guard units and ferried to Korea.

The early technical problems of close air support in Korea were largely resolved when South Korean airfields became available for jet operations and when F-84E Thunderjets, with improved payload and range, came into service towards the end of 1950. Yet as long as fighter-bombers had only a limited loiter time over the battle lines, command and control was of crucial importance to their success. Accordingly, very efficient methods of control were improvised, which remained in force for the duration of the war. One such was the forward air controller, mounted on a radio-equipped jeep and attached to each US infantry regiment. The major innovation of Korea, however, was the airborne controller. Using the radio call-sign 'Mosquito', these controllers orbited the battle area in T-6 piston-engined trainers for periods of up to three hours. Not only did they reconnoitre enemy positions and direct the fighter-bombers in their airstrikes, but they also provided an efficient communications link between frontline ground forces and the joint operations centre responsible for allocating air support missions. Forward Air Control (FAC) became a critical element in close support.

Although the Mosquito controllers were generally acknowledged to be a success, senior American officers believed that the slow and low-flying FAC aircraft would be too vulnerable to be used in a future conflict. Consequently the airborne FAC found no

place in the USAF's permanent organisation and, when American forces were committed to Vietnam in the mid-1960s, airborne FAC units had again to be improvised. The need for such control over South Vietnam, where there were no fixed battle lines, was even more pressing than it had been in Korea. As North Vietnamese Army and Viet Cong units were adept at camouflage and at sheltering among the civilian population, the task of the airborne FAC was greatly complicated. One solution to the problem was to allocate FACs to each Vietnamese province, as well as to field formations. This allowed the controller to familiarise himself with the normal pattern of life within his area and therefore be better able to spot any unusual activity that could betray enemy troop movements. The FAC aircraft were certainly vulnerable to groundfire when operating over South Vietnam. Pilots of 0-1s and 0-2s were unarmed apart from such personal weapons as carbines and sidearms and their aircraft had inadequate armour protection. The OV-10 Bronco, which reached Vietnam during 1968, was better equipped in both respects, but the low-flying FAC's best guarantee of safety was the realisation by

Top: Two Lockheed F-80s of the 8th Fighter-Bomber Wing take off during the Korean War. The F-80 was the usual aeroplane used for close support missions during this war. Above centre: An A-1 Skyraider prepares to take off from the USS *Oriskany* off Vietnam in September 1966. The Skyraider proved to be an exceptionally good aeroplane for close air support missions during the Vietnam War. Above: Two OV-10A Broncos armed with rocketpods fly in search of Viet Cong activity.

the communist forces that he could retaliate to any groundfire by calling in an airstrike.

There was certainly no shortage of tactical airpower in South Vietnam during the years of American involvement in the war. On average some 800 sorties were flown each day in support of ground forces, the greater part of this effort coming from the USAF, with Marine aviation units supporting their own ground forces in the I Corps area in the north and the Vietnamese Air Force taking on an increasing share of this work as the policy of 'Vietnamization' took effect from 1968. Although the piston-engined A-1 Skyraiders and the slower jets such as the A-37 and F-5A were best suited to ground-attack missions in South Vietnam, it was the faster jets which bore the brunt of the work. In 1969, for example, F-100 Super Sabres flew 52,699 close-support missions, and F-4 Phantoms flew 19,185 missions, while A-1s flew only 2055 and A-37s 8305 missions. These statistics clearly show that the USAF was forced to fight a counter-insurgency war in Southeast Asia with aircraft which were, for the most part, designed for the very different conditions of a major war in Europe. Without the help of the FAC's target marking, a high-performance jet like the Phantom stood little chance of spotting and successfully attacking the fleeting targets presented by the insurgents, unless communist forces launched large-scale conventional attacks, as in 1972. Nor were the powerful US jet aircraft to find an adequate response to communist night raids; diving attacks by the light of flares were very risky, for the pilot could easily miscalculate his altitude and fly into the ground.

The peculiar problems of close support in Vietnam led to many imaginative solutions, including the deployment of transport aircraft armed with broadsides of machine guns, the development of attack helicopters to a hitherto unheard-of level, and occasionally (as at Khe Sanh in 1968) the use of heavy bombers dropping their loads within 1km of friendly forces. These were all, however, a part of the realisation that conventional close support by high-performance fighter-bombers was insufficient in this unconventional war.

In 1967, the Israeli Defence Forces demonstrated a close coordination between forces on the ground and in the air; the early battles in the Sinai were the scene of closely integrated assaults on Egyptian positions by Israeli tank columns and Fouga Magisters that were summoned by the Israeli brigade commanders. Forward air controllers operated with the leading Israeli elements on the ground.

The close-support capabilities of the Arab forces in 1967 were hampered by the Israeli airstrikes on the first day of the war and never recovered. The Yom Kippur War of 1973, however, saw the renaissance of Arab airpower: the Syrians used aircraft to attack Israeli troop concentrations on the Golan Heights while the Egyptians attacked targets behind the Bar-Lev Line. As the Israeli Air Force entered the fighting, the Arab aircraft retired behind their air defence lines: these caused heavy losses to Israeli aircraft operating in support of troops on the ground and the Israeli brigade commanders became more circumspect in summoning air support. The main lesson drawn from this was to integrate artillery more closely with the armoured columns, and the 1982 invasion of the Lebanon saw a switch to artillery fire in support of assaults rather than airstrikes.

Harriers and lasers

Ground-attack aircraft did not contribute greatly to the 1982 conflict in the South Atlantic or to the Gulf War. A single squadron of RAF Harriers was despatched to the Falklands to provide close support for ground forces and they flew a total of 126 sorties (many of them from the deck of HMS *Hermes*). However, their efforts were somewhat hampered by the lack of adequate reconnaissance and the need to fly at very low level to evade Argentinian gun and missile defences, although a notable innovation of the campaign was the use of laser target-designators by forward air controllers.

The lack of effective ground-attack missions by either of the combatant air forces in the Gulf War is less easily explained. Iran has a substantial force of F-4 and F-5 fighters, well suited to such missions, and despite problems of spares availability and lack of qualified maintenance personnel, has managed to keep significant numbers of them operational. Iraq is in an even stronger position, with Soviet Flogger and Fitter attack aircraft serving alongside Western-supplied Mirage F1 and Hunter fighter-bombers. Yet since these far from negligible air forces have exerted virtually no influence on the land war, one can only conclude that their operators lack the necessary skills to employ them effectively.

It can be seen, therefore, that the role of the fighter-bomber in warfare since 1945 has by no means been as impressive as might have been imagined. A high level of technical skill, adequate technology, good organisation and suitable geography are necessary for this breed of weapons system to achieve the devastating results of which it is capable; and not all these factors can be guaranteed in modern warfare.

Anthony Robinson

DIESEL-ELECTRIC SUBMARINES

Since the era of the nuclear-powered submarine began with the successful trials of USS *Nautilus* in 1955, the conventionally-powered (diesel-electric) submarine has often been ignored. Attention has been focused on the more fashionable SSN (sub-surface nuclear), even though conventional submarines played a decisive role in sea warfare during World War II and are still capable of fulfilling all the functions of a modern submarine – not only attacks on surface vessels, but also 'hunter-killer' operations against other submarines and the launching of missiles against land targets. The main problem encountered in submarine operations during World War II, the need for submarines to surface so that air could be provided for the diesel generators to recharge the boats' electric batteries, has been overcome by snorkelling – taking in air while still submerged. This has meant that diesel-electric submarines can remain under water for the duration of their mission just like nuclear submarines, although their radius of action remains limited by the eventual need to refuel.

The diesel-electric submarine does in fact possess several advantages over the SSN. In particular, its propulsion system is quieter and can be shut down when the submarine is under threat; the nuclear submarine needs to keep its reactor cool at all times, involving a pumping action detectable to enemy sonars. The diesel-electric system consists of an electric propulsion motor fed by a lead-acid battery; the recharging of the battery is carried out by diesel generators. To reduce noise to a minimum, the engines are resiliently mounted on flexible supports and the engine rooms may be lined with sound-proofing material. The propulsion system is inevitably to the aft of the hull, while living accommodation is toward the bows.

Another advantage of a diesel-electric submarine is its smaller crew. This advantage is increased by the use of automation in equipment on the submarine, primarily in the area of operational systems – such as the propulsion and rudder control – with the intention of reducing the amount of attention necessary to ensure the smooth running of these systems. The Swedish Navy has particularly concentrated on automating the equipment on board its submarines to a high degree.

The main armament of the submarine is still the torpedo; most submarines now in service have between six and 10 torpedo tubes, normally for firing 21in torpedoes, sometimes divided into two sets, in the bows and aft. In the future, torpedoes will be supplemented or replaced by anti-ship missiles like the Harpoon. World War II submarines mounted a

Previous page: HMS *Sealion* of the Porpoise class. Top: The Soviet Whiskey class is in service with many nations' navies. Above: Two Foxtrot-class submarines of the Soviet Navy show the flag in Dar Es Salaam. Below: A Soviet Golf I with the hatch of one of its SS-N-4 missile tubes open.

Foxtrot class (1958)

Complement 75 officers and men
Dimensions Length 91·5m (300ft); beam 8m (26ft); draught 6·1m (20ft)
Displacement 1950/2500 tons (surface/submerged)

Propulsion Three diesels, 6000bhp; three electrics, 6000hp
Speed 18/16 knots (surface/submerged)

Armament Six 533mm torpedo tubes in bows; four 406mm torpedo tubes in stern

gun on deck, but this has been deleted from more recent models because of its adverse effect on the streamlining of the boat underwater. Some conventional submarines have been converted to carry cruise or ballistic missiles. The main sensor of submarines is sonar, used to detect both targets and enemy threats.

The operator of the world's largest conventionally-powered submarine fleet is the Soviet Union with over 150 in service in 1983. This is an inheritance of the Soviet naval policy before the massive expansion of the 1960s; until then resources were devoted to the production of an essentially defensive navy consisting largely of small attack craft and submarines.

The first Soviet submarines of the postwar era were the Whiskey class, based on captured plans of the German Type XXI U-boat; these would probably have been effective in operations against convoys like their German cousins. Some 240 were built between 1951 and 1957, coming in six different types, depending on the number of guns carried. About 20 Whiskey-class boats have been converted to carry SS-N-3 cruise missiles and four others were converted to radar picket boats; two others have been turned into oceanographic research boats.

Contemporaries of the Whiskey class were the Quebec class and the Zulu class. The Quebec class was built between 1954 and 1957 and was intended for operation in the confined coastal waters of the Baltic. Eighteen were built and it is thought that this class is not highly regarded. The Zulu-class boats were very large and long-range submarines intended both to operate against convoys and to act as reconnaissance ships; 26 were built in 1955 and six were converted to fire SS-N-4 ballistic missiles. Like the Whiskey class, the Zulu and Quebec classes were based on German plans.

The Soviet Union began constructing nuclear submarines in the late 1950s and the Romeo class, which was originally planned to be built in large numbers as a successor to the Whiskey class, eventually numbered only 18 boats, built between 1956 and 1961 as an interim measure, possibly in case the nuclear-propelled November class proved to be a failure. The Romeo class was a development of the Whiskey class

with a modified conning-tower and Hercules and Feliks sonars. Complementing and contemporary with it was the Foxtrot class which was designed as an improved Zulu. About 60 were built between 1958 and 1967 and it seems to be regarded as a very successful product. Lessons learnt from the production of the Zulu ballistic missile conversions were applied to the Golf class which, like the Zulu conversions, has SS-N-4 (SS-N-5 in later models) ballistic missiles mounted in the fin; the Golf-class boats were built between 1958 and 1962.

A successor to the Whiskey-class missile boats was the Juliet class built between 1962 and 1967. These are much less noisy boats since the SS-N-3 missiles are mounted in tubes that are flush with the hull. Sixteen were built.

An unusual class of vessels is the Bravo class; these boats are similar in appearance and shape to American and British SSNs. Only four were built between 1966 and 1970, and one is attached to each of the major Soviet fleets. They are presumably training vessels for anti-submarine warfare, perhaps the Soviet Navy's equivalent of the US Air Force 'Aggressors' programme.

In 1973 a new Soviet submarine was revealed at the Soviet fleet review in Sebastopol. The Tango class comprises 16 boats which seem to be designed to operate in shallow waters as scouts and hunter-killers. Production of these was stopped in the later 1970s when the Kilo class was begun. These boats are being built on the Pacific coast of the USSR; two units are at present operational, and appear to be undergoing extensive testing. The Soviet conventional fleet is rounded out by the single-boat India class and the Lima class which are strictly oceanographic boats.

The Soviet Union has achieved some success in exporting its conventional submarines. The Romeo class have proved very popular with the Chinese who have themselves built most of their own fleet of 76 boats, as well as providing North Korea with four of these; the North Koreans have gone on to produce about eight of their own. Egypt operates Romeo and Whiskey boats, Libya and India Foxtrot-class boats, Bulgaria Romeo class only, and Poland Whiskey

Above: One of the newer classes of Soviet diesel-electric submarines is the Tango class; as long as a Foxtrot, the class is wider and requires a smaller crew, indicating a higher degree of automation.

Top: The *Daphne*, first of the French Daphne class of patrol submarines. Above: the *Casma*, a West German-manufactured Type 209 patrol submarine of the Peruvian Navy.

class. There have been reports of Tango-class boats going to India, but none have been delivered.

The three most important submarine classes built in Western Europe are the Daphne class of France, the Type 209 class of Germany and the UK's Oberon class. These have had great success in the armaments market, are in service with many navies, and are highly respected by naval journalists and naval personnel.

The Daphne class has its origins in the ubiquitous Type XXI U-boats, since the first postwar French submarine, the Narval class, was based on this design. The Arethuse class which followed was a small hunter-killer type. The Daphne class was based on experience from both of these designs; it is in service with the French, South African, Pakistani, Spanish and Portuguese navies. This class may have problems with sea-keeping, as two have been lost in mysterious circumstances. The successor class to the Daphnes, the Agosta class, has been in service since 1977 and is designed to operate in distant waters.

The German Navy began work on a postwar submarine fleet in 1954, with the design of small boats for Baltic operations. The first U-boats of the postwar era entered service in the early 1960s; although there were problems with non-magnetic steel hulls that corroded badly and forced the scrapping of the first two boats, later models proved satisfactory and the Type 205, Type 206 and Type 207 boats remain in service in the 1980s. The experience gained from these was used in building the larger Type 209 which is in service with the Greek, West German, Brazilian, Chilean, Venezuelan, Ecuadorian, Colombian, Peruvian, Turkish and Indonesian navies. They were designed not to require too many technical skills from their crews and yet to carry sophisticated electronic equipment.

The British Oberon class are an improved Porpoise class (the first postwar British submarines) and have been exported to Australia, Brazil, Canada and Chile as well as serving with the British Navy. They are designed for deep diving, long range, habitability and extremely quiet operation. They will be replaced in

Oberon class (1959)

Complement 69 officers and men
Dimensions Length 90m (295ft); beam 8·1m (26ft); draught 5·5m (18ft)
Displacement 2030/2410 tons (surface/submerged)

Propulsion Two diesels, 3680bhp; two electrics, 6000hp
Speed 12/17 knots (surface/submerged)

Armament Eight 21in torpedo tubes (six in bow, two in stern)

the Royal Navy by the Type 2400 class in the late 1980s and early 1990s. The Type 2400 will have a teardrop hull like those of nuclear submarines and a high degree of automation which will reduce the crew from the Oberon's 69 to only 46. The torpedo tubes will be capable of firing Harpoon missiles.

The Japanese Maritime Self-Defence Force has three submarine classes currently in service: Ooshio, Uzushio and Yuushio. These have teardrop hulls, which give faster and quieter underwater capabilities; the Uzushio and the Yuushio classes have the torpedo tubes mounted amidships so that a large sonar array can be fitted. High-quality steel is used to allow for greater diving depths.

The United States no longer has any diesel-electric submarines operational with its active fleet and those in the reserve fleet are being slowly phased out. Apart from a large number of ex-US submarines of the World War II era in service with South American navies, the other nations with diesel-electric submarines are Denmark, Italy, the Netherlands, Sweden and Yugoslavia. Most of these are descendents of the Type XXI, but the Yugoslav boats were developed from a sunken Italian submarine that the Yugoslavs raised and rebuilt.

Productive experimentation with the propulsion system may result in further major advances in conventionally-powered submarine design, while reduction of hull fittings and smoothing of the shape of hull and conning tower have probably yielded all improvements possible to provide quieter and faster running. The aim of any future developments of the conventionally-powered submarine will be to reduce the time spent at or near the surface to an absolute minimum, preferably none. This may prove an important field of armaments research, because the conventional submarine has one important advantage over the SSN – lower cost.

Top: HMS *Otus*, a Royal Navy attack submarine of the Oberon class. Above centre: An Uzushio-class patrol submarine of the Japanese Maritime Self-Defence Force. Below centre: A Royal Norwegian Navy West German-built Type 207 Kobben-class patrol submarine. Above: A Zwaardvis-class patrol submarine of the Royal Netherlands Navy on exercise in the North Sea. Left: A Soviet Juliet-class submarine, armed with 4 SS-N-3 missiles.

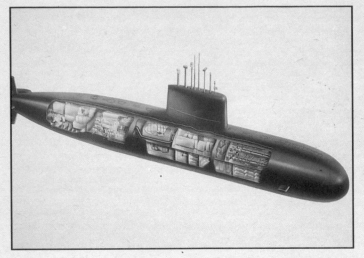

Top left: A cutaway of the British Type 2400, the class intended to replace the Oberon class in the 1990s. Top right: A Swedish Hajen class submarine emerges from its pen somewhere in the Baltic. Above: The Danish submarine *Narvahlen*. Below: The name ship of the Italian Sauro class underway in the Mediterranean. Left: The Italian submarine *Leonardo da Vinci* shows its multi-bladed propeller (designed for quieter running) during its launch.

N. SAURO

Dollars and dictators
US involvement in Latin America

Ever since 1823, when President James Monroe warned the European powers to keep out of the Americas, the United States has claimed the right to exert exclusive authority over the nations to its south. At the turn of the century the occupation of Cuba (1898), the annexation of Puerto Rico (1898) and the sponsoring of the breakaway Republic of Panama, formerly a province of Colombia (1903), signalled US readiness to back its claim with forceful action, while active intervention was officially endorsed in 1904, when President Theodore Roosevelt announced that his country would exercise 'international police power' in cases of 'chronic wrongdoing or an impotence which results in a general loosening of the ties of civilised society'. Over the following three decades Central America and the Caribbean became a familiar stamping ground for US troops, deployed at various times in Mexico, Cuba, Panama, Haiti, the Dominican Republic and Nicaragua, while the US government made and unmade governments throughout the area.

At first such interventions were justified, as by President Taft in 1912, on moral grounds; inevitably, though, the economic self-interest which had been present from the start came increasingly to the fore. US business interests followed the flag: looking back on his military career in 1935, General Smedley Butler candidly described himself as 'a high-class muscleman for Big Business, for Wall Street and for

Left: The United States inevitably dominated the close relationship between the North and South American neighbours, but US cultural, economic and political power did not always win friends and influence people. Military intervention and support for right-wing military dictatorships undermined Washington's claims to be defending democracy against revolution.

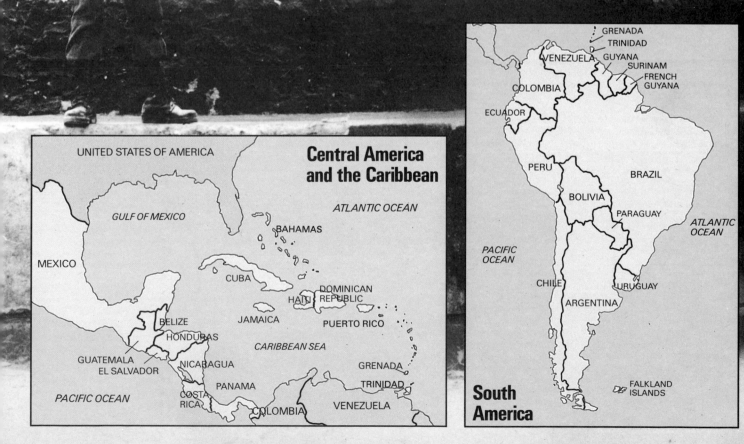

Top: General Augusto Pinochet, leader of the military junta which overthrew President Salvador Allende of Chile (above) in September 1973. US opposition to the left-wing Popular Unity government of Allende led to a CIA-backed destabilisation campaign which contributed to the conditions that made the military coup possible.

Below: US military instructors in Honduras. The Sandinista victory in Nicaragua prompted a huge increase in US military aid to its allies in Central America, and US troops were on semi-permanent 'manoeuvres' in Honduras.

the bankers'.

In the 1930s under the 'Good Neighbour' policy announced by President Franklin Roosevelt in 1933, emphasis was switched away from armed intervention to the promotion and support of local dictators throughout Central America and the Caribbean. Some, such as Rafael Trujillo in the Dominican Republic and Anastasio Somoza in Nicaragua, got their start as commanders of a US-created National Guard. Others, such as Fulgencio Batista in Cuba and Hernández Martínez in El Salvador, became dependable allies of the United States once in office. All proved harsh and intolerant, and in the end ruled without any semblance of popular support.

During the 1940s, a number of important developments occurred. First, the United States emerged as a world power. Second, it began to define its interests, in global terms, in opposition to those of the Soviet Union, and to assess conflicts within the Americas within the context of the 'Cold War'. Third, it sought to extend its diplomatic and economic power across mainland South America. And fourth, US ties with the repressive dictatorships south of its borders increasingly became an embarrassment to a state claiming to defend the values of democracy against the challenge of the Soviet bloc.

Nationalist governments which put US economic interests at risk in their pursuit of social justice were denounced as communistic and Soviet-controlled, as was that of Jacobo Arbenz in Guatemala, overthrown in a coup masterminded and funded by the CIA in 1954. But in the same period the United States threw its support behind democratisation in Brazil in 1945 and in Bolivia after the revolution of 1952. A consistent pattern appeared to be emerging when Colombia and Venezuela were prompted towards democracy in 1958, but the situation in the region changed dramatically at the end of that year, when Fidel Castro swept to power in Cuba as the dictatorship of Batista crumbled while the US government dithered in the wings.

The consolidation of the Cuban revolution and its rapid shift into the Soviet orbit has been the major factor behind US intervention in the region ever since. US policy has been pulled simultaneously in two opposing directions: on one side is the awareness that social reform and democratisation are essential in the long run if the underlying conditions of poverty and repression which make revolution attractive are to be removed; on the other is the need to support conservative allies and build up friendly armies in order to protect US interests in the short term, to prevent radical opponents of the US from gaining ground. There has always been too great a gulf between who the US government's friends are, and who it would like them to be.

The problems the United States has faced are clearly seen in the failure of the Alliance for Progress, launched by President Kennedy as a direct response to the Cuban revolution. Its reformist impulse was rapidly lost as the armies built up across Central and South America and trained in the task of counter-insurgency tired of the moderate politicians sponsored by their paymasters and took power for themselves, justifying themselves by claiming that drastic methods were needed to root out the guerrilla movements that had sprung up across the region in the wake of Castro's success in Cuba. The threat these movements posed was never substantial, but the US soon abandoned its commitment to reform. In the wake of the botched attempt to defeat the Cuban revolution at the Bay of Pigs in 1961, President Kennedy sponsored the overthrow of the democratically elected President Juan Bosch of the Dominican Republic, while his successor, President Johnson, supported and swiftly welcomed the coup which overthrew President João Goulart of Brazil in 1964, and sent 20,000 US troops back to the Dominican Republic in 1965 to prevent Bosch from returning to power.

Business before reform

Developments such as these, in the aftermath of the Cuban revolution, set the scene for US relations with Central and South America in the 1970s and 1980s. The overriding goal became the prevention, at all costs, of the appearance of another Cuba in the Americas. Sporadic attempts to promote or support reform broke down continually as old allies reacted with hostility, or new forces threatened too radical a departure from the status quo. The situation was further complicated by suspicion arising out of long-standing US links with the most conservative business and political interests throughout the region, and by the refusal of local armed forces, greatly strengthened by US aid and by the licence given them by the doctrines of counter-insurgency to play a dominant role in domestic affairs, to heed the urgency of social reform. Given its record, it was not easy for the United States to pose as the agent of democracy and social reform in the region.

The dilemmas facing the United States in South America over the last two decades are best seen in the case of Chile. In the early 1960s concern that the conservatives who ruled the country would prove unable to resist the power and appeal of the left coalition headed by Salvador Allende, a Marxist doctor with lengthy parliamentary experience, led the US to back the newly prominent Christian Democrat leader Eduardo Frei, in the hope that he would provide an attractive reformist alternative to socialism. To this end millions of dollars were poured into Chile to back Frei's presidential campaign in 1964, and in the wake of his resounding victory he was encouraged to pursue land reform and other progressive measures. But the results were not those for which the US had hoped. Frei's 'Revolution in Liberty' weakened under pressure from the right in the country and from conservative elements in his own party, the most committed reformers moved to the left as they saw

Fall of a democracy

Months of instability preceded the 1973 coup which overthrew President Salvador Allende of Chile. His Popular Unity coalition failed to gain a clear majority in the 1973 congressional elections, and a national lorry-drivers' strike contributed to the country's runaway inflation. Increasingly isolated, Allende attempted to neutralise the armed forces by including a number of senior officers in his government. By September, however, the heads of Chile's armed forces and paramilitary Carabiñeros had joined together in a plot to seize power, and in the early hours of 11 September, naval personnel occupied key points in the port of Valparaiso.

By 0730 hours, tanks were taking up positions around the Moneda Presidential Palace in the capital, Santiago, where Allende was defended by a small group of his personal bodyguards. Shooting began at approximately 0930 hours, and at 1130 hours after Allende had repeatedly refused to surrender Chilean Air Force Hawker Hunters bombed the palace. At 1400 hours, Allende ordered his staff to cease resistance and then, alone in his office, committed suicide.

Fighting continued for several days, with scattered pockets of left-wing resistance around the Santiago Technical State University and in the capital's industrial suburbs. The security forces arrested tens of thousands of the Popular Unity government's supporters, and the National Stadium became a notorious concentration camp, in which large numbers of people were tortured and murdered. Two US students interned in the stadium during the first week after the coup reported witnessing up to 500 executions.

The new military junta was headed by General Augusto Pinochet, commander-in-chief of the army, who gradually eclipsed his colleagues, assuming the title of supreme chief of state in June 1974, and of president in December 1974.

their hopes frustrated and in 1970 the Chileans elected Allende, by the narrowest of margins, as president.

Although the Allende government had been democratically elected, and was committed to a reform programme broadly similar to that adopted by Frei (with US blessing) in 1964, the new rulers faced unremitting hostility from the United States. US agencies promoted economic destabilisation and funded civil disorder, while stepping up aid to the armed forces. They achieved their goal in September 1973, when General Augusto Pinochet seized power at the head of a military junta. The bloodshed which accompanied and followed the coup, along with the curtailing of civil liberties and the widespread use of repression and torture, inevitably reinforced the impression that despite the lip-service paid to democratic reform, the United States would tolerate any action, and any regime, however harsh, which could present itself as being fundamentally 'opposed to communism'.

By the mid-1970s dictatorships were proliferating in Central and South America. But at the same time a reaction was beginning to the cynical 'realism' of the Nixon-Kissinger years. Defeat in Vietnam. Congres-

Right: A Chilean Hawker Hunter bombs the presidential palace during the 1973 coup. Above: Troops arrest supporters of the Allende regime during the reign of terror which followed the coup.

sional investigations into the human rights records of US military allies in the Americas, criticism in the wake of revelations regarding covert action against the Allende regime, and eventually the election of President Carter in 1976 led to a shift of emphasis once again in US policy. The Panama Canal Treaty of 1977, US pressure to guarantee free elections in the Dominican Republic in 1978, and the prominent role given to human rights considerations in assessing the disbursement of aid were all facets of an approach which appeared once again to be sensitive to what Carter's National Security Advisor Zbigniew Brzezinski called 'the mounting desire in Central America for greater social justice and national dignity'.

Although the new perspective was hesitant, and virtually abandoned before Carter left office, it had an unsettling effect, in Central America at least. This was first clear in Nicaragua, where the dictator Anastasio Somoza, younger son of the first Somoza, was toppled from power on 19 July 1979 after a protracted popular uprising led by the Frente Sandinista de Liberación Nacional (FSLN), during which the US had vacillated between renewed support for the dictator and increasingly desperate attempts to find a safe reformist alternative. Then, in El Salvador, US intervention played a significant part in prompting the coup by junior officers in October 1979 that ousted the military dictator General Carlos Humberto Romero, and started the process which developed into the civil war of the 1980s.

The US administration of Ronald Reagan that took office in 1981 abandoned any serious concern for human rights, but in other respects, despite its harsh rhetoric, it tended to follow on where President Carter left off, seeking to establish democratic rule which could be presented as reformist in those countries where it could make its influence felt, while using all means short of direct invasion by its own troops to bring about the downfall of the Sandinista regime and the defeat of the guerrillas in El Salvador. The key development of the period, in Central America at least, was the massive military build-up that accompanied this process, culminating in virtually continuous joint manoeuvres that kept thousands of US troops in Honduras (a state that borders on Nicaragua and El Salvador), and the provision of military aid to El Salvador to the extent of $200 million in 1984 alone.

The achievements of the Reagan administration were distinctly mixed. The campaign against Nicaragua failed to elicit much support either in Congress or among the people of the United States, while the majority of the nations of Latin America itself were hostile. Attempts to demonstrate high levels of Cuban and Soviet involvement through Nicaragua in the conflict in El Salvador have repeatedly failed to come up with positive evidence, and in any case the trickle of arms that might come through such routes is nothing compared to the massive flow into the region from the US itself. Covert funding established an army 15,000 strong on the borders of Nicaragua, Nicaraguan harbours were mined in blatant disregard for international law, and private US citizens were allowed to participate in attacks on the government of Nicaragua. On this front, despite the serious damage done to the Nicaraguan economy, the United States has been losing the propaganda war, while its divided 'Contra' allies have found little support inside Nicaragua. In El Salvador, despite the infusion of aid, the war has reached a state of deadlock.

It was on the political front that Reagan's policy made some progress, in pursuing a campaign to replace open military dictatorship with controlled and guided democracy. The results of this policy were seen in Honduras, where an elected government came to power in 1982, in El Salvador, where a lengthy process of democratisation culminated with the election of José Napoleón Duarte as president in 1984, and in Guatemala, where a constituent assembly made provision for elections in 1985. It remains to be seen whether these efforts at democratisation will not in the end prove as great a destabilising factor as similar experiments have in the past. In the meantime, the invasion of Grenada by US troops in 1983 stands as a reminder that the United States has not ruled out the use of direct force where it estimates that the chances of an easy victory are high.

Paul Cammack

Below: Cleaning up the backyard, men of the US 82nd Airborne Division establishing a bridgehead during the 1983 invasion of Grenada. Popular in the US, the invasion was condemned by some of America's closest allies.

Sandinistas against Somoza

Revolution in Nicaragua

At 4.30 am on 17 July 1979, President Anastasio Somoza Debayle of Nicaragua, along with several close political allies and senior military officers, boarded a plane in the capital, Managua, bound for Miami. For Nicaragua it was the end of a bitter and bloody revolutionary war in which it has been estimated that between 40,000 and 50,000 Nicaraguans died. Two days later, Nicaraguans awoke to the sound of Radio Sandino broadcasting triumphant slogans as the first victorious rebel columns of the Frente Sandinista de Liberación Nacional (FSLN) entered the capital.

The Sandinista revolution in Nicaragua had been a long time in coming. Along the pattern of most Central American societies, Nicaragua consisted of a large and totally impoverished peasant population dominated economically and politically by a tiny minority of extremely wealthy landowning families. The first two decades of the 20th century had seen a considerable quantity of American investment in mining and agriculture poured into Nicaragua, and to protect these investments came a force of US Marines. Possessing the only competent fighting force in the country at the time, the US was in a position effectively to control the turbulent Nicaraguan political situation and look after its growing economic interests. But the US presence also served to engender an intensely nationalist armed movement demanding an end to all foreign interference in Nicaraguan affairs. This Ejercito Defensor de la Soberania Nacional (EDSN) became engaged in the late 1920s in a war against the US Marines and the newly-formed Nicaraguan National Guard. The EDSN was commanded by the romantic and legendary figure of Augusto Cesar Sandino (from whom the Sandinistas take their name). Realising that conventional military action was impossible against the superior firepower of the US forces, he prosecuted a guerrilla war from his stronghold in the inhospitable mountains in the northwest of the country. From the bleak and inaccessible peak of El Chipote Sandino's army fought for six years and by 1933 the war had spread through 10 of Nicaragua's 16 provinces. Unable to secure a victory against the rebels and under considerable pressure in the US to end the war, the Marines withdrew, leaving the security of the country in the hands of the 2500-strong National Guard.

Sandino immediately accepted a ceasefire and peace negotiations began between the EDSN and

Above right: Augusto Cesar Sandino, whose name was adopted by the guerrilla movement which fought its way to power in Nicaragua during the late 1970s. A rebel leader, Sandino was assassinated by Somoza Garcia's National Guard in 1934. Somoza (right), a former US Marine, became head of the American-backed National Guard and dictator of Nicaragua. Below: US Marines arrive in the provincial town of Matagalpa during the US occupation of Nicaragua which lasted from 1927 to 1933.

Top: Carlos Fonseca, a co-founder of the FSLN. Above: General Anastasio Somoza Debayle, who took power in 1967, exploited the country through the National Guard, which administered large sectors of the economy. Below: The Guard was no match for the determined fighters of the FSLN, and by June 1979, it was defending Managua.

Anastasio Somoza Garcia, the youthful commander of the National Guard. As the negotiations proceeded, relations between the Guard and the EDSN deteriorated. Pre-empting a further outbreak of hostilities, the Guard assassinated Sandino and several of his generals during the fourth round of peace talks in Managua in 1934. A campaign of ruthless pacification was mounted and the EDSN guerrillas, now leaderless and with their popular cause removed by the US withdrawal, were wiped out. But the seeds of *Sandinismo* had been sown and rebel military operations were to resume again 25 years later, not this time against foreign domination in Nicaragua but against an internal force, the corrupt military dictatorship of the Somoza family.

Between Sandino's death and the re-emergence of armed opposition in the late 1950s, the Somoza family established complete control over the economic, political and military institutions of Nicaragua. Somoza Garcia had wasted no time in seizing power in a coup in 1935; after his assassination in 1956, he was succeeded by his son Luis, who was in his turn succeeded by his brother Anastasio Somoza Debayle in May 1967. Between them the Somozas wielded immense power. They had accumulated a massive personal fortune – US sources estimated Somoza's wealth at $900 million on his arrival in Miami in 1979 – the presidency was firmly in their hands and, above all, they controlled the means to keep it, the National Guard.

It has been said of Nicaragua that it was 'a country invaded by its own army' – not an army restricted to the maintenance of external security, but an army that permeated much wider fields of governmental and administrative processes in the country. The Guard numbered some 10,000 troops in the 1970s, many of whom had passed through US military training programmes including the US Army Infantry and Ranger

School, the Military Police School and the Army Command and General Staff School. Weapons and equipment were modern. The Guard arsenal included considerable quantities of US-supplied kit – Garand rifles, M16 assault rifles, M101 150mm artillery, M4 medium tanks – and this was supplemented by shipments of Israeli Galil assault rifles, Uzi sub-machine guns, rockets and anti-aircraft weaponry. Considerable quantities of Somoza's personal money and Nicaraguan public funds were lavished on the Guard, while its officers enjoyed great social prestige, many of them securing important government posts on their retirement from active duty. So effective was this system that extreme personal loyalty to the Somoza regime remained steadfastly intact throughout the Guard for the whole period of Somoza domination.

The narrow concentration of power in the hands of the Somoza family and the contempt they showed for the Nicaraguan constitution provoked opposition to the regime among the privileged sector of Nicaraguan society, expressed politically through the Conservative and Liberal Parties. Both these parties spawned abortive attempts at armed uprisings in the 1940s, and many of the middle-class intellectual guerrilla fighters who took up arms against Somoza in the late 1950s came from the Liberal Party's youth wing. It was the Somozas' alienation of the Nicaraguan bourgeoisie by their reliance on repression, their refusal to share power and their failure to respect the business aspirations of the professional middle class, that was eventually to cement a united opposition front with the poverty-stricken peasants and *barrio* (slum) dwellers and spark off a full-scale civil war between Somoza's Guard and virtually the rest of Nicaragua.

The Sandinista movement originated in the early 1960s. In July 1961, three former university students, Carlos Fonseca, Silvio Mayorga and Thomas Borge,

met in the Honduran capital Tegucigalpa with the aim of establishing a revolutionary movement to topple Somoza. Small ill-armed Conservative-sponsored guerrilla raids across the Honduran border over the previous three years had amounted to little more than pinpricks in the hide of *Somocismo*, but spurred on by the example of the Cuban guerrilla war against the Batista regime, the students founded the FSLN in 1962. Small-scale guerrilla actions continued while the nascent FSLN looked for support among the working classes of Nicaragua, but with no financial support from abroad to buy weapons and food, the early guerrilla units had to struggle to survive in the northern mountains where their hero and mentor Sandino had waged war against the Americans. Apart from the rigours of the hard life in the barren mountains, they also suffered a number of costly defeats in their early clashes with the National Guard. But slowly the ranks of the FSLN began to swell and arms caches were established on the proceeds of extremely dangerous bank raids and tiny personal donations from their sympathisers.

Out of isolation

It was the massacre of several hundred people by the National Guard at a Conservative-organised demonstration outside the National Palace in Managua on 22 January 1967 that was to give the still fragile FSLN the impetus it needed. The Sandinista leadership judged the time right to consolidate a guerrilla army at Mount Pancasan near Matagalpa, bringing the war away from the isolated border region and placing it firmly in central Nicaragua. At the end of August, however, the National Guard unearthed the guerrilla columns at Pancasan and the FSLN suffered a severe military defeat in which Silvio Mayorga was killed.

Despite this severe setback, the FSLN continued its search for support, concentrating more on the inhabitants of the cities' *barrios*, but what networks were established were in constant danger of exposure through Somoza's informer net, the *orejas* ('ears'). In 1970 the prospect remained bleak for the FSLN and after a great deal of self-examination the leadership decided to take the movement underground.

Guerrilla activity remained dormant for the next four years while the FSLN worked through student organisations and trade unions to gain recruits and propagate the political aims of the underground leadership. Between 1970 and 1974 strikes, demonstrations and protests became increasingly frequent and with the pressures of a deteriorating economic situation in Nicaragua, FSLN ideology began to take a firm root in the country. Widespread disillusion with Somoza was further intensified in the aftermath of the disastrous 1972 earthquake which devastated most of the centre of Managua. The National Guard openly looted the ruins and a force of US troops had to be called in to maintain order. Rumours abounded that much of the $30 million of international aid that poured into Managua after the disaster was pocketed by the Guard and the construction work that started to rebuild the city was contracted to Somoza-owned building companies.

At the end of 1974 the FSLN broke cover. On 27 December a Sandinista commando unit of 13 guerrillas launched a raid that humiliated the regime and brought the Sandinista cause back into the light. Armed with M1 carbines, 0·22in hunting rifles and a

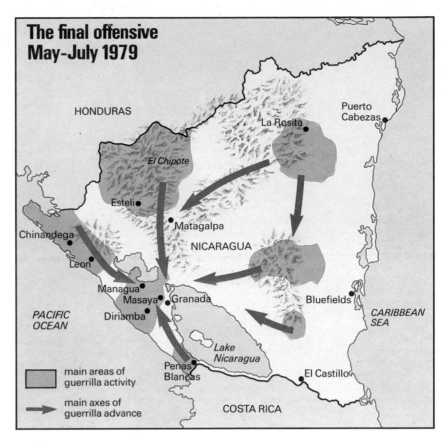

The final offensive May-July 1979

HONDURAS

La Rosita

Puerto Cabezas

El Chipote

Esteli

Matagalpa

Chinandega

NICARAGUA

Leon

Managua

Masaya Granada

Bluefields

CARIBBEAN SEA

Diriamba

PACIFIC OCEAN

Lake Nicaragua

Penas Blancas

El Castillo

COSTA RICA

☐ main areas of guerrilla activity

→ main axes of guerrilla advance

motley collection of smallarms and grenades, the group burst in on a reception being held for the US ambassador Turner B. Shelton in Managua and took the guests hostage. After a 60-hour siege Somoza had no alternative but to accept the FSLN demands – political prisoners including Daniel Ortega of the FSLN national leadership were released, a $2 million ransom was paid and wage increases for the Nicaraguan industrial and agricultural workers were agreed to. Accompanied by 18 prisoners, the successful commandos flew out to Havana in Cuba.

Somoza's reaction to the raid was to impose what amounted to a state of siege in Nicaragua which was to last for nearly three years. Martial law was declared, strict censorship was imposed and a brutally repressive counter-insurgency campaign was mounted by the Guard against the guerrillas in the Matagalpa

Below: Sandinista guerrillas manning a recoilless rifle during the FSLN 'final offensive' of 1979.

mountains. The 'search and destroy' operations were augmented by air force bombing and the use of napalm and defoliants; peasant villages in the guerrilla areas were destroyed and concentration camps set up. In the face of this ferocious backlash many of the FSLN were forced to seek sanctuary in Costa Rica and those that remained were effectively contained. In 1976, the FSLN lost another of its founder members, General-Secretary Carlos Fonseca, who was killed in an exchange of fire with a Guard patrol near Zinica, and it seemed that the movement was in peril of being wiped out.

Mass popular insurrection

In July 1977, however, Somoza suffered a heart-attack and, taking advantage of his condition, the guerrillas renewed their offensive in October with outright attacks on Guard units in Managua and the main provincial towns. A split within the FSLN itself had also resulted in a change of tactics from a prolonged guerrilla war of attrition to mass popular insurrection. Its previously narrow Marxist base was broadened to embrace the disaffected but non-communist Nicaraguan middle classes who were by now totally disillusioned with Somoza and the harsh rigours of the state of siege. Rioting broke out in January 1978 as crowds attacked US and Somoza-linked buildings in Managua following Somoza's assassination of Pedro Joaquin Chamorro, the outspoken editor of the newspaper *La Prensa*. The riots were immediately followed by a two-week general strike which brought out employers as much as their work-forces. Throughout 1978 armed upheavals, barricade-building and street-fighting flared in the cities and *barrios* throughout Nicaragua. Hostilities were further exacerbated by the Guard's excessive use of force in quelling these disturbances.

Most feared were the Guard's elite units. These included the Brigadas Especiales Contra Actos de Terrorismo, which swooped into the towns in their orange jeeps and worked in conjunction with informers to root out anti-government sympathisers, and the notoriously savage Escuela de Entrenamiento Basico de Infanteria (EEBI). The EEBI was set up in 1978 under the direct command of Anastasio Somoza Portocarrero, son of Somoza Debayle, and was trained by Michael 'Mike the Merc' Echannis and his South Vietnamese mercenary assistant Nguyen Van Nguyen. Indoctrinated with a fierce hatred for what amounted to most of the Nicaraguan population, the

EEBI slogan *somos tigres* – we are tigers – struck fear into the hearts even of other National Guard units, so savage were their techniques.

Nothing, however, could check the advance of the insurgency. On 22 August 1978 another major blow was struck against the regime when the senior FSLN commander Eden Pastora, known as 'Commander Zero', mounted a 25-strong commando raid 'Operation Pigsty' against the National Palace in Managua. Senior politicians and congressmen were taken hostage and again the guerrillas got away unhindered, this time to Panama, with a $500,000 ransom and the release of more than 50 FSLN political prisoners. The attack on the palace immediately emboldened the various opposition factions – on the popular level the inhabitants of Matagalpa rose in open revolt while the Broad Opposition Front, composed of professionals and middle-class anti-Somoza elements, organised another general strike. Rioting and armed insurrection spread rapidly in September through the cities of Matagalpa, Masaya, Leon, Chinandega and Esteli as the inhabitants fought openly with what weapons they could lay their hands on against the National Guard.

With the cities in revolt, Somoza and the FSLN were now at open war with each other. The Nicaraguan Air Force bombed whole towns while Guard ground forces pounded the *barrios* with artillery and rocket fire. Eventually the towns were subdued, but although the FSLN was temporarily defeated, the war continued with a renewed guerrilla offensive in February 1979 against the towns of Diriamba, Masaya, Leon and Granada, followed by further assaults in March against towns in the north.

In May 1979 the final offensive against Somoza was launched on seven main battle fronts and one by one the towns and cities of Nicaragua fell to the advancing Sandinistas. On 9 June, the inhabitants of Managua took to the streets. Barricades were erected. In a last gesture of defiance Somoza took personal command of the counter-attack in the capital as the Guard shelled the *barrios orientales*, the heart of the insurrection, and aircraft and helicopter gunships bombed and strafed the rebel positions. Exhausted from three weeks of continuous fighting, the guerrillas withdrew from Managua on 27 June, but within two weeks the advancing Sandinista columns had the capital surrounded. Advance units entered the city on 13 July.

For Somoza it was all over. A last-ditch attempt to obtain military support from El Salvador and Guatemala failed, and on 17 July he resigned and fled to Miami. The next day opposition from the National Guard crumbled and the Sandinista Junta of National Reconstruction flew into Leon from Costa Rica.

Somocismo was dead, Anastasio Somoza himself being assassinated in Paraguay in September 1980. In its place the new five-member Sandinista junta was faced with the task of reassembling the country ravaged by a year of all-out civil war. But the war was far from over, as US efforts to destabilise what appeared to the Reagan administration as a major communist threat in the 'backyard' resulted in the emergence of armed Contra groups and the battle for Nicaragua continued. **Jonathan Reed**

Far left: Preparing petrol bombs in Matagalpa. Left: A Sandinista sniper waits for another patrol. Above: The legendary 'Commander Zero', Eden Pastora, whose commando raid on the National Palace in August 1978 humiliated the Somoza regime. Right: FSLN troops enter Managua.

The roots of the social conflict which led to the outbreak of open civil war in El Salvador in 1979 went back over 100 years. Between 1879 and 1882, three successive land reforms abolished collective ownership of the land from which the peasants scraped a subsistence living, and substituted a free market in land and labour. The result was the emergence of an economy based upon the export of coffee, and an extremely unequal pattern of land ownership. It made possible the creation of a powerful landed elite, usually known as the '14 families', which controlled a densely-settled peasantry.

The first major confrontation between the peasantry and the elite came in 1932, in the wake of the coup of December 1931 that had ousted the progressive President Arturo Araujo, who had held office a mere nine months. A hastily-organised popular uprising was easily crushed by the army under General Her-

nández Martínez, and an estimated 30,000 peasants were massacred as the landed elite re-imposed its grip upon the countryside. General Martínez ruled in dictatorial style until 1944, when a five-month democratic interlude ended in a military coup and a return to army rule, which continued until another brief period of democratic government between October 1960 and January 1961, ended by a further military coup in which the United States was directly involved.

Between 1961 and October 1979, El Salvador was ruled by the army-dominated Partido de Conciliación Nacional (PCN). During this period a degree of industrialisation based on the capital, San Salvador, produced a growing urban working class. At the same time, rapid population growth intensified pressure on the already densely settled land. The result was a dramatic increase in the number of landless peasants – from 12 per cent in 1961 to an estimated 65 per cent 20

Above left: Guerrillas of the left-wing FMLN engage an army patrol during street-fighting in El Salvador. By 1980, military repression had driven most of the country's opposition groups to armed rebellion. Above: FMLN guerrillas during an ambush on the vital Pan-American Highway. The rebels were able to gain control of large areas of the north and northeast, forcing the government troops onto the defensive.

lvador

years later.

The political impact of these developments was first felt in San Salvador, where José Napoleón Duarte, the candidate of the Partido Democrático Cristiano (PDC), which had been founded in 1960, was elected mayor in 1964. Political mobilisation and electoral competition were furthered by the foundation of the social-democratic Movimiento Nacional Revolucionario (MNR) led by Guillermo Ungo in 1968, and in the following year of the Unión Nacional Democrática, a front for the banned Partido Comunista Salvadoreño (PCS). These three political groups joined together to contest the 1972 presidential elections as the Unión Nacional Opositora (UNO), with Duarte as their candidate. Early returns showed an overwhelming victory for the opposition coalition, but President Sánchez Hernández was determined to hand over power to his designated military successor,

Colonel Arturo Armando Molina. He therefore imposed a news-blackout and announced that Molina had won a narrow victory. Taken aback by the scale of this fraud, progressive junior officers launched a coup attempt against Molina. It failed, and Duarte was snatched by the security forces from the home of a diplomat with whom he had sought asylum, beaten and bundled onto an aeroplane bound for Venezuela.

The events of 1972 – a decisive demonstration that the army was not prepared to lose power through the ballot-box – began a process of radicalisation which continued throughout the 1970s. UNO struggled on to contest the elections of 1977; once again, massive fraud kept UNO out of power, but this time substantial elements of the democratic opposition responded to the increasing repression and the blocking of all democratic change by deciding to take up arms against the regime. The relative complexity of the guerrilla alliance which later emerged was explained by the diverse political origins of the various groups, and by the different stages at which they joined the armed struggle.

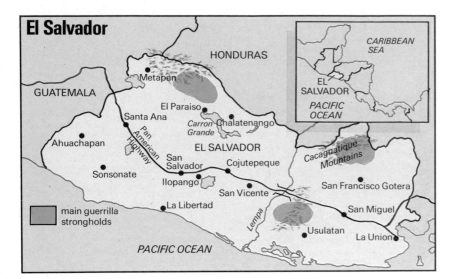

Far left: President Napoleón Duarte, whose attempt to construct a democratic alternative to the ultra-right military and the guerrilla left was challenged by Roberto D'Aubuisson (left), leader of the Arena party and alleged head of the death squads. Below: A group of ERP guerrilla fighters. The ERP was one of the most effective guerrilla groups.

The communist PCS had been involved briefly in an unsuccessful guerrilla campaign during the early 1960s, from which it had drawn the lesson that it would be more profitable to pursue its goals through electoral alliances. But in 1970, a group led by Salvador Cayetano Carpio broke away from the PCS to form the first of the guerrilla groups, which emerged in 1972 as the Fuerzas Populares de Liberación–Farabundo Martí (FPL–FM), operating from a base in the northwestern province of Chalatenango. Farabundo Martí, after whom the new group was named, had been a leading member of the PCS who had been executed during the 1932 uprising.

Radicalised urban supporters of the christian democrat PDC, disillusioned by the events of 1972, formed the Ejército Revolucionario Popular (ERP), which though initially committed to a Guevarist strategy of revolution carried out by a small guerrilla elite, subsequently adopted the aim of a mass insurrection. A dissident faction of the ERP formed the Fuerzas Armadas de la Resistencia Nacional (FARN) during the mid-1970s, and became increasingly committed to the creation of a broad opposition alliance. While the ERP set about establishing a base in the northeastern province of Morazán, FARN caught public attention with a series of highly lucrative kidnappings in the late 1970s. In November 1978, for example, two British bank executives were kidnapped, only being released the following July in return for a £4 million ransom.

Opting for armed resistance

The fourth of the guerrilla groups to emerge was the Partido Revolucionario de los Trabajadores Centroamericanos (PRTC), founded in 1975 and making its existence as a fighting force known in 1979. The array of guerrilla organisations was completed in 1980, when the PCS finally abandoned its stubborn faith in the electoral process and opted for armed struggle. Far from initiating the civil war, the orthodox communists were the last to join it.

By 1979 then, the political situation in El Salvador had undergone a rapid and startling transformation. Under Colonel Molina (1972-1977), the ruling military had continued to pursue its policy of repression, but had also introduced a number of limited reforms. These only contributed to the gathering crisis, however, by provoking the development of a number of extreme right-wing political and paramilitary groups, determined to resist change. The landowning elite refused to accept a minor land-reform programme promoted by the United States, and Molina was forced to accept as his successor General Carlos Humberto Romero, the hardline minister of defence and head of the paramilitary rural security network, Organización Democrática Nacionalista (Orden). Under Romero the right-wing death squads, such as the Unión Guerrera Blanca (UGB), extended their operations, and the already extremely poor human-rights record in El Salvador deteriorated in dramatic fashion.

The sequence of events leading to open civil war was precipitated by the 'reformist' coup of 15 October 1979, in which Romero was overthrown by junior officers led by Colonel Adolfo Arnaldo Majano. At first, the democratic forces of UNO welcomed the new regime, and MNR leader Ungo accepted an invitation to join the junta, but it soon became clear that the security forces would block all reform. As the

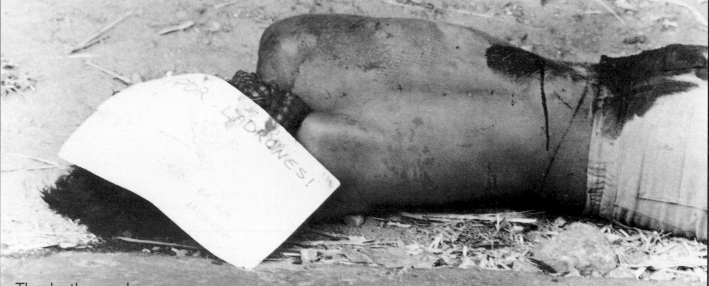

The death squads

Above: A body in the street, and a message from the death squads.

Between 1979 and 1984, over 30,000 people lost their lives as a result of the civil war in El Salvador – an estimated three-quarters of them civilian victims of right-wing death squads. Operating under a variety of grandiose and gruesome titles, such as the Fuerzas Armadas de Liberación Nacional-Guerra de Exterminación (FALANGE), or the Escuadrón de la Muerte (EM), the death squads were often little more than a front for members of the security forces, supplementing their already fairly indiscriminate repression of suspected supporters of the left-wing opposition with a freelance campaign of kidnapping, torture and murder.

As well as the 30,000-strong armed forces, there were a number of police and security organisations in El Salvador, all ultimately responsible to the minister of defence and national security. Of these, members of both the Treasury Police and the National Guard were deeply implicated in the activities of the death squads. In December 1980, for example, three American nuns and a woman missionary were sexually assaulted and murdered. Six members of the National Guard were subsequently arrested for the crime, but pressure from the armed forces and the extreme right prevented them from ever appearing before a court.

The death squads first became active during the mid-1970s, at the time when left-wing guerrilla groups were mounting a series of kidnappings and assassinations. In June 1977, the Unión Guerrera Blanca, which accused sections of the Catholic church of collaborating with the leftists, issued a warning that all Jesuits had one month to leave the country or be 'executed'. It adopted the slogan: 'Be a patriot! Kill a priest!' On 27 November 1980, a school in which leaders of the opposition FDR were preparing for a press conference was surrounded by police and troops. A group of some 20 heavily-armed men in plain-clothes entered the building and arrested five members of the opposition whose bodies, tortured and mutilated, were later found on the shores of Lake Ilopango. Responsibility for the murders was later claimed by a group styling itself the Brigada Maximiliano Hernández Martínez. This particular death squad had gained notoriety as a result of an earlier incident, in which the beheaded bodies of four young men were dumped in one of the capital's main streets along with leaflets proclaiming 'Long live El Salvador! Long live the massacre of 1932!'

The majority of deaths were the work of the semi-official 'Orden', however. This had been established in 1968 as a paramilitary network of informers and armed auxiliaries in order to back up the National Guard. Orden was closely associated with the former National Guard major and intelligence chief, Roberto 'Bob' D'Aubuisson, head of the ultra-right-wing Arena party.

D'Aubuisson was the alleged head of the El Salvador death squads, and was named by former US ambassador Robert White as being responsible for the murder in 1980 of Archbishop Oscar Romero. No evidence of direct involvement was ever produced, however, and D'Aubuisson stood as a candidate in the 1984 presidential elections against José Napoleón Duarte.

Left: An army execution squad searches the pockets of its victims during counter-insurgency operations in an El Salvador village. Wholesale and indiscriminate killings during 'search and destroy' operations by government forces led to world-wide condemnation and strengthened guerrilla support among the peasants.

paramilitary groups stepped up their activities, the junta fell apart. During 1980, the reformers were driven out and replaced by individuals prepared to collaborate with the hard-line approach of the armed forces. The most striking change was the return of Duarte, former leader of UNO and himself previously a victim of the arbitrary actions of the military. Duarte entered the junta in March 1980, and became its head in December.

By that time the battle lines had been drawn up and the civil war was well under way. The unarmed opposition groups had been progressively radicalised by the brutal repression of peaceful political activities. The climax came on 22 January 1980 when a 250,000-strong march through San Salvador ended with unarmed demonstrators being massacred by the security forces on the steps of the cathedral. Two months later Archbishop Oscar Romero, an outspoken critic of the government and the extreme right,

was assassinated by a member of a death squad as he celebrated mass. Faced with these outrages, the MNR and the christian democrats joined with other opposition groups linked to student and trade union organisations to form the Frente Democrático Revolucionario (FDR).

The PCS, meanwhile, had put its name to a joint communique with the FPL and FARN, issued on 10 January 1980, calling for an armed popular revolution. The guerrilla groups finally united on a permanent basis on 21 October with the formation of the Frente Farabundo Martí de Liberación Nacional (FMLN). The FDR pledged its support to the armed struggle when six of its leaders were assassinated late in November 1980 during the severe repression which followed a series of general strikes which it had organised.

Fighting increased throughout 1980, and allegations of direct Cuban and Nicaraguan backing for the

FDR-FMLN led to a rapid increase in US military assistance to El Salvador. In spite of a temporary halt to supplies of 'non-lethal' military equipment imposed by President Carter after the murder of three American nuns by members of the El Salvador National Guard in December 1980, aid was resumed in January 1981, and extended for the first time to include 'lethal' items such as M16 rifles and Huey UH-1H helicopters.

Guerrilla pressure increased, however. During the spring of 1981 fighting centred around the province of Morazán, and army casualties were particularly heavy. The FDR-FMLN also mounted a series of bomb and sabotage attacks in and around the capital, and electricity supplies to large parts of San Salvador

Above: Men of the elite American trained Atlacatl Battalion in hot pursuit of a guerrilla unit after an ambush on the Pan-American Highway in July 1984.

were temporarily cut off. By May 1981, the guerrillas claimed control of substantial areas of Morazán, Chalatenango, Cabañas and San Vicente Provinces, and by June the army had been forced to withdraw from its key communications base near the Chichontepec volcano, east of San Salvador.

The government counter-offensive which opened on 8 July was spearheaded by the elite American-trained Atlacatl Battalion. During this operation, which was intended to clear Cabañas and Chalatenango of rebel forces, large numbers of peasants were forced to seek refuge across the Honduran border by the indiscriminate use of bombing by government forces. There were also widespread allegations that army units were massacring innocent peasants whom they suspected of sympathising with the guerrillas.

While US backing for the El Salvador government prevented the FDR-FMLN from successfully launching the kind of all-out national offensive which had brought the Sandinistas victory in Nicaragua in 1979, the government forces were unable to prevent the guerrillas from consolidating their control of many areas, especially in the north and northeast. By late 1981, it had become apparent that neither side was strong enough to gain an early victory, and that the civil war would be long and costly. While casualties

of the war and the murder campaigns of the right-wing death squads mounted, a systematic FDR-FMLN campaign of economic sabotage hit El Salvador very severely. During 1981, the rebels destroyed 25 major bridges, including the strategic Golden Bridge over the Lempa River on 15 October. The guerrillas also staged a number of operations designed to demonstrate the inability of the government to exercise effective control over important towns and highways.

One of the guerrillas' most spectacular successes came on 27 January 1982, when some 100 rebels attacked the airbase at Ilopango, east of San Salvador, destroying an estimated 50 per cent of the Salvadorean Air Force. The United States swiftly made good the losses, however, and provided El Salvador with $55 million-worth of emergency military aid. The new US-supplied equipment included C-123 transports, Cessna 0-2 reconnaissance aircraft and a number of Huey UH-1H helicopters.

Operation Well-Being

Despite American assistance, the El Salvador Army was unable to seize the strategic initiative, and continued to react to guerrilla activities by launching large, clumsy and generally unsuccessful search-and-destroy operations which did little damage to the guerrillas, but alienated peasant support. FDR-FMLN forces continued to be able to occupy many rural towns, retreating when the army arrived and returning when it withdrew. In June 1983, however, the government initiated a 'National Campaign Plan', which attempted to replace the discredited sledge-hammer approach to counter-insurgency with a Vietnam-type pacification programme, adopted on the recommendation of US advisers. The new policy was tested in Operation Well-Being, which was launched on 10 June, with the army seeking to make contact with and destroy guerrilla forces in San Vicente Province. The rebels failed to oblige, however, and though the army was able to reoccupy previously guerrilla-held territory, there were no decisive engagements. During July, on the other hand, large guerrilla units inflicted heavy casualties on government troops on several occasions. While the rebels had spread uncertainty and demoralisation among government troops in the past by releasing their prisoners, by the summer of 1983 few prisoners were being taken by either side.

In the search for a solution to the situation, the United States consistently backed Duarte, describing him as a centrist between the extremes of the FDR-FMLN on the one side and the right-wing on the other, represented by Major 'Bob' D'Aubuisson, a former Salvadorean intelligence chief. After a series of elections in which the FDR could only have participated at the risk of physical annihilation, Duarte finally emerged as president in May 1983. This improved the national image of El Salvador, and the US Reagan administration was able to counter criticism of its Central American policy and continue the supply of military equipment to the regime. But though the El Salvador Air Force, in particular, was able to deploy much greater firepower during 1984, the threat of a new and more dangerous guerrilla offensive was widely discussed, and in October President Duarte, backed by Washington, opened peace negotiations with the FDR-FMLN. The depth of the conflict inside El Salvador, however, made any permanent solution to the crisis unlikely. **Paul Cammack**

Key Weapons

THE F-86
SABRE

The North American F-86 Sabre was arguably the best of the early jet fighters. Not only did it establish air superiority for the UN forces during the Korean War with more than 10 communist MiG-15s claimed destroyed for every Sabre lost, but it also equipped the fighter forces of virtually all Western nations at the height of the Cold War. The Sabre design was originally based on that of the North American Company's FJ-1 Fury straight-wing naval fighter and was intended as a successor to the first-generation P-80 and P-84 jet fighters. However, it soon became apparent that such an aircraft would be incapable of reaching the 967km/h (600mph) maximum speed specified by the US Army Air Force (USAAF) in May 1945. Consequently the aircraft was entirely redesigned with swept-back wings in the light of German research work that had been captured at the end of World War II and made available to American aircraft manufacturers. The outcome was a fighter which was capable of a maximum speed of 1086km/h (675mph) in level flight and could exceed the speed of sound in a shallow dive.

The prototype XP-86 first flew on 1 October 1947 and production F-86s reached the US Air Force (USAF) 1st Fighter Group in February 1949 when the aircraft was given the name Sabre. The early model F-86A (the designation F for fighter had replaced P for pursuit in 1948) was powered by a 2360kg (5200lb) thrust General Electric J47 turbojet. In order to improve the low-speed handling characteristics of the fighter, whose 35 degree swept-back wing was optimised for high-speed flight, automatic wing leading-edge slats were fitted which would open to delay the onset of a stall. Other advanced control features included power-boosted ailerons, which remained operable at speeds that would 'freeze' manually-operated surfaces, and hydraulically-powered speed brakes fitted to the sides of the rear fuselage. The cockpit was pressurised and its bubble canopy provided the pilot with an excellent all-round view. However, the F-86's armament of six 0·5in machine guns – the same as a P-51 Mustang – was less satisfactory; the weight of a three-second burst was 7kg (15lb) compared to the 18kg (40lb) three-second burst of the MiG-15's 37mm and two 23mm cannon. The unsatisfactory performance of the Mk 18 gunsight of the early Sabres further exacerbated the faults with the armament until a new sight, the more effective A-1CM, was introduced, linked to a ranging radar mounted in the lip of the Sabre's nose intake.

By the end of 1950 three USAF fighter groups were operating the F-86A and one of these (the 4th Fighter Group, later retitled the 4th Fighter-Interceptor Wing) was hurriedly deployed to Korea with the appearance of communist Chinese-piloted MiG-15s in the fighting. On 17 December 1950 Sabres and MiG-15s met in combat for the first time in an area south of the Yalu River, later christened 'MiG Alley'. The outcome was a victory for the USAF and the first of the 792 MiGs claimed by Sabre pilots. This enormous total suggests that the F-86 was a totally superior aeroplane to the MiG-15, but in fact the MiG was faster at some altitudes, had a better rate of climb and, as has been seen, heavier armament (although the rate of fire was slower). Therefore, while the superior tactical skills of the USAF pilots in Korea, combined with the good handling qualities and rate of roll of the Sabre, ensured that the threat of communist Chinese jet fighters was suppressed, it was apparent that the

Previous page: A 'fluid four' flight of F-86 Sabres belonging to the 51st Fighter-Interceptor Wing somewhere in Korea. Top: These F-86As, destined for the 4th Fighter-Interceptor Wing, are waiting to be delivered from the North American factory at Los Angeles. Above: This F-86E has two 'kills' credited as indicated by the stars on the fuselage.

Above right: The F-86H; this is one of the first 113 models of that type as indicated by the armament of six 0·5in machine guns. Inset left: An Italian Air Force F-86E. Inset right: An F-86H armed with the standard armament of four 20mm cannon. Right: Three F-86s of the 51st Fighter-Interceptor Wing flying through a Korean mountain range.

North American F-86F Sabre

Type Single-seat air-superiority fighter and fighter-bomber
Dimensions Span 11·91m (39ft 1in); length 11·44m (37ft 6in); height 4·48m (14ft 8in)
Weight Empty 4970kg (10,950lb); maximum take-off 9350kg (20,610lb)
Powerplant One 2680kg (5910lb) thrust General Electric J47-GE-27 turbojet

Performance Maximum speed at 11,000m (36,000ft) Mach 0·9, or 965 km/h (600mph)
Range Combat radius 740km (460 miles); ferry range 2454km (1525 miles)
Ceiling 15,000m (49,200ft)

Armament Six 0·5in M3 machine guns with 267 rounds of ammunition per gun; up to 910kg (2000lb) of ordnance on four underwing hardpoints, including AIM-9 Sidewinder AAMs, bombs, rockets, napalm tanks, or a tactical nuclear weapon

premier USAF fighter had shortcomings which required urgent action to rectify.

The F-86E model of the Sabre, which reached the combat theatre with the 51st Fighter-Interceptor Wing in October 1951, was a refined development of the F-86A, with an 'all flying' tail (in which the entire horizontal tail surface pivoted to act as an elevator) and fully-powered flight controls. These improvements in controllability did nothing to alleviate the Sabre's most serious problem, which was an inferior high altitude top speed in comparison with the MiG-15. This shortcoming was tackled by the F-86F, which first appeared in Korea in June 1952 and thereafter rapidly supplanted the earlier Sabre models with the 4th and 51st Fighter-Interceptor Wings. The F-86F was powered by the 2680kg (5910lb) thrust J47-GE-27, which provided an additional 320kg (700lb) of thrust, and was fitted with the new '6-3' wing. This wing was so called because it incorporated an extended leading-edge, which increased the wing's chord by 6in (15cm) at the root and 3in (7·5cm) at the tip. The improvements in performance conferred by these modifications were dramatic; maximum operating altitude was increased by 1220m (4000ft) to a combat ceiling of 15,850m (52,000ft), and both rate of climb and maximum speed were appreciably greater. One backward step was the deletion of the wing leading-edge slats, which resulted in difficult low-speed handling characteristics, and in 1955 the USAF directed that slats be retro-fitted to all F-86Fs. This model, unlike earlier Sabres, had a useful ground-attack secondary capability. Four underwing pylons could carry an assortment of ordn-

ance, including bombs, napalm tanks, rockets and tactical nuclear weapons. A number of F-86Fs were experimentally fitted with a 20mm cannon armament, but most retained the unsatisfactory 0·5in machine guns.

In addition to re-equipping the 4th and 51st Fighter-Interceptor Wings in Korea, F-86Fs were also supplied to the 8th and 18th Fighter-Bomber Wings and No. 2 Squadron South African Air Force before hostilities ceased. Although the demands of the 'hot war' in Korea were an absolute priority, the tensions between the Warsaw Pact and Nato in Europe and a much exaggerated perceived threat to the United States from Soviet long-range strategic bombers created urgent demands elsewhere for high-performance fighters. Accordingly Sabre production was accelerated, with two North American factories in the United States building the type and a third production line being established by Canadair in Canada. Over 1000 F-86E and F fighters were accepted into service by the USAF in fiscal year 1953 and at the peak of its service in 1955 Sabres equipped 44 wings of the USAF. By this time most of the early-model F-86E and F Sabres had been phased out of frontline service with the USAF, to be passed on to the reserve units of the Air National Guard or to more than a score of allied and friendly air forces under the Military Assistance Program. There remained the F-86H fighter-bomber and F-86D and L all-weather interceptor versions of the Sabre; these served on with active-duty USAF units until the early 1960s.

Although the USAF had intended to use the F-86H Sabre as an air-superiority fighter, it proved unsuited to this role and was to specialise in ground-attack and

Above: Four Canadair Sabre 4s belonging to No. 92 Squadron of the RAF begin a loop manoeuvre. Right: Two RAF Canadair Sabre 4s taking off from their airfield.

Below: A South African Canadair Sabre 6 displays its weapons' capability.

tactical nuclear strike missions. The F-86H differed from earlier Sabres in its powerplant, a 4050kg (8920lb) thrust General Electric J73-GE-3 engine; as this required a larger air intake, modifications had to be made to the fuselage and these presented an opportunity to provide increased internal fuel tankage. The extra drag from the new fuselage largely offset the benefits of increased thrust from the J73 engine. Furthermore, the F-86H's greater loaded weight led to a high wing-loading, which together

Top: A Canadair Sabre 5 belonging to the Royal Canadian Air Force (RCAF); this is one of 370 models built for the RCAF. Above: An Australian-built Sabre armed with two 30mm Aden cannon. Commonwealth Aircraft Corporation built 112 Sabre variants and this example belongs to the Malaysian Air Force.

Above: One of the two F-86D prototypes. Right: An F-86D in flight near Edwards air force base in California. The F-86D was the all-weather interceptor F-86, identifiable by the prominent nose radar. It was armed with 2·75in Mighty Mouse rockets in place of the machine guns.

with poor engine performance at altitude ruled out the type's employment in air-to-air combat. However, it proved to be an effective ground-attack aircraft, not least because the Sabre's machine gun armament was at last replaced by a quartet of 20mm cannon. By 1958 the F-86H had been retired from active duty with the USAF in favour of the F-100 Super Sabre.

In 1953 the Sabre entered service with the USAF's Air Defense Command as an all-weather interceptor, responsible for the defence of the American homeland. The F-86D version intended for this role was produced in considerable numbers (2504 were accepted by the USAF between 1951 and 1955) and in mid-1955 F-86Ds made up more than 70 per cent of Air Defense Command's interceptor force. Its flight performance was considerably better than that of the two-seat F-89 and F-94 interceptors. However, in order to compensate for the lack of a second crew member, the fighter's fire-control system was automated and this complex equipment was unreliable and fragile. In theory, the nose-mounted radar and the E-4 fire-control system linked to an autopilot could compute a target's position, set up a collision-course attack and then fire salvoes of 2·75in rockets when the target had closed to a distance of 460m (500 yds). Yet despite numerous modification programmes this equipment was never entirely satisfactory. However, the threat from Soviet strategic bombers was mistakenly believed to be so serious that the USAF persevered with this unpromising interceptor as the best system immediately available. In 1956 the F-86L began to replace the D-model. The new aircraft was fitted with a data-link, which allowed interceptions to be directed automatically from ground-control stations. A third variant, the F-86K, was a simplified all-weather interceptor, armed with four 20mm cannon and two AIM-9B Sidewinder AAMs.

The USAF was the major Sabre operator and eventually accepted a total of 5893 of these fighters into service. A parallel design, the FJ-2/4 Fury was built as a carrier fighter for the US Navy. Among numerous foreign operators of the type were the West German Luftwaffe and the Royal Air Force, which flew the Sabre as a stop-gap fighter pending availability of the Hunter. The Pakistani Air Force flew F-86Fs in combat against the Indian Air Force during the wars of 1965 and 1971, and Nationalist Chinese Sabres fought with communist Chinese jets over Quemoy in the late 1950s. A total of more than 9000 Sabres were produced, including licence production in Canada, Australia, Italy and Japan, and it was undoubtedly one of the classic fighter aircraft of aviation history.

Above: A flight of Royal Norwegian Air Force F-86Ks. This variant of the F-86 was designed to provide Nato air forces with an all-weather fighter.

Below: An F-86D belonging to an Air National Guard (ANG) unit. The F-86 remained in ANG service until 1970.

Stalemate in Ulster

Northern Ireland, 1978-84

In August 1978 Roy Mason, the secretary of state for Northern Ireland, announced the establishment, with generous government assistance, of a major sports-car factory by the Delorean Motor Company on a site near West Belfast. This was hailed as a substantial economic coup which would provide 2000 badly-needed jobs. Although the factory was built and went into production in record time, the venture proved to be an unmitigated disaster. By 1982 the company had collapsed leaving debts of £100 million. But the Delorean example reflects both a continuing belief that part of Northern Ireland's problems stem from economic and social deprivation, and also an apparently unquenchable hope that support for terrorism can be bought off with jobs, that violence can be 'killed with kindness'. Since Northern Ireland suffers over 20 per cent unemployment, this is an understandable attitude.

The encouragement of economic development is but part of the three-fold approach which the British government has adopted in attempting to 'solve' the Northern Ireland problem. The other two policy elements are security – the enforcement of law and order – and repeated efforts to secure a political framework for the Protestant and Catholic communities to share power. In terms of security, both Roy Mason and Humphrey Atkins, his successor after the Conservative election victory in June 1979, persevered with the 'Ulsterisation' policies begun in the mid-1970s. The General Officer Commanding between 1977 and 1979, Sir Timothy Creasey, however, believed that the practice of 'police primacy' was impeding an efficient security operation and 'tying soldiers' hands' in the battle against the terrorists. By

contrast, Sir Kenneth Newman, the chief constable, thought that a tough, predominantly military effort would be disastrous.

The murder of Lord Mountbatten near his holiday home in the Irish Republic and the death of 18 soldiers at Warrenpoint, County Down, on the same day in August 1979 prompted a reappraisal of security policy. The government decided not to change the Ulsterisation policy, but eased the tension between army and police by appointing Sir Maurice Oldfield to be 'security coordinater'. Oldfield's background was in neither the military nor the police, but in the intelligence services, and he was popularly believed to have been the model for John Le Carré's fictional spymaster, George Smiley. Oldfield's appointment, and the arrival of new men – Sir Richard Lawson and Jack Hermon – to head the army and police, restored a cooperative atmosphere to the security forces. Oldfield stayed until late 1980 and was replaced by another senior official with intelligence experience, but police primacy had finally been established and the post of coordinator effectively lapsed during 1981.

Like previous secretaries of state, Atkins engaged in a 'political initiative'. Early in 1980 he arranged a conference to discuss possible new political structures, but the talks were boycotted by the Official Unionist Party (OUP) and they broke down without agreement during the summer. By this time, however, the secretary of state was becoming preoccupied with the deteriorating situation in the Province's prisons.

Since 1976 prisoners in the 'H-Blocks' (so called because of their design) at the Maze and Magilligan

Below: The funeral, with full paramilitary honours, of Provisional IRA hunger striker Bobby Sands, who died in the Maze prison on 5 May 1981. The ability of the Provisionals still to mount such a public display in the 1980s demonstrated their power of endurance, even in the face of highly successful operations by the security forces.

prisons had been protesting against the abolition of 'special category' status for convicted terrorists. The relatively low-key 'blanket protest', in which prisoners refused to wear prison clothes, gradually gathered strength until in 1980 some 300 protesters (out of a total prison population of 2500) were participating. Outside the prisons the Republican 'H-Block Information Centre' mounted a publicity campaign in Ireland and elsewhere to secure support for 'political status'.

When the authorities refused to move on the question of political status, in October 1980 the protesters at the Maze began a series of selective hunger strikes. The hunger strike is a particularly emotive weapon in the Irish nationalist armoury. It has been used at intervals throughout this century against both British and Irish governments. Typified as an act of selfless moral courage, the hunger strike can generate emotional public support to an extent that violent action can never do. It also raises acute difficulties for the government, who are put on the defensive and, if they refuse to concede the strikers' demands, run the risk of appearing heartless and intransigent. In late 1980 there was a great wave of Catholic sympathy for the protest and a series of large demonstrations both north and south of the border. Only as the first striker seemed on the point of death was an unexpected compromise over prison clothing reached and the strike ended on 18 December.

Martyrs to the cause

In the New Year, however, the agreement broke down and on 1 March 1981 Bobby Sands, the Provisional commanding officer in the Maze, began a solitary fast. At intervals of about a fortnight further prisoners, carefully chosen from a wide geographical spread of home districts so as to achieve maximum impact, joined the strike. Early in April Sands' protest was given a massive boost by his election as MP for the border constituency of Fermanagh and South Tyrone. On 5 May he died after 66 days without food. Nine more hunger strikers starved themselves to death between 12 May and 20 August 1981.

Each death was marked by bouts of rioting in Belfast and Londonderry although the Provisional leadership reined in terrorist action somewhat lest violence should erode the widespread popular support for the H-Block campaign. Nevertheless, on 19 May 1981 five soldiers of the Royal Green Jackets were killed near Camlough, south Armagh – the most serious single attack since the Warrenpoint killings.

Deaths in Ulster 1969-84

	1969	1972	1975	1978	1980	Total: July 1969-October 1984
Army	0	103	14	14	3	379
UDR	–	26	6	7	4	147
RUC	1	17	11	10	4	200
Civilian	12	322	216	50	15	1686

On the political side, two H-Block candidates were elected to the Dublin parliament in the June general election. Sands' successor in Fermanagh and South Tyrone, after a by-election in August, was another Provisional nominee, Owen Carron. Yet in the face of the British government's steadfast refusal to concede political status, the hunger strikes gradually ran out of steam. The campaign was called off in October after the remaining six strikers' families, strongly supported by Catholic churchmen, announced that they would request medical intervention if a striker neared death. The new secretary of state, James Prior, who succeeded Atkins in September, was able to help the Provisionals save a little face by offering some minor concessions on prison conditions.

The chief legacy of the hunger strikes, other than bitterness and increased community polarisation, was the Provisionals' move towards a more political stance. The by-election victories in Fermanagh and South Tyrone demonstrated the potential of electoral campaigning. They did not, however, plan to lay down their guns. At the Provisional Sinn Fein *Ard*

Below: A protest outside the courts in Belfast against the controversial use of 'supergrass' informers which severely hit both Republican and Loyalist paramilitary groups and led to a large number of successful convictions for terrorist offences. Below left: The H-Blocks of the Maze prison contain some of Northern Ireland's most dangerous terrorists.

Above: British troops on patrol in Northern Ireland had become part of everyday life for the people of that war-torn province. Above right: A fortress-like British Army observation post. Although the need for such defences remained, the number of British Army casualties was much lower in the 1978-84 period than earlier in the Troubles.

Below right: Prime Ministers Margaret Thatcher of Britain and Garret Fitzgerald of Ireland at a summit meeting on 7 November 1983. Though Anglo-Irish security cooperation improved, there was little progress toward a political initiative to settle the Northern Ireland problem.

Feis (conference) in Dublin in November 1981 the organisation's publicity officer Danny Morrison dramatically outlined a double strategy, 'with a ballot paper in one hand and an Armalite rifle in the other'. Terrorist attacks have continued, although the number of deaths has dropped – 108 people died in 1981, the year of the hunger strikes, but in 1983 the total was 74, the second lowest since 1970.

On the political side Provisional Sinn Fein (the legal party wing of the Provisional IRA) challenged the constitutionalist Social Democratic and Labour Party (SDLP) for leadership of the Catholic community. They polled 10 per cent of the votes in the October 1982 Northern Ireland Assembly elections and 13 per cent in the 1983 general election, when Gerry Adams won West Belfast constituency. In the 1984 European elections, however, their share of the vote increased no further and the SDLP (with 22 per cent of the vote) remains as yet the leading Catholic party. One problem which arises from the Provisionals' two-pronged strategy is the comparative incompatibility of political and military action. While they are committed to violent methods, their constituency of political support will remain largely limited to the hard Republican core of the Catholic community – who do not constitute enough votes to defeat the SDLP.

Within the Provisionals there is a tension between those who want to develop the political side and those who wish to stick with a military strategy. After the Harrods bomb, which killed five and injured 90 in London just before Christmas 1983, the Provisionals announced that the action had not been authorised. They apparently had no such qualms, however, about the bomb attack on the Grand Hotel at Brighton in October 1984 which almost killed Prime Minister Thatcher.

The Provisionals' rivals in terror, the Irish National Liberation Army (INLA), have never had any doubts about the most violent tactics. Supposedly led by the so-called 'mad dog' Dominic McGlinchey, they have maintained an unequivocably military stance and do not hesitate to engage in sectarian assassinations. Their most spectacular attack was the car bomb which killed the Conservative Northern Ireland spokesman, Airey Neave, at the House of Commons in March 1979. In a particularly horrifying incident in November 1983, INLA gunmen burst into a Gospel Hall in Darkley, County Armagh, during a service and fired on the congregation with automatic weapons. Three men were killed and seven injured.

After Darkley, in protest against what they believed to be a weak government attitude towards security, the Official Unionists withdrew from participation in the Northern Ireland Assembly. In Octo-

ber 1982 James Prior had set up the elected Assembly as an advisory body, but in the hope that sufficient cross-community support could be forthcoming to give it some executive powers. But the nationalist parties refused to take part and only the two Unionist Parties (Paisley's Democratic Unionist Party and the OUP), together with the moderate Alliance Party have attended Assembly sessions. Without nationalist cooperation the body will remain powerless.

Institutional innovation has not been confined to representative and administrative bodies, but has also affected the judicial process. At an early stage in the 'Troubles' it was found virtually impossible to maintain a conventional system of trial by jury because of the problem of intimidation, both of witnesses and jurors. In 1973 the government adopted the recommendations of a commission chaired by Lord Diplock and for the duration of the emergency established a system of non-jury trials for specifically terrorist offences – the so-called 'Diplock courts'. In the Irish Republic a similar non-jury 'Special Criminal Court' has operated since 1972. In order to compensate for the reluctance of witnesses to give prosecution evidence, the new courts also established the easier admissibility of confessions and this consequently put considerable pressure on the police to extract such statements from suspects.

During the late 1970s there was a growing number of complaints about police interrogation techniques. In 1975 there were 180 allegations of ill-treatment, and in 1977 there were 671. In May 1978 an Amnesty International report detailed 78 cases of alleged abuses. The government responded by setting up the Bennett Committee into Police Interrogation Procedures, which reported in March 1979. The committee noted that some injuries sustained by prisoners while in police custody were not self-inflicted. It was undoubtedly true, as the chief constable admitted, that there were some 'bad apples' in the Royal Ulster Constabulary (RUC). Bennett proposed a number of safeguards, such as the installation of closed-circuit TV in interview rooms, and independent medical examinations. Since their introduction the number of complaints alleging ill-treatment has markedly declined.

Another development in the courts has been the use of 'supergrasses' – informers granted some immunity from prosecution in return for giving evidence against former colleagues. In the first supergrass trial to be concluded (during April 1983) 14 Loyalists received life sentences for over 60 crimes. In August 35 persons were convicted on the basis of statements made by Christopher Black, a former Provisional. One of the most important informants was another ex-Provisional, Robert Quigley, whose information led to the arrest of over 70 people during 1983. In May 1984 nine Londonderry men and women convicted on his evidence were sentenced to a total of 1000 years' imprisonment for a wide variety of terrorist offences.

The practice of using supergrasses has been vigorously resisted by both Republicans and Loyalists. The technique has undoubtedly damaged the terrorist organisations; by mid-1984 it was estimated that about 450 persons had been charged on supergrass evidence. In 1983 the wife and stepfather of informer Harry Kirkpatrick were kidnapped by the INLA in an effort to persuade Kirkpatrick and other potential informers to stay loyal to their terrorist colleagues. Both people were later released unharmed. The use of supergrasses, however, and the conviction of persons on the sometimes uncorroborated evidence of paid

Below: Sinn Fein leader Gerry Adams (left) and Martin Galvin of the pro-IRA American group Noraid at the 12 August 1984 rally in Belfast at which Sean Downes was killed. Right: The sequence of events that led to Downes' death: he rushes forward (above) as the RUC attempt to arrest Galvin who had been banned from entering Ulster, and an RUC man fires a plastic bullet at point-blank range (right). Downes' body (far right) shows the massive damage that plastic bullets could inflict at close range.

informants, does run the serious risk of undermining faith in the whole judicial system if the practice is misused.

One clear development from the late 1970s onwards was an increase in Anglo-Irish consultation and cooperation, which was powerfully boosted by the shocked Southern Irish reaction to the Mountbatten murder. But cooperation has not developed entirely smoothly. The spread of H-Block agitation into the Republic strained relations. A much more serious breach occurred during the Falklands crisis in 1982, when the Dublin government broke away from the EEC policy of support for Britain and refused to back economic sanctions against Argentina. Gradually the governments have repaired the links and at a meeting in November 1983 Margaret Thatcher and the Irish prime minister, Dr Garret FitzGerald, reaffirmed their joint commitment to defeat the men of violence.

Cooperation over the border

Although much of the Anglo-Irish security cooperation has been at a day-to-day, unspectacular but vital level, such as regular meetings between the RUC and the Irish police, the Dublin government has also made some notable moves to counter Loyalist accusations that the Republic is a 'safe haven' for terrorists. In 1976 the Irish parliament introduced a Criminal Law Jurisdiction Act which allowed people to be tried in the Republic for offences committed in the United Kingdom. The first convictions were secured in December 1981, when two Provisionals who had escaped from Crumlin Road jail in Belfast were sentenced to 10 years' imprisonment in Dublin. In July 1982 Gerard Tuite was convicted on evidence supplied from Scotland Yard for possessing explosives in London. The Republic has also begun to extradite suspects to Northern Ireland. Dominic McGlinchey, who was captured on 17 March 1984 after a dramatic period on the run, was almost immediately handed over to the RUC. Nevertheless, when 38 Republican prisoners escaped from the Maze in a deeply embarrassing breakdown of security in September 1983, it was believed that most of the 19 men not quickly recaptured had taken refuge in the Republic.

In September 1984 James Prior gave up the job of Northern Ireland Secretary and was replaced by Douglas Hurd. By late 1984, although cross-border security cooperation remained satisfactory, and could possibly even be improved further, the political and security scene was otherwise not very encouraging. The Assembly remained largely an irrelevance. The death of Sean Downes on 12 August 1984, after being hit by a plastic bullet at a Provisional rally to mark the anniversary of internment, added force to existing worries about the use of plastic bullets for crowd control. The event was also televised around the world and evoked memories of the first civil rights demonstrations in the late 1960s. It was as if nothing had changed. On the same day, sombrely marking the comprehensive nature of political violence in Northern Ireland, Sergeant William McDonald of the RUC died nine months after being seriously injured by a Provisionals' bomb set off during a social studies class in the Ulster Polytechnic. After the bombing at the Conservative Party conference at Brighton on 12 October 1984, no one in Britain was likely to forget that the Northern Ireland problem continued to be unsolved.   **Keith Jeffery**

Warrenpoint

The IRA ambush the Paras

On the same August Bank Holiday – 27 August 1979 – that Lord Mountbatten was assassinated at Mullaghmore in the Irish Republic, the British Army suffered its heaviest casualty toll from a single incident in Ireland since 1921 at Warrenpoint in County Down, Northern Ireland. Eighteen soldiers were killed in a neatly executed double ambush carried out with two huge bombs and supporting gunfire. It was an obvious military victory for the IRA and it brought them added credit because Mullaghmore and Warrenpoint were seen as a deliberately-executed double attack conceived by a fiendishly cunning central command in response to accusations that it was defeated. In fact a great deal of luck contributed to the heavy casualty toll at Warrenpoint and the timing of the two attacks was almost certainly coincidental.

Warrenpoint was another incident in a long line of IRA lorry and culvert bombs aimed at passing patrols or military convoys. Any road that periodically carries troop movements is at risk from these tactics and roads close to the border with the Irish Republic are prime targets because of the proximity of a relatively safe haven. The successive governments in Dublin have opposed the IRA but the application of resources for a policing of the border with Northern Ireland comparable in scale to the British effort would impose a severe strain on the Irish economy. Added to this is a ponderous, slow-motion form of communication between the security forces of the Irish Republic and the United Kingdom and that makes it difficult for a quick reaction force to be mobilised south of the border to prevent a terrorist's getaway.

Arranging an ambush

The road through Warrenpoint leads to the British barracks at Newry and it runs just metres from the border. The stretch upon which the IRA executed their ambush is a good dual-carriageway divided from the Irish Republic by the narrow waters of Carlingford Lough. The garrison at Newry was one company strong – at this time, C Company, the 2nd Battalion, Parachute Regiment (2 Para) – and the IRA knew that the garrison was relieved at intervals. When this happened the relief company would come speeding down the road in soft-skinned vehicles – a tempting target, but only if the attacker could be very precise in his timing. It would be a matter of seconds before the relief convoy was past any danger point, so the terrorists needed good observation posts south of the border and a reliable, instant detonation system to be sure of causing carnage.

The IRA chose bombs that would be detonated by radio signal. Although this met all the criteria for precise control, it was not infallible; British counter-

Below: The wreckage of an army truck in which six men of the 2nd Battalion, the Parachute Regiment were killed in the first stage of the IRA attack at Warrenpoint on 27 August 1979. A second explosion brought the death toll to 18.

measures included sweeping the radio spectrum with strong signals at intervals and this had resulted in occasions where terrorists were blown up as they carried a bomb to its destination. At Warrenpoint, either by good luck or clever management of the detonator mechanism, the IRA managed unscathed to drive a trailer-load of hay concealing about 250kg (560lb) of explosive into a lay-by alongside the road; there it waited, ostensibly broken down. Even more dangerous was a second load of explosives packed into a ruined gate lodge about 400m (440yd) down the road. The terrorists knew well enough the sort of procedures British soldiers would automatically adopt after the explosion of the first device and hoped to catch them with the second when they redeployed to hard cover.

The plan worked perfectly. A three-vehicle convoy carrying men from 2 Para came rolling down the road to Newry. The Land Rover in front and the first four-tonne lorry passed the trailer and as the second four-tonne lorry drew abreast the terrorists set off the device; six men were killed instantly. It was a devastating blow but the men under attack were trained infantry and they immediately began to shake out into a long-rehearsed anti-ambush drill.

The survivors of the unlucky convoy numbered off and began attending to the injured; members of the 2 Para machine-gun platoon soon arrived on the scene from Newry and blocked off the road to civilian traffic. Already the ruined gate lodge was being used as convenient hard cover and the paratroopers were peering out from behind its pillars and walls, unaware of the over 500kg (1120lb) of explosive packed into a pillar. The second target must have been tempting but the IRA radio controller either gambled on the arrival of more men and equipment, or just possibly, was having difficulty making the detonating radio signal work.

As the minutes ticked by more and more British soldiers arrived at the danger area: C Company's commander, an airborne medical team and soldiers from the 1st Battalion, Queen's Own Highlanders, along with that battalion's commander. By this time a large concentration of men and equipment had formed around the gate lodge. A Wessex helicopter with the wounded aboard began taking off and then the second device was detonated; gunfire from across Carlingford Lough raked the scene.

Returning fire

A further 12 men were killed but the helicopter full of wounded managed to pull itself clear and, although damaged, flew to its base at Bessborough. The Highlanders' lieutenant-colonel and a lance-corporal were killed, as were the paratroop major commanding C Company and nine other ranks. For 15 minutes or so the surviving paratroopers took cover behind hedges and returned the IRA's fire but the only man killed in the shooting was an innocent English tourist on a fishing holiday in the Irish Republic.

The main results of the incidents of 27 August were the introduction of a security coordinator for Northern Ireland, Sir Maurice Oldfield, and a decision to accelerate the handing over of high-profile security duties to an expanded Royal Ulster Constabulary (RUC). The Warrenpoint incident, although to be counted among the successes of the IRA, was marked by the professionalism of regular soldiers in the face of two morale-shattering blows. **Peter Banyard**

Votes and violence

New strategies for the Republican terrorists

In the autumn of 1975, a shaky truce between the Provisional IRA and the British Army, agreed during the previous winter, finally broke down under the pressure of a rising tide of violent incidents. In reality there had been no peace – 196 civilians had been killed in the first nine months of the year, mostly in a vicious succession of 'tit-for-tat' sectarian attacks by Protestant paramilitaries and the Provisionals. But the Provisionals' leadership had nourished some hope that the truce might be a first step towards a British withdrawal. The complete breakdown of the flimsy agreement revealed the bankruptcy of this wishful thinking, which had been born of war-weariness and serious defeats at the hands of the security forces. By October 1975 the Provisionals were engaged in a bloody feud with the Official IRA, as well as in the continuing sectarian violence which they themselves admitted was chaotic and pointless. The ageing die-hard leadership, represented by such men as Seamus Twomey, could not disguise its paucity of ideas for continuing the struggle, since the British had refused to be cudgeled out of Ulster.

Among younger Provisionals, however, new ideas were emerging both for a long-term strategy to sustain a prolonged struggle, and for coping with the immedi-ate pressing problems – how to counter the security forces' success in penetrating and decimating the IRA's loose organisation of 'battalions' and 'brigades', and how to win back popular support in Catholic areas alienated by the years of terrorism. The centre for new thinking was, ironically, Ulster's prisons, where many Provisionals were cooped up together with time on their hands for reading and discussion. Here the works of revolutionary theorists were studied and practical experiences discussed.

One man inside the Maze prison at this time was to emerge as the leading individual in the reconstruction of the Provisional IRA – he was Gerry Adams. Having joined the old IRA in 1965, Adams had sided with the Provisionals during the split of 1969. He had been a trusted 'brigade' and 'battalion' commander during the bombing campaigns of the early 1970s, until his arrest in 1973. He proved the most influential proponent of the view that the Provisionals could only succeed in a continued terrorist war if they also led a political and social revolution in the Catholic areas of the Province.

Adams publicised his views through the propaganda organ of the Provisionals' Belfast Brigade, *Republican News*, in a series of articles published between

Above: Gerry Adams after his election as MP for West Belfast in 1983. Adams advocated combining participation in elections with a campaign of selective terrorism.

Leading figures of the British establishment were targets of Republican terrorism. Above right: The car in which Conservative MP Airey Neave was assassinated by the INLA in March 1979. Right: A body is lifted from the sea after the murder of Lord Mountbatten by the Provisionals in August 1979.

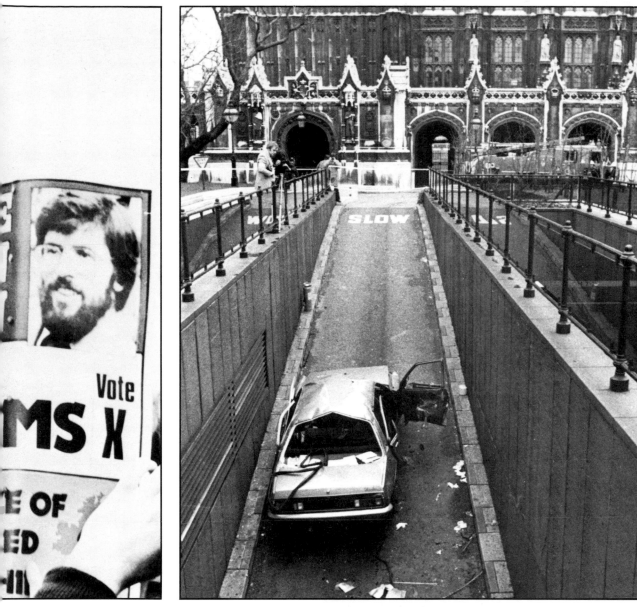

1975 and early 1977. The IRA, he suggested, was unlikely simply to bomb and shoot Britain into defeat. It needed to place itself at the head of a far-reaching popular movement which would agitate in every corner of Catholic life. This, Adams thought, could ensure for the IRA survival, support and eventual success: 'We need a complete fusing of our political and military activity . . . it affects us all. Each of us can examine ways of broadening the local Republican war machine into an alternative to the Brit system. An alternative spearheaded by the IRA.'

By requiring that the military and political activities of the IRA be fused, Gerry Adams was laying the ground for what has now become known as the 'ballot-bomb' strategy of the IRA and its political front, Sinn Fein. From now on, political agitation should supplement a more selective, precise and controlled terrorist war.

In another document written in prison, but not published, Adams and others ruled on what kind of IRA should fulfill this new role. Certainly, it could not resemble the shambolic, wild Provisional organisation which had merely battered Ulster to pieces and was, anyway, steeped in British intelligence penetration. Gerry Adams and a group of like-minded prisoners drew up the blueprint for a streamlined IRA – a blueprint which is credited with rescuing the Provisionals from the brink of defeat. Their organisation would now be modelled on a tight cell structure, which had been found effective by other urban guerrilla groups – disciplined and durable against espionage and interrogation. That, at least, was the plan.

During 1977, with Adams released from prison in February, the reorganisation of the Provisionals was well underway. Adams himself quickly became 'director of publicity' and, in the summer, 'northern officer commanding', with a post on the Provisionals' Army Council. Other radicals were soon slotted into key positions in Belfast, although elsewhere in the Provisional organisation the response to the new approach was more mixed. In the rural areas there was no point in attempting to create secret cells of guerrillas where everyone knew who the IRA men were anyway. South of the border, in the Republic, more traditional IRA attitudes were widespread, but the Dublin men could only look on. By the end of 1977, Adams had become the Provisionals' chief of staff.

Tightening up

Introducing the new cell structure for the Provisionals in Belfast was a task simplified by the depletion of the organisation's numbers during the previous two years through casualties, arrests and low recruitment. Already a much smaller group than in 1972, the Belfast IRA had only to tighten up its operational procedures. Weapons were now to be issued to individuals only for specific authorised operations, almost exclusively restricted to attacks on the security forces or the fire-bombing of commercial premises. Gone were the large indiscriminate car-bombs that had paralysed Ulster's city centres, which had so damaged the IRA's image with the Catholic population. The Provisionals wished to present themselves as an army that respected civilian life fighting against an army of occupation – though events like the La Mon restaurant fire-bombing in February 1978 in which 12 people were burnt to death were still liable to seriously hamper this quest for popularity.

One essential part of the new regime in the IRA was the tightening up of discipline within the organisation. Men carrying out unauthorised operations or failing to return weapons after completing an attack were liable to 'trial' and punishment – in some cases, execution. This crackdown also extended to the population of staunchly Republican areas. Since 1971 in much of west Belfast normal policing had been non-existent and it had been IRA policy to take over responsibility for order, imposing its own arbitrary law enforcement. During 1977, however, the Provisionals attempted to adopt their 'people's police' function more seriously. The result was a sharp rise in the savage corporal punishment they employed – the dropping of concrete blocks on knees and elbows, or the blowing off of kneecaps by bullets. One night in September 1977, 23 youths were lined up against a wall and 'kneecapped' in a narrow back street which earned the nickname 'Kneecap Alley'. In all 126 kneecappings were recorded that year, double the figure for any year since.

The Provisionals worked hard to legitimise this policy – Sinn Fein kept record cards of the crimes and sentences – but inevitably it provoked opposition. Crime, unsurprisingly, declined, but in 1978 a leading Provisional admitted that the IRA had used 'crude

and somewhat barbarous methods'.

The Provisionals' concern with their image was not only dictated by the need for popular support at home, but also by their dependence on arms and finance from the Irish community in the United States. The potentially most damaging aspect of the Provisionals' new line in this connection was the apparent Marxist tendency that their political thinking espoused. After the appointment of Adams as vice-president of Provisional Sinn Fein in the autumn of 1978, marking the fusing of the movement's military and political strategy, the newspapers branded the organisation as 'hard left'. Yet any suggestion of Marxism was anathema to most Catholics in Ireland or the United States, and to many in the ranks of the Provisionals – the original split in the IRA that had created the Provisionals had, after all, had as one of its main motives an objection to the Official IRA's Marxist line.

In June 1979, Adams delivered the traditional oration at the Bowdenstone graveside of the Irish Patriot, Wolfe Tone, in terms that suggested a left-wing position. 'We are opposed to big-business,' said Adams, 'to multi-nationalism . . . , to sectarianism and to the maintenance of a privileged class.' In fact, his speech was perhaps more of an Irish nationalist expression of hostility to all manifestations of British involvement in Ireland than true Marxism, but his later assertion that he knew of 'no one in Sinn Fein

Above: Masked members of the INLA train in the back-alleys of Belfast. The INLA, formed in 1976, posed a serious threat to the security forces, and engaged in a number of vicious sectarian attacks, such as when the congregation of a Protestant church in Armagh was sprayed with automatic fire in November 1983, killing three and injuring seven.

Right: Bernadette Devlin McAliskey, a prominent civil rights campaigner of the late 1960s and a former Westminster MP, consistently denounced sectarian murders carried out by Republican paramilitary groups, and argued for a broad-based political coalition to achieve a united Ireland. Her attitudes showed the degree of opposition to the Provisionals that existed even among Catholic Nationalists.

who is a Marxist or would be influenced by Marxism' cannot be accepted at face value.

Whatever its precise ideology, the Provisionals' increased operational efficiency was evident by 1979. Even before the assassination of Lord Mountbatten and the Warrenpoint massacre of 27 August, the Commander of Land Forces in Ulster, Major-General James Glover, had produced a flattering reassessment of the IRA. He warned that: 'We can expect more precise targeting of prestige targets', and conceded that: 'Our evidence of the calibre of the rank-and-file terrorist does not support the view that they are merely mindless hooligans drawn from the ranks of the unemployed and unemployable.' In effect, the British Army regarded the IRA as a formidable enemy.

The political option

On the other side, however, Gerry Adams realised that military force alone could never achieve a British withdrawal. His long-term aim was to sit down with the British and negotiate their withdrawal on the basis of strong political support among the Catholic population. It was in 1981 that the ballot-bomb strategy needed to achieve this aim first got under way.

The hunger strikes of that year were a considerable propaganda victory. To demonstrate the popular support for the strikers, the first of them, Bobby Sands, was chosen to stand in a parliamentary by-election in Fermanagh and South Tyrone in April 1981, and won the seat with a staggering 30,000 votes. Subsequent elections were to show that the support was not just a sentimental reaction to a particular situation. At the Northern Ireland Assembly elections in May 1982, Sinn Fein won five seats. A year later, in May 1983, Gerry Adams himself won the West Belfast seat in the Westminster parliament, defeating the moderate MP, Gerry Fitt; Province-wide, Sinn Fein received 102,000 votes, only 25,000 behind their non-violent rivals for the Catholic vote, the Social Democratic and Labour Party (SDLP).

In November 1983 Gerry Adams became president of Sinn Fein, in place of Rory O'Brady, the only member of the old Provisional leadership still with a position of power. Yet from the time of Adams achieving this pinnacle of influence in the IRA, a certain decline in the success of the policies he advocated could be discerned. Maintaining the balance between terrorist action on the one hand and the pursuit of political respectability on the other was far from easy. A considerable element in the Provisionals still doubted the value of the electoral strategy, and the fall in the Sinn Fein vote in the European elections of June 1984 tended to confirm suspicions that it could never reach a sufficient level to achieve its objectives. At the same time, the authorities use of 'supergrasses' won renewed successes against the Provisionals, despite the supposedly secure cell structure.

The attempt to assassinate Prime Minister Margaret Thatcher at Brighton in October 1984 did not constitute a change of strategy – the Provisionals have never stopped attacks on political figures and military targets in Britain – but it did confirm the continuing impasse in which the IRA finds itself, capable of carrying out spectacular terrorist coups and of winning substantial Catholic support, and yet still no nearer forcing a British withdrawal from Northern Ireland by either military or political pressure.

John Ware and Edward Vulliamy

Above: Bobby Sands, whose death in May 1981 gave the Provisional IRA a new martyr and awakened widespread sympathy amongst the Catholic population of Northern Ireland. The new strategy launched with his election to Westminster in April 1981 was not universally popular within the IRA, however, and there remained a conflict between the needs of electoral popularity and the continued campaign of terrorist violence.

Garrison duties

The British Army in Northern Ireland

At the end of Operation Lionheart, British Army of the Rhine's summer exercise of 1984, a West German brigadier paid a tribute to the British soldier. He had been impressed by the British infantry's flexibility and operational skilfulness with small detachments, and said: 'We envy you your experience in the Falklands and Northern Ireland.' These conflicts have provided the British Army with a recent combat experience, which most of the armies in Nato lack.

The nature of operations in Northern Ireland has particularly developed the skills of infantry and of junior commanders in control of small bodies of men. Although at the peak of the conflict in 1972, reserves of infantry were inadequate and gunners and technicians were pressed into an infantry role, the declining level of terrorist activity, improved administration and a growing role for the Royal Ulster Constabulary (RUC) and the Ulster Defence Regiment (UDR) ensured by 1977 that there were enough infantrymen to cope with infantry tasks. There are, of course, soldiers from all the army's corps in Ulster, but the business of making contact with terrorists or maintaining internal security is now the business of the infantry.

As the RUC has taken back the role of policing most of the Province since 1976, army foot patrols in urban areas have been largely phased out. The front-line role of the RUC has helped to reduce the army's casualty rate significantly, as has the general drop in the level of violence. Between 1971 and 1974 232 soldiers were killed in Ulster; for 1980 to 1983, the figure was down to 44. Yet the Province can still be a hard school for the development of the leadership qualities of NCOs, especially in the border areas, where small detachments of seven or eight men may patrol the dangerous countryside or wait in hides for some sign of terrorist activity. As often as possible officers will lead these units, but all ranks have absolute confidence in the ability of the junior commanders, as well as the professionalism to organise themselves effectively if the commander should become a casualty. It is a habit inspired by rigorous training, but it is in Northern Ireland that this self-reliance has been established and there is no doubt that it would be of great value in any other theatre of war. This professionalism has its basis in the high morale of the all-volunteer British Army.

The stoic acceptance of danger is rather different from taking pleasure in the conditions of service in Ulster. In the early 1970s the lack of proper accommodation made a soldier's life there grim indeed, with a serious shortage of beds, lavatories and washing facilities. By 1978 the situation had been vastly improved but was still far from luxurious – particularly for the roulement battalions on a short tour of duty. The Province has a regular garrison of close to 4000 men and this is provided by battalions on an 18-month tour of duty. All other soldiers in Ulster are on a four-month tour. The demands of the different lengths of duty vary considerably.

On a long tour as part of the garrison, servicemen have their wives and families with them. For this to be possible without great strain facing an enemy which regards women and children as a legitimate target, the regular garrison is stationed in barracks among predominantly Loyalist sections of the community. This provides a degree of safety and normality so that, although garrison soldiers spend much of their time in the field on security duty, they have some sort of family or social life to return to. However, this is never without anxiety and occasional tragedy as the bomb in the 'Droppin Well' discotheque frequented by soldiers of the Cheshire Regiment demonstrated in 1983. The need to be constantly alert and the resulting restriction on normal life make a tour of garrison duty in Ulster far from popular.

Attitudes to a short tour are more mixed. Because families do not accompany a short tour, soldiers can be stationed among hostile and dangerous sections of the community. In some places – such as Crossmag-

Below: Unable to enjoy the normal recreations of garrison life on mainland Britain, the troops in Northern Ireland look forward to the visits of entertainers, for whom security is understandably tight.

Regiment in the front line

The Ulster Defence Regiment (UDR) was established on 1 January 1970 as a result of the Hunt Report, which had been published in October 1969. The report had recommended that the predominantly Protestant Royal Ulster Constabulary be disarmed, and that its notoriously sectarian auxiliary force, the armed B-Specials, be disbanded. The report recommended the creation of a well-trained militia under army control. By 1 April 1970, seven battalions of the new regiment had been founded, and by the following September there were a total of 11 battalions, each territorially based in the Province's six counties and major cities. Great efforts were made to attract Catholic recruits, but initially only some 18 per cent of the UDR were Catholic, and by 1980 that figure had slumped to an estimated two per cent. The aim of creating a non-sectarian force with the support and confidence of both Northern Irish communities was undermined during the UDR's early years by the large number of its intake who were former members of the B-Specials. There were repeated allegations that some members of the UDR maintained close links with Protestant paramilitary groups, and

several UDR men have been convicted of sectarian terrorist offences.

In spite of these problems, the UDR was gradually transformed from an under-equipped poor-relation of the regular troops into the frontline military back-up for the civilian RUC. The regiment maintains over 40 bases in eight tactical operational areas with its headquarters at Theipval Barracks, Lisburn. Training and key administrative positions are assigned to regular servicemen on a two-year posting with the UDR, and the commanding officer, a brigadier, is advised by a six-man civilian council composed of three Catholics and three Protestants.

One-third of the UDR is full-time and two-thirds part-time soldiers. The part-timers are allowed to carry weapons for self-defence while off-duty. Living within the Northern Ireland community, the members of the UDR are uniquely vulnerable to terrorist assassination attacks, and between January 1970 and October 1984, 147 members of the UDR were killed, many while off-duty. The largest regiment in the British Army, the UDR also holds the distinction of having served the longest unbroken period of active duty totalling 15 years by the end of 1984.

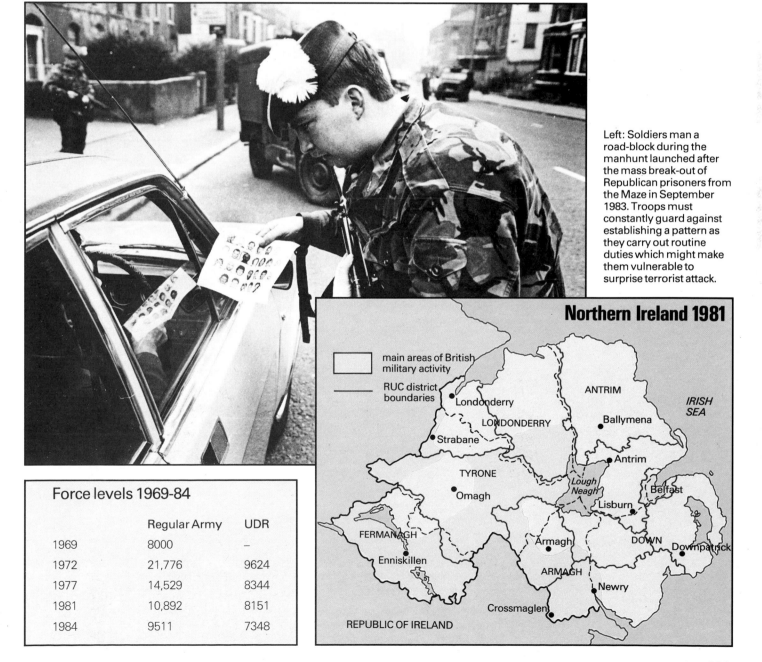

Left: Soldiers man a road-block during the manhunt launched after the mass break-out of Republican prisoners from the Maze in September 1983. Troops must constantly guard against establishing a pattern as they carry out routine duties which might make them vulnerable to surprise terrorist attack.

Force levels 1969-84

	Regular Army	UDR
1969	8000	–
1972	21,776	9624
1977	14,529	8344
1981	10,892	8151
1984	9511	7348

Northern Ireland 1981

☐ main areas of British military activity

— RUC district boundaries

ANTRIM
IRISH SEA
Londonderry
LONDONDERRY
Ballymena
Strabane
Antrim
TYRONE
Lough Neagh
Belfast
Omagh
Lisburn
FERMANAGH
Armagh
DOWN
Downpatrick
Enniskillen
ARMAGH
Newry
Crossmaglen
REPUBLIC OF IRELAND

len – they exist in virtual forts protected by fencing which is proof against rocket attack. In these circumstances there is no social life outside the garrison unit and there is little doubt that it is this factor, rather than the danger, which is most galling to soldiers on a short tour. To some it is a minor irritation to be set against the satisfaction of being engaged in real soldiering where professional skills are put to vital use day after day but, to others, it is tedious. Entertainment is limited to reading, television and video films so that existence becomes a monotony of 'getting your scoff down your neck and getting your head down'. In this atmosphere patrolling can be a relief and, perhaps strangely, the opportunity to save money which comes from having few ways of spending it, is often welcome.

All this is a far cry from the early days of the present troubles. At that time most units were fully stretched in violent confrontation with rioting mobs. Riot is still a danger in the Province but it is usually snuffed out quickly. The struggle against the armed IRA, meanwhile, has become a more covert affair. Patrols are as invisible as possible and use their ears and eyes to gather information which may enable them to ambush the terrorists. A very typical example would be the Royal Green Jackets' Operation Vehement of June 1981 in which the command wire of a suspected bomb was discovered and a hidden patrol of Riflemen watching the command end of the wire were able to photograph three men preparing to use it. The men were arrested by the RUC and, as a result of their information, five would-be bombers were convicted in a Belfast Court 15 months later. Undramatic

perhaps, but the very essence of counter-insurgency warfare in Ulster.

The emphasis on intelligence work means that search operations have taken on even more importance. In towns, search teams operating in a district inspect all abandoned buildings, open ground, alleys and houses. Some searches can be very large, such as one conducted on 6 September 1979 when contingents from the 1st and 3rd Battalions, Royal Anglian Regiment, and the 1st Battalion, Green Howards operated in the New Lodge district of Belfast. Over 100 soldiers took part formed into eight search teams; arms, ammunition and explosives were found.

Search operations in the countryside can take many days and will involve dogs, aerial photography and support. Farmhouses, fields, hedges, and conspicuous features such as trees, culverts and bridges are inspected, sometimes with excellent results. On 10 December 1978, for example, a well searched by a patrol of the 1st Battalion, Gloucestershire Regiment, yielded 295kg (650lb) of explosives, bomb-making equipment, a rifle, a pistol and ammunition.

The British Army's role in Northern Ireland between 1978 and 1984 could cautiously be characterised as successful. Techniques in countering armed guerrilla insurgency and sectarian disorder have improved immeasurably and the situation over those years never threatened to go out of control. Yet the army is still forced to perform an internal security role in Northern Ireland with concomitant loss of life. It is to the advantage of the British Army only in that the techniques of soldiering are being learnt in one of the hard places of the world. **Peter Banyard**

Below: Exhausted by the physical and emotional strain of a patrol, two soldiers of the Royal Welsh Regiment catch up on some sleep. In constant danger of terrorist attack the British Army faces the prospect of many more years of duty in Northern Ireland.

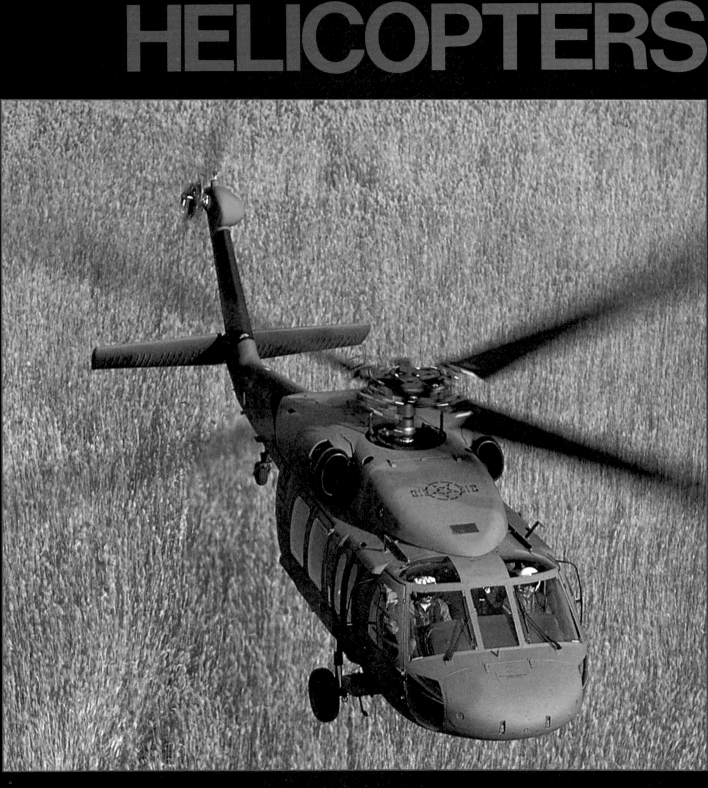

The helicopter may be said to have come of age as a weapon during the American involvement in Southeast Asia between 1962 and 1972. Indeed, it can be argued that the Vietnam War could not have been fought at all without rotary-winged aircraft. The campaign also highlighted the vital nature of logistics in modern warfare and it is in this least glamorous of roles that the helicopter excels: hauling troops and supplies in and out of the battle zone, evacuating casualties, providing airborne command posts, acting as courier and VIP transports alongside a myriad of more mundane but necessary tasks. The term 'utility helicopter' is actually a specific American service designation of specific types but has come to be regarded as an umbrella term encompassing all military rotorcraft used predominantly for light transport.

The Sikorsky S-55 was one of the first helicopters to be used in action, serving as a transport and for casualty evacuation during the Korean War. Two major variants were produced, differing mainly in the engine used: the H-19A with a 600hp Pratt & Whitney R-1340-57 engine and the H-19B with the Wright R-1300-3 engine that produced 700hp. The standard helicopter in the US armed services during the 1950s, it was also built in Britain under licence as the Westland Whirlwind. Apart from Korea, it has seen action in Algeria, Indochina and Malaysia, and with the Israeli Defence Forces.

Without doubt, the most familiar 'utility' type is the Bell UH-1 Iroquois. Known universally as the 'Huey' (because of its original service designation – HU-1), the helicopter first flew, as the Bell XH-40, on 22 October 1956. The first production model, the UH-1A, entered service with the US Army in June 1959. Powered by a 770hp T53-L-1A turboshaft, the aircraft had a flight crew of three and could carry a maximum of four passengers. Production of the model amounted to approximately 170 examples and the UH-1A was the first Huey to see combat in Vietnam, first used operationally there in 1962.

Even as the UH-1A was entering service, the US Army had a requirement for a more powerful version. This emerged in 1960 as the UH-1B. In the new model, the T53-L-1A powerplant was replaced by the 960shp T53-L-5. Even this increase in power was considered insufficient and late production examples were fitted with L-11 engines, offering 1100shp. Bell developed a commercial variant of the UH-1B known as the Model 204 and the Italian Agusta concern

produced such aircraft under licence as the AB-204B, a number of which were supplied to the Italian and other armed forces.

The US Army employed the UH-1B mainly as a gunship in Vietnam, a role for which the next model, the UH-1C, was specifically tailored. Transportation again came to the fore, however, with the UH-1D which entered service during August 1963. In the D, Bell began to utilise the basic design's potential to the full. The 1100shp T53-L-11 was used as a powerplant driving a 14·6m (48ft) diameter main rotor and the main cabin was lengthened to accommodate a maximum of 12 men. A grand total of 2561 UH-1Ds were produced for the US Army, many of which were re-engined to UH-1H standard during their service lives. As with the UH-1B, the D was built under licence by foreign producers, in this case Agusta in Italy (as the AB-205) and Dornier in West Germany.

The next major transport model was the UH-1H (the intervening two models, the UH-1E and F, were tailored respectively for use by the US Marine Corps as an assault support helicopter and for the USAF in the missile-site support role). The UH-1H proved to be the most widely produced variant of the whole family, a total of 4850 examples being built for the US services between September 1967 and July 1982. Essentially similar to the UH-1D, the H employed the T53-L-13 power unit, rated at 1400shp. These two variants (the D and the H) formed the backbone of the US Army's assault transport capability in Vietnam

Previous page: A UH-60 Black Hawk, the US Army's latest utility helicopter. It also comes in an electronic counter-measures version, the EH-60A. Above: Westland Whirlwinds over a mine in Malaya. The Malayan Emergency saw the first use of helicopters in counter-insurgency operations.

Below: A UH-1D helicopter in the Casevac (casualty evacuation) role in the Mekong Delta, 1967. The most valuable operation the helicopter performs is in getting wounded men to medical attention more rapidly than was possible previously.

Above: A Huey UH-1E of the US Marine Corps with a chin gun turret. Below: US Special Forces troops in Vietnam prepare to move out on UH-1H Hueys with door-mounted M60 machine guns. The helicopter's ability to provide highly mobile fire support, albeit from a vulnerable platform, brought a new dimension to warfare.

and like its predecessors, the UH-1H was produced under licence, this time in Italy, Japan and Taiwan.

With the creation of the H model, development of the Huey family switched away from the domestic military to foreign customers. During 1968, the Canadian government ordered a twin-engined derivative under the designation CH-135. Using a 14·6m (48ft) diameter main rotor, the CH-135 is powered by a PT-6T3 Turbo Twin Pac unit which comprises two coupled turboshafts, offering a combined rating of 1800shp, and is capable of lifting a maximum of 14 passengers. Known to Bell as the Model 212, the type

was taken up by the USAF, the US Navy and the US Marine Corps under the designation UH-1N and has been produced under licence in Italy as the AB-212.

Even more powerful was the Model 214 which was produced specifically for Iran prior to the Shah's fall in 1979. Produced in two versions, the Model 214 was first ordered in December 1972 and a total of over 300 aircraft had been delivered by the beginning of the Iranian revolution. Power for the 214 is provided by a 2930shp LTC4B-8D turboshaft and Bell continue to market the type in a civilian version known as the Biglifter, an indication of its capabilities.

In all, the Huey family has served with the armed forces of no less than 79 countries and has been used in almost as many roles, ranging from basic transportation, through gunship and search-and-rescue models to the specialised anti-submarine warfare variants developed by Agusta.

The UH-1 is being replaced in US Army service by the Sikorsky UH-60 Black Hawk. Developed from the late 1960s, the Black Hawk is designed to fulfill the service's UTTAS (Utility Tactical Transport Aircraft System) requirement and entered service with the 101st Airborne Division in 1979. Building on combat experience with the Huey, the UH-60 carries extensive navigational aids, communications and electronic counter-measures gear and incorporates a much greater degree of 'survivability'. With a flight crew of three, the Black Hawk can carry an 11-man infantry squad, four litters for casualty evacuation or a 3628kg (8000lb) externally-slung cargo load. The Black Hawk saw combat during the US invasion of Grenada and was in contention for orders from the British and Australian Armies.

Outside the United States, Europe is a prolific manufacturer of this class of helicopter, with one, the Aérospatiale Alouette, rivalling the Huey in the extent of its service. First flown in March 1955, the Alouette family is an extensive one, military applications concentrating on the SA 313/318 Alouette II, SA 315 Lama and the SA 316/319 Alouette III models. The Alouette II sub-variants differ in the type of engine used (SA 313: one 360shp Turbomeca Artouste II turboshaft; SA 318: one 360shp Astazou IIA unit). Production of the five-seat 'twos' ended in 1975 by which time some 1000 SA 313s and around 300 SA 318s had been delivered; the type has served

with the armed forces of 32 countries. The Alouette II also formed the basis of the 'hot and high' Lama which was a joint venture between Aérospatiale and the Indian HAL company (which calls it the Cheetah). The Lama uses the Alouette II's airframe combined with the SA 316's engine and was built specifically for service with India's armed forces.

The Alouette III differs from the earlier type in being a seven-seater and the two sub-variants again differ in their use of the Artouste (in the SA 316) or the Astazou (in the SA 319) powerplants. Production of the 'threes' ended in 1977, by which time some 1450

Above centre: A section of British infantry debark from a Lynx. Above right: A British Westland Scout hovers in a forest glade. Right: A French Milan anti-tank missile team leaps from a Puma. Far right: Royal Marines race across HMS *Bulwark* to their Westland Wessexes.

Above: Alouette IIIs of the Netherlands' Army. The Alouette III has seen action with French, Rhodesian and South African Forces. Left: A British Gazelle passes over an Amerindian temple in Belize.

Right: UH-60A helicopters of the US Central Command (Rapid Deployment Force) on an exercise in 1982. The Black Hawk first entered service in 1979.

examples had been produced for around 51 military customers. The SA 319 was also produced under licence in India where it is known as the Chetak. All of the military Alouettes have provision for a wide range of equipment including strap-on armament, rescue hoists, ski and float undercarriages and simple search radar.

France followed up the Alouette with a joint Aéro-spatiale/Westland helicopter, the Gazelle. Originally a French design, the Gazelle became the subject of a multi-national production agreement in February 1967. A high performance five-seater powered by a single Astazou turboshaft, the Gazelle is operated by all three branches of Britain's armed services and by the French Army, has been exported to at least 11 other countries, and is produced under licence in Yugoslavia. The Gazelle illustrates graphically the current European trend away from 'utility' types to what can best be described as 'battlefield' helicopters.

Whilst it can be used as a light transport, the armies of France and Britain use it predominantly as an air observation post/command and control platform or as a true anti-armour gunship.

The same is true to an extent of the Westland/ Aérospatiale Lynx, another product of Anglo-French cooperation in the 1960s. Bigger than the Gazelle, the Lynx uses two 1120shp Gem 41 turboshafts and has been developed in both naval and land-based versions. The major user of the land version is the British Army, in whose service it is designated the Lynx AH-1. Capable of carrying a squad of 10 men, the Lynx can also be used for anti-armour operations, search and rescue, reconnaissance, armed escort, casualty evacuation and command and control missions. To fit it for the more offensive tasks, the Lynx can carry a wide range of weaponry and complementary sighting systems; it has proved so successful in the anti-armour role that a dedicated

gunship model, the Lynx 3, has been developed, first being exhibited in 1984.

Alongside their frontline helicopters, the British Army and Marines continue to operate a limited number of elderly Westland Scout and Wessex helicopters. The diminutive Scout first flew on 4 August 1960 and, powered by a 685shp Nimbus 101/102 turboshaft, can carry up to three passengers or a stretcher in addition to a flight crew of two. The Wessex is a derivative of the Sikorsky S-58 powered by coupled Gnome turboshafts offering a power output of 1550shp. Ten variants of the design were produced of which two, the RAF's HC-2 and the Royal Marines' HU-5 had a transport role. Capable of lifting up to 16 men or 1814kg (4000lb), the Wessex has seen extensive service in Northern Ireland alongside Scout observation posts.

Within the Soviet bloc, the Warsaw Pact countries make great use of military helicopters, the majority of

their utility types coming from the design bureau of Mikhail Mil. The earliest of his designs still in service, the Mi-4 Hound, entered service during 1953. Similar to the American Sikorsky S-55, the Mi-4 is powered by a single 1700hp ASh-82V radial engine and, in its Hound-A transport form, can carry a maximum of 14 passengers. Developed in several versions, including the Hound-B anti-submarine warfare model and the Hound-C electronic countermeasures platform, production of the Mi-4 is believed to have ended in the early 1960s, by which time at least 3000 had been built. Despite its age, the Hound remains in relatively large-scale use throughout the Warsaw Pact and with the armed forces of a number of 'client' states.

The Mi-8 is a development from the Mi-4, although it has little in common with its predecessor. Instead of a four-blade rotor it uses one with five, powered by two 1500shp Isotov TV-2-1117A turboshafts. Rear-loading doors enable the whole of the cabin to be used in transporting equipment. The Mi-8 can carry rocket or cannon pods and the windows are reportedly provided with pivots from which the up to 32 passengers can fire their smallarms.

Further down the size scale comes the Mi-2 Hoplite which first flew in September 1961. Powered by two 431shp GTD-350P turboshafts, the Mi-2 can carry a maximum of eight passengers. In 1964, production of the Hoplite was transferred to Poland, and by 1981 some 4000 examples had been built, an estimated 2000 of which went to the military. The type is the Warsaw Pact's standard training and liaison helicopter and it has been supplied to at least five operators in the Third World.

Above: A Mil Mi-8 Hip of the Soviet Army in a European camouflage scheme. The Hip is in service with Warsaw Pact nations and the armed forces of other Soviet-supplied nations. The Hip was used for helicopter assaults during the 1973 Yom Kippur War with mixed results.

Right: An Mi-8 armed as a gunship takes off from its base in Afghanistan, August 1983. The Mi-8 Hip is often used as a gunship when the Mi-24 Hind is not available. They can also be equipped for aerial minelaying and it is reported that Aeroflot Mi-8s have been used in this role in Afghanistan.

Balance of terror
The superpower arms race, 1975-84

Once the Soviet Union had established a credible capacity to strike targets in the United States with nuclear warheads in the 1960s, the superpowers entered a new era of strategic thinking, in which both such a time-honoured concept as military superiority and newer concepts like 'nuclear deterrence' were called into question. The existence of mutually assured destruction (MAD) suggested that having more missiles or bombers than your enemy no longer conferred military superiority upon your forces, since all the nuclear strike capacity above a certain computable level was mere overkill – useless to prevent your own destruction or achieve anything describable as 'victory'. On the other hand, the fact that a total nuclear exchange was recognised to be mutually suicidal cast doubt upon the reality of nuclear deterrence – if nuclear weapons were, by their nature, unusable by either side, then was not a return to conventional conflict inevitable?

From the contemplation of such strategic conundrums a number of different lines of thought developed. One was that the United States, which in the early 1960s enjoyed a massive strategic nuclear superiority over the Soviet Union, had no need to maintain this lead, since its nuclear capacity was already more than adequate to inflict unacceptable damage on Russia, and the Soviets could not be prevented from deploying a similar capacity against America. By the early 1970s Soviet nuclear forces had almost closed the gap, without provoking a significant US response.

It was also perceived, however, that to allow either superpower to gain a decisive advantage in the nuclear confrontation, especially by the deployment of an effective defence system against ballistic missiles, would have a disastrous impact on the delicate balance of terror, tempting either a first strike by the superpower which felt it had achieved an advantage, or a pre-emptive strike by the other side which felt threatened.

Above: The East German crew of a pair of Soviet-built Goa SA-3 anti-aircraft missiles hurriedly put on their NBC (nuclear, biological, chemical) suits during Warsaw Pact manoeuvres. The danger of any conventional conflict between the Warsaw Pact and Nato in Europe escalating through the use of tactical nuclear, biological or chemical weapons to an all-out nuclear exchange is an essential element of mutual deterrence, but posed new problems as the arms race of the 1970s and 1980s undermined the balance of terror.

Left: The Trident missile represents the third generation of US submarine-launched ballistic missiles (SLBMs). The destructive power of the SLBM can be measured by the fact that a single US submarine carrying SLBMs has enough warheads to destroy every Soviet city with a population over 150,000.

The Superpower Balance

	1974		1979		1984	
	USA	USSR	USA	USSR	USA	USSR
ARMY						
Personnel	782,000	1,800,000	750,800	1,825,000	780,000	1,840,000
Tanks	9500	50,000	10,500	50,000	12,000	51,000
AFVs	23,000	50,000	22,000	55,000	19,000	70,000
Artillery/Missiles	29,000	48,000	30,000	50,000	33,000	54,000
Aircraft (inc. helicopters)	11,000	–	8500	–	9500	4100
NAVY						
Personnel	551,000	475,000	524,200	433,000	564,000	490,000
Principal Combat Surface Ships	177	221	180	275	206	293
Attack Submarines	73	245	80	248	99	278
Combat Aircraft	1900	715	1100	870	1800	1100
MARINES						
Personnel	196,000	17,000	184,000	12,000	196,000	16,000
AIR FORCE						
Personnel	645,000	400,000	563,000	475,000	594,500	400,000
Combat Aircraft	5000	5350	3400	4350	3700	3260
OFFENSIVE STRATEGIC NUCLEAR FORCES						
SLBMs	656	720	656	1028	592	981
ICBMs	1054	1575	1054	1398	1037	1398
Bombers	441	140	381	156	297	143

engaged in major breakthroughs in technology which were to fundamentally alter the terms of the strategic debate.

The crucial new development was the production of missiles with a far greater accuracy than anything previously seen, combined with multiple warheads. The Polaris A-3 SLBM, first deployed in 1964, had been equipped with a multiple re-entry vehicle (MRV) scattering three warheads about its target zone, but it was only in 1968 that the Americans had begun experiments with a new generation of weapons to be fitted with multiple independently-targetable re-entry vehicles (MIRVs), giving an extremely high level of accuracy for each individual warhead. The first missile system with MIRVs to be deployed was the Poseidon C-3 SLBM 1971, but for other technical reasons Poseidon was not capable of great accuracy. However, the Minuteman III land-based ICBM system deployed in 1977 or the Soviet SS-18 (model 2) of the same period could deliver each MIRV to within about 400m (440yd) of a target at intercontinental range.

Winning a nuclear exchange

The effect of these new missiles was to make a 'counter-force' strike, aimed at disabling the enemy's nuclear strike force, a real possibility. Each MIRV would stand a good chance of taking out a hardened missile silo, and with each SS-18, for example, having 8-10 MIRVs, the potential was enormous. According to some American estimates, the 300 or so SS-18s deployed by the Russians could destroy perhaps 93 per cent of US missile silos, although America's nuclear bombers and submarines would remain intact. This seemed to present a serious chance of actually winning a nuclear exchange through an effective first strike, given a superpower's readiness to accept a considerable level of damage in the inevitable nuclear reply from the enemy. It also opened the way to consideration of the use of the strategic nuclear armoury as weapons playing a role in a large-scale war on more conventional military lines – that is, instead of being seen as a blackmail threat

Above: US tanks in a West German town during an exercise in 1982. In the event of a war between Nato and the Warsaw Pact, West and East Germany would almost certainly be devastated by tactical nuclear strikes. Below: US Huey Cobra helicopters during Operation Lionheart, the Nato exercise in autumn 1984. The development of precision-guided munitions and accurate sighting technology may make a conventional defence of Western Europe possible.

The most important provisions of the first Strategic Arms Limitation Talks agreement (SALT I) signed in 1972, and its detailed protocol agreed in 1974, addressed themselves to these issues. Seeing that there was no advantage to be gained by the deployment of endlessly increasing numbers of nuclear delivery systems, the United States and the Soviet Union agreed to an upper limit for their intercontinental ballistic missiles (ICBMs) and submarine-launched ballistic missiles (SLBMs), which effectively gave parity to the two sides. At the same time, the agreement limited the deployment of anti-ballistic missile (ABM) systems to 100 for each country, recognising the principle that the nuclear balance could only exist if both sides remained vulnerable to attack.

Although agreement between the superpowers on these points was important, however, and showed the progress made in detente during the early 1970s, SALT I restricted itself to consideration of the numbers of delivery systems, making no provision as to their quality. But by 1974 the superpowers were

setting limits to the enemy's action, they could be restricted to accurate attacks on specific military and industrial targets without precipitating a total holocaust. In January 1974 US Secretary of Defense James Schlesinger heralded this new era of strategic doctrine with the statement that 'immediate massive retaliation against Soviet cities was no longer to be the president's only option and possibly not the principal option.' Originally rejected by the Carter administration in 1977, the targeting of US missiles away from Soviet cities and onto military objectives was reconfirmed by Presidential Directive 59 in the summer of 1980.

This approach, blurring the distinction between the strategic and tactical use of nuclear weapons, was encouraged by a second technological advance – the American development, beginning in the mid-1970s, of highly accurate cruise missiles with good chances of penetrating enemy defences by low-level flight. Capable of delivery from sea, air or mobile land platforms, cruise missiles greatly complicated the nuclear picture.

American progress in technology was by no means limited to the field of missiles in the 1970s. With the B-1 bomber, the United States created the first supersonic aircraft specifically designed for strategic bombing. The B-1 project ran into much hostile criticism which led President Jimmy Carter to cancel production of the aircraft in 1977, but testing of the prototype continued. Another controversial development was the enhanced radiation weapon (ERW), known popularly as the neutron bomb – a misleading name, since the ERW was designed for deployment as an artillery shell. The outcry that greeted Carter's announcement that ERWs would be deployed in Europe was a response to the weapon's extraordinary characteristic of killing people while leaving inorganic matter, such as houses or war material, intact – an effect achieved through reducing the blast and heat output of a nuclear explosion to almost zero, while increasing radiation. Branded by the Soviets as 'the ultimate capitalist weapon' aimed to preserve property at the expense of human beings, it was designed in fact for use against massed Soviet armoured formations in Europe, or possibly for urban fighting to help retake a Soviet-occupied city. The unpopularity of ERW in Europe prevented its deployment there (at least officially), although production went ahead. It showed once again the growing tendency in the West to regard nuclear weapons as potentially usable at battlefield or tactical level without an escalation to a strategic exchange – an idea apparently consistently rejected by the Soviets, who seem to have held to the view that any major war would involve nuclear weapons, and that any nuclear exchange would inevitably reach the highest level.

As usual, Soviet technology was not as innovative as the American equivalent in the 1970s, but the Russians did begin experiments with particle-beam and laser technology in the hope of developing an effective anti-ballistic missile defence, presumably through the stationing of satellite platforms for them in orbit. Although this was a long-term project with no immediate possibility for implementation, it inevitably appeared threatening from the American side of the fence.

Such new technology as the increased accuracy and MIRVing of missiles or the development of cruise were in themselves destabilising, but they

Below: The USS *Nimitz*, one of the US Navy's most powerful modern aircraft carriers. Vessels such as the *Nimitz* form the core of the formidable US carrier battle-groups, which not only give the US a powerful global intervention capability, but also represent the key to Western naval strategy in such vital theatres as the North Atlantic.

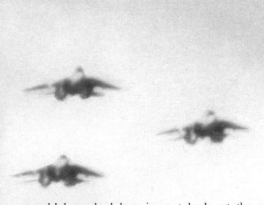

would have had less impact had not the general climate of superpower relations deteriorated so rapidly in the late 1970s. The SALT negotiations continued, addressing themselves to the new technology by including MIRVs and cruise missiles in the numbers game, but the second SALT treaty (SALT II) embodying these broader controls and agreed in 1979, was never to be ratified in the US Senate. By that time, American opinion had come to feel that the United States was getting very much the worse of a profound shift in the world balance of power, and that the arms limitation talks had provided a smoke-screen for a massive expansion of Soviet military might.

The Soviet advance

This perception of a Soviet advance was not limited to nuclear weapons, although the Soviet Union had clearly made great strides under SALT I – expanding its nuclear installations right up to the limit laid down in the treaty – and its position could easily be described as one of superiority if the figures were read the appropriate way – for example, Soviet ICBMs carried much larger warheads than their US equivalents, so that in megatonnage the Soviets far outstripped the Americans. Much American attention was concentrated, however, on the expansion of Soviet conventional forces as a direct challenge to the West's position worldwide.

One of the most obvious areas of Soviet military build-up was in naval forces, which by the mid-1970s had been completely transformed from the predominantly coastal defence force of the Stalin period to a formidable instrument for the global projection of

maritime power. Under Admiral Sergei Gorshkov, units of the Soviet fleet began to operate in all the oceans of the world. The first Kiev-class carrier, which became operational in 1976, indicated an intention to develop a capability to project airpower at sea, both in the anti-submarine role, and also in order to be able to deploy increasingly large naval formations to challenge the formidable US carrier battle groups. Likewise, the introduction of the Ivan Rogov class of amphibious assault ships, capable of carrying up to a battalion of naval infantry; the Kirov class of nuclear-powered, missile-armed battle cruisers; and the Slava class of cruisers, armed with an impressive battery of SS-N-12 missile launchers, represented a trend towards a new balance of naval forces, which undermined the previous dominance of the United States. US observers linked the Soviet naval expansion to its involvement in Angola, Ethiopia and, finally, Afghanistan, and made of the two together a formidable image of a consistent policy of global expansion.

It was in the European theatre, however, that the most bitterly controversial issue was to arise. Since

Above: The Soviet aircraft carrier *Kiev* during its first operational cruise in the Mediterranean in July 1976. The *Kiev* represented the growth of a new Soviet challenge to US naval supremacy, masterminded by Admiral Sergei Gorshkov, who stressed the need for the Soviet Union to acquire a powerful blue-water navy.
Below: The air traffic control centre of the American aircraft carrier USS *Dwight D. Eisenhower*. Western technological superiority continued to outweigh the growth in Soviet numbers, but seemed an increasingly dubious advantage as new weapons systems became more and more expensive and difficult to maintain.

World War II, Europe had remained the vital pivot of the superpower balance. On the Western side, the United States was seen as the essential counterweight to Soviet regional predominance; from the Eastern side, Western Europe was viewed as a potential forward base for American action against the Soviet Union. By 1977, some West European leaders, most notably Chancellor Helmut Schmidt of West Germany, had become extremely disturbed by the growing Soviet strength in the European theatre. The Warsaw Pact had long enjoyed a substantial numerical superiority in armour and infantry, offset by the technical superiority of Nato equipment – although even this technical advantage was to be put in question as such weapons as the T72 tank and the Hind gunship came into service. What worried Schmidt most, however, was the growing Soviet nuclear force directed at Western Europe. In 1977 the Soviet Union began deployment of the SS-20 intermediate range nuclear missile, with a three-MIRV payload, to replace its existing ageing tactical missiles and supplement the Backfire and Su-24 bombers.

In December 1979, in an effort to redress the balance of theatre nuclear weapons in Europe and to tie the United States more solidly into the defence of the region, it was agreed at a Nato summit that 464 land-based cruise missiles and 180 Pershing IIs would be installed in the UK, West Germany, Italy, Belgium and Holland. The Soviet response to this decision was extremely hostile – and perhaps understandably so. It was all very well for the United States to distinguish between these 'tactical' missiles and strategic forces, but it was a fact that cruise missiles in Europe would be able to strike the Soviet Union, whereas SS-20s could not reach the United States.

Upgrading military strength

The inauguration of President Ronald Reagan's first administration in 1981 confirmed the West's new commitment to the upgrading of its military strength. The superpower talks envisaged as part of the SALT process went ahead – the Strategic Arms Reduction Talks (START) and the Intermediate Range Nuclear Forces (INF) talks – but in an atmosphere of mounting suspicion and hostility they stood little chance of success. President Reagan pressed ahead with the new generation of armaments which had been delayed in the indecisive atmosphere of the late 1970s. The B-1 bomber went into production and the administration debated plans to deploy the replacement for Minuteman, the Peacekeeper ICBM (better known under its experimental designation MX).

The debate which raged over the basing-mode for the Peacekeeper highlighted the point nuclear technology had reached. It was argued that if the missiles were based in conventional silos, however much they might be reinforced, they would be too vulnerable to a Soviet first strike. The original plan for a race-track deployment – in which the missiles would have moved around an underground track punctuated by silos, leaving the enemy with no idea which silo should be hit to take out the missile – was abandoned because of its expense and its ecological effects (it would have involved digging up vast areas of the American west). After other plans for road-borne, airborne or 'dense-pack' basing had been abandoned, it was finally decided to deploy the Peacekeeper in extra-reinforced Minuteman silos, although this left the original problem of the weapon's vulnerability

Above: President Ronald Reagan, whose abrasive attitude towards the Soviet Union provoked fears of a superpower conflict. Right: Helmut Schmidt, a prime mover behind the deployment of cruise and Pershing II missiles to Europe. Below: A Tomahawk cruise missile launcher; the mobility of these weapons was meant to guarantee their survival in a nuclear exchange.

unsolved. In this mode, Peacekeeper deployment should begin in 1986.

What was clear about the Peacekeeper basing-mode debate was that it undoubtedly involved thinking the unthinkable – how to fight and win a nuclear war. After all, it could hardly be argued that the theoretical possibility of a nuclear first strike disabling ICBMs undermined the US nuclear deterrent – the Americans had too many other strings to their bow – but it could affect the outcome of a nuclear exchange in the sophisticated 'war-winning' scenarios now being considered by influential US strategists.

Yet despite a number of incautious public statements by Reagan and his advisers – one especially unfortunate in suggesting the possibility of a nuclear war limited to Europe – it was obvious that they were not enamoured of the prospect of a nuclear conflict. They did feel, however, that emphasising their readiness to 'go nuclear' if necessary would restrain Soviet actions. They were also determined if possible to restore a decisive American lead in armaments such as had existed two decades before, or at least to reverse the advantage that they believed the Soviets had gained. In the view of the Reagan administration, if there were to be negotiations it must be the Soviets who made concessions – a view epitomised by Reagan's offer of the 'zero option' in 1981 which asked the Russians to delete their SS-20s in return for the West keeping its forces at existing levels.

The exchange of proposals and counter-proposals by the superpowers that accompanied the countdown to Pershing II and cruise deployment in Europe was more by way of a propaganda effort on both sides than a genuine effort at negotiations. In 1983, deployment went ahead and the START talks broke down, as the Soviets tried to demonstrate how strongly they felt about this new Western pressure. The adverse Soviet reaction was echoed by the response of the European nuclear disarmament movement, which regarded the new deployment as bringing closer the threat of nuclear war in Europe.

To some extent, their anxiety was quite widely shared in Western European governments. There was still great interest in the possibility of a more effective conventional defence of Europe which would validate the non-nuclear option. The United States was as keen on improving its conventional as its nuclear position, and the 1980s saw the introduction of a new generation of Nato main battle tanks, the M1 Abrams

By the 1980s both superpowers had already moved into the exploitation of outer space for military purposes. The US space-shuttle, photographed here from a satellite, was backed by the Pentagon for its military potential.

and Leopard II, the M-2 Bradley mobile infantry combat vehicle (MICV) and the Hughes AH-64 helicopter, among a host of other expensive systems. Much hope was vested in emergent technologies (ET) for the future, with such prospects as the widespread use of robotics, already seen in the development of remotely piloted vehicles (RPVs), the transformation of communications (direct manpack satellite links for infantrymen, for example), and revolutionary armour (notably 'active' armour which explodes in response to attack, minimising penetration). It was argued that with a decisive technological advantage restored – supposing the Russians to be incapable of catching up – the West would be able to establish a favourable conventional balance obviating the need to 'go nuclear'.

But a worrying image persisted of technology proceeding with its own momentum and of strategy in some disarray. New nuclear systems continued to appear. By 1984 the United States had begun replacing its Poseidon SLBMs with Trident – having almost double the range, an accuracy which made it the first SLBM with counterforce potential, and the possibility of carrying a manoeuvrable re-entry vehicle (MARV) payload to ensure better penetration of enemy defences. The Soviet Union was also upgrading its SLBMs, introducing the SS-N-18 in 1978 and the longer-range SS-N-20 in huge Typhoon-class submarines in the 1980s.

On 23 March 1983 President Reagan delivered his controversial 'Star Wars' speech, in which he proposed the development of a space-based ballistic missile defence system, perhaps setting the scene for the 21st century arms race. Space vehicles were already serving many military purposes (it was reported that most of the objectives behind the space-shuttle programme were military), and the F-15 was being groomed as a satellite destroyer.

President Reagan appeared set on the pursuit of military superiority, but it remained unclear what real sense this could have in the nuclear age. Nuclear and conventional weapons of ever greater accuracy, sophistication and cost have succeeded one another, with no clear rational strategic plan for their use. The United States could correctly feel that in the 1980s the initiative in superpower relations had returned to their side, after the Soviet advances of the 1970s, but even the Reagan administration could not be sure that US interests were best served by keeping Russia threatened and insecure. **Graham Brewer**

Poland and the Pact

Solidarity shakes the Soviet Union

Even at the height of Poland's own brand of Stalinism under Boleslaw Bierut during the early 1950s, it was clear that there were limits to how far the Polish people would be led down the road to socialism. The Catholic Church, which had survived the four partitions of Poland as the focal symbol of Polish nationalism and cultural identity, came under attack from the Communist Polish United Workers' Party (PUWP), which saw it as a rival centre of influence; but it was not subject to the degree of repression practised in some of the other Eastern European People's Democracies and in the Soviet Union. In fact, by depriving the Church of its very large holdings of land, the communist regime removed a source of friction between priest and peasant.

Though Poland attempted to emulate the Soviet model by rapid development of a heavy industrial base, the collectivisation of agriculture was not pressed to its conclusion, so that by 1955 only 9.2 per cent of arable land had been collectivised. Polish agriculture remained dominated by small private peasants and under-investment was a continual weakness. The return to power of Wladyslaw Gomulka in October 1956 seemed to offer the

promise of a democratisation of the overcentralised Polish state; Gomulka's de-Stalinisation was not thoroughgoing, however, and the PUWP increasingly became an association of managers and bureaucrats preoccupied by economic growth. Unwilling to provoke outright opposition, the communist regime avoided many necessary but unpopular economic measures, but in December 1970, the government grasped the nettle.

The announcement of large price increases, particularly severe on food, provoked a wave of strikes and demonstrations which, after incidents in which workers were fired on and killed, led to the replacement of Gomulka as first secretary of the PUWP by Edward Gierek, a former miner who appealed for restraint as the only way to avert a 'national tragedy' (which in the coded language of Polish politics stood for Soviet intervention). Political reform soon proved to mean the restoration of Party control over the independent workers, and, as under Gomulka, attention was again concentrated upon achieving rapid economic growth.

Gierek embarked upon an astonishing programme of economic expansion with Western credits and

Top: A strike meeting organised by the Polish free trade union movement Solidarity, whose birth posed a direct challenge to the power of the unpopular communist regime and threatened to provoke a Soviet military intervention. Above: Riot police face demonstrators in Gdansk on 1 May 1983.

Above: Striking Polish workers attack an army truck during violent clashes with security forces in the northern seaport of Gdansk in December 1970. The 1970 confrontation brought Edward Gierek (below left) to power promising reforms. His programme of rapid economic expansion ran into problems during the mid-1970s, leading to renewed unrest and opposition.

1970s, and by 1980 the debt to Western banks had reached a staggering $17 billion, requiring a repayment of some $5 billion in that year alone. The deflationary economic policies necessitated by this situation made a clash between government and people inevitable.

In July 1980, the Polish government was again forced to remove a number of food subsidies, and again strikes broke out in a number of industrial centres, but the spark which set off the prairie-fire of revolt which soon swept across Poland was struck in the Baltic seaport of Gdansk, scene of some of the bitterest confrontations of December 1970. On 14 August 1980, workers at the Lenin shipyard in Gdansk struck in support of the reinstatement of a crane-driver, dismissed for membership of the illegal Free Trade Union of the Coast. The leader of the strike was Lech Walesa, an electrician who had himself been sacked from the Lenin Yard in 1976 for trade union activities.

The right to strike

By 15 August, the strike had spread to the Paris Commune shipyard in neighbouring Gydnia, and soon delegates from striking factories throughout the region were establishing an Inter-Factory Strike Committee in the conference hall of the Lenin Yard. The strikers, supported by the Catholic Church, put forward a number of demands, including a wage rise of 2000 zloties, the abolition of censorship, and free trade unions with the right to strike and access to the media. The new mood of optimistic nationalism which had been created by the election of the Polish Cardinal Karol Wojytyla as Pope John Paul II in October 1978 and his visit to Poland in June 1979, contributed greatly to the rapid spread of the free trade union movement from the Baltic ports to the rest of Poland in a matter of days. The government had no choice but to negotiate with the strikers in a glare of publicity totally unprecedented in Eastern Europe.

On Sunday 31 August, the Polish government was forced to sign the historic Gdansk agreement, which recognised the workers' right to form free trade unions. By stubbornly attempting to limit the application of the new agreement to the Baltic region, the government ensured that the crisis smouldered on into the winter of 1980-81 as strikes throughout Poland forced it step-by-step to accept a series of increasingly wide-ranging demands put forward by the new independent trade union, Solidarity.

The crisis extended to the PUWP itself, and as thousands of rank-and-file Party members joined Solidarity, Gierek, a broken man, suffered a heart attack and was replaced as first secretary by Stanislaw Kania on 5 September. Kania, who had been Party secretary responsible for security and the armed forces, had consistently opposed the use of force against striking workers, as had the minister of defence, General Wojciech Jaruzelski. There were those in the PUWP leadership who were pressing for a harder line against Solidarity, however, and the emergence of these rival factions within the Party promoted its gradual disintegration.

Criticism of the events in Poland became increasingly violent in the Soviet, East German and Czechoslovak press, and Poland's Warsaw Pact allies attacked Kania's policy of limited concessions as a surrender to 'creeping counter-revolution'. On

industrial equipment, and by 1972, Poland had the third highest rate of economic growth in the world, though from a very low base. The 1973-74 oil crisis and the resulting world economic dislocation hit Poland especially hard, and caught her in a trap more common in the underdeveloped Third World than in industrialised Europe. The Polish economy now had to be wholly geared to the repayment of the spiralling debts owed to the West, and the Polish people were again asked to tighten their belts as the export market drew off the products of the country's new industry and potentially rich agriculture in order to earn the foreign exchange necessary to stave off total bankruptcy.

The Gierek administration received a sharp warning in June 1976, when an attempt to impose a heavy increase in meat prices led to protest strikes and riots that threatened to escalate into a repeat of December 1970. In the wake of the incidents of 1976, a number of dissident groups emerged, the most prominent of which was the Committee for the Defence of Workers' Rights (KOR), led by Jacek Kuron, a former member of the PUWP. Poland's economic crisis deepened during the worldwide recession of the late

25 November 1980, the US State Department announced that Soviet units stationed along the border with Poland had been placed on a higher state of alert than normal, and on 2 December, East Germany closed areas bordering Poland to Western military attaches. The US reported that Soviet forces in the western districts of the USSR, in Czechoslovakia and the German Democratic Republic amounting to some 30 divisions were taking up positions from which they could launch an invasion of Poland. At a Warsaw Pact summit meeting held in Moscow on 5 December, Kania came under severe attack for his alleged failure to deal firmly with the crisis, and was forced to promise a crack-down on dissident groups associated with Solidarity.

On 11 February 1981, the Polish prime minister, Jozef Pinkowski, resigned and was replaced by General Jaruzelski, who retained his position as minister of defence. Jaruzelski had fought alongside the Red Army during World War II in the ranks of the Soviet-organised Polish First Army, and had taken part in the liberation of Warsaw in 1944. It was known that he had opposed the use of troops against strikers in 1970 and 1976, and his appointment was received optimistically by many members of Solidarity, including Walesa. The Soviet Union also seemed reassured, and criticism of the Polish situation in the Soviet press temporarily diminished.

A number of KOR activists and leaders of right-wing nationalist organisations were arrested in order to reassure the regime's Warsaw Pact critics, but the sheer strength of support for Solidarity forced the government to make one of its greatest concessions on 12 May, when the Warsaw District Court accepted the legal registration of Rural Solidarity, an independent organisation of Poland's conservative private peasants. The emergence of what was virtually an independent non-communist peasants' party after 35 years of communist domination had been strongly resisted by the PUWP and awakened grave fears in Moscow. Those fears were reinforced during the weeks which preceded the 9th Congress of the

PUWP which had been set for 14 July 1981.

Pro-Solidarity critics of the leadership within the PUWP pressed for and won the election of delegates by secret ballot, ensuring that many members of the current Central Committee were not even congress delegates. There was also a great deal of pressure for a reform of the structure of the Party, and for the creation of a new 'horizontal' organisation which would allow contact between local Party organisations without Politburo control. Kania was able to avert what appeared to Moscow as the dissolution of the PUWP, but though re-elected by the congress, was forced to resign as first secretary on 18 October. The new Party leader was General Jaruzelski.

Jaruzelski appealed to the patriotism of the Polish people, and promised to make the improvement of food supplies and industrial efficiency his first priority. The strikes and protests of the preceding year had seriously affected Polish industrial production, making it even more difficult to service the country's huge foreign debts and intensifying the hardships of the Polish people. On 23 October, Jaruzelski announced that members of the armed forces would be appointed to key positions throughout the economy and administration in order to ensure the

Above: Lech Walesa, leader of Solidarity, flanked by his advisers, KOR leader Jacek Kuron (right), and Bogdan Geremek (left). A Gdansk electrician, Walesa provided a charismatic style of leadership that inspired the Polish working class, but came under increasing criticism within Solidarity.

Below left: Strikers pray together with supporters at the gate of the Lenin shipyard in Gdansk in August 1980. The election of the Polish Pope John Paul II in 1978 and his visit to Poland in 1979 were an inspiration to the strongly Catholic Polish opposition.

Above: General Wojciech Jaruzelski (second from right) confers with his Warsaw Pact colleagues, the commander-in-chief of Warsaw Pact forces, Soviet Marshal Victor Kulikov (far left), and East German minister of defence General Heinz Hoffmann (second from left) during the March 1982 'Friendship 82' manoeuvres held in Poland. Below: A Soviet Marine Infantry BTR-60PB APC landing on the Polish coast during the 'Soyuz 81' Warsaw Pact exercises, which were widely thought to be a signal to the Poles of the Soviet Union's readiness to intervene.

unhindered transport of food supplies, to combat waste and black market speculation, and to resolve local disputes. On 4 November Jaruzelski held private talks with Lech Walesa and the leader of the Polish Catholic Church, Cardinal Jozef Glemp, in an effort to reach a compromise solution that would avert the disintegration of the country and the risk of Soviet intervention.

Walesa, however, had come under increasing criticism within the leadership of Solidarity from militants who distrusted his moderation and what they saw as an inconsistent and autocratic style in negotiations with the government. At a meeting of the national leadership of Solidarity on 11-12 December, it was agreed to conduct a national referendum on 15 January on the issue of no confidence in the Polish government. Solidarity now appeared to be making the bid for political power which the hard-liners in the PUWP and Moscow had all along predicted; Soviet intervention seemed imminent. The response of General Jaruzelski was drastic and immediate. At 0200 hours on the morning of 13 December, troops and police surrounded the hotel in Gdansk where the Solidarity leadership was meeting, arresting everyone, including Walesa.

The following morning, Jaruzelski announced over the radio that a state of martial law had been declared. Both Solidarity and the official trade unions were banned, and internment without trial was introduced. Tanks appeared on the streets of Warsaw and Gdansk, but hundreds of thousands of workers took part in strikes and demonstrations against the suppression of Solidarity. In Gdansk, up to 13,000 workers occupied the Lenin shipyard, and troops were sent in to clear the Huta Warszawa steel mill near Warsaw. By 28 December, however, the Military Council for National Salvation headed by General Jaruzelski announced that for the first time since August 1979, there were no strikes in Poland.

Coming almost on the second anniversary of the Soviet intervention in Afghanistan, the introduction of martial law in Poland led to a worsening of the new Cold War that was clearly developing in the early 1980s. The Reagan administration accused the Soviet Union of direct responsibility for the tragic events in Poland and imposed economic sanctions on both countries. American efforts to persuade the European Nato governments to adopt a similarly hard line led to friction within the alliance, however.

Resisting martial law

Although Solidarity had been forced underground and an estimated 5000 of its leading members interned, it continued to organise resistance to martial law. There were frequent clashes between demonstrators and the riot police (Zomo), and a crowd of over 10,000 was dispersed with water cannon and baton charges in the centre of Warsaw on 3 May 1982. As part of their efforts to promote national reconciliation, the martial law authorities gradually raised a number of restrictions, and by July 1982 only 637 detainees, including Lech Walesa, remained in internment. In spite of this, the anniversary of the birth of Solidarity in August was marked by mass demonstrations throughout the country, and there were violent clashes in a number of places. The workers remained loyal to Solidarity, and when new official trade unions were introduced by decree in October 1982, they remained empty shells.

On 31 December 1982, martial law was suspended and the remaining detainees released. Walesa, who had been released on 12 November, became the target of a government campaign to discredit him, and he was arrested and interrogated on a number of occasions. His prestige remained enormous, however, and he continued to proclaim his support for the banned Solidarity. The situation seemed to have stabilised with the communist regime in control of the apparatus of power and the people again without any independent voice. A few courageous individuals did speak out, though, including a Catholic priest, Father Jerzy Popieluszko, whose pro-Solidarity sermons made him a key figure in the opposition to the Jaruzelski regime. His murder in October 1984 by three officers of the Polish secret police resulted in the re-emergence of opposition to the government, revealing the total failure of the communist administration to legitimate its authority. Walesa and the Catholic church counselled restraint, however, and the immediate crisis seemed to have been averted. All sides appeared to recognise that stability was a pre-condition of a peaceful solution to the Polish crisis.

Walter Hoffmann

Satellites and computers

The new espionage of the 1980s

A popular misconception exists that to be a spy is to work in a highly glamorous profession – composed of a colourful group of highly resourceful men and women. In actual fact the life of an intelligence operative is generally far from dramatic. Even agents on secret foreign missions do not advertise themselves in the manner of James Bond because to do so would be to destroy the purpose of their mission and their credibility; to remain anonymous is the desire of every 'secret' agent. Technological change has also undercut the 'James Bond' image of the secret agent that has become so popular since the 1960s. Satellites operating from outer space now add a formidable supplement to air reconnaissance capabilities; monitoring stations intercept communications by using

Above: GCHQ, the nerve-centre of Britain's vital signals intelligence network. Although most intelligence is now electronically gathered, the infiltration of GCHQ by Soviet spy Geoffrey Prime indicates the continued importance of the classic methods of intelligence.

sensitive listening devices. Indeed it is sometimes suggested that machines will eventually oust men from the 'front line' of spying altogether. This technological struggle – a vital factor in the wider arms race – has become increasingly important.

But in the same way that men still fight wars though machines help them to fight, so it is inconceivable that satellite cameras will completely replace the secret agent. Observation from space or high flying aircraft does provide very comprehensive intelligence of a

Right: Anthony Blunt, publicly exposed in 1980 as a Soviet spy who had infiltrated Britain's MI5 during World War II. Even during his days of active work for the Soviet GRU, signals intelligence was of crucial importance, and monitoring of signals traffic between Moscow and the Soviet embassy in Washington during the late 1940s helped to focus suspicion upon Blunt's fellow agent, Kim Philby.

Below: A USAF SR-71A Blackbird high-altitude reconnaissance aircraft. The Nicaraguan government alleged in November 1984 that Blackbirds were being used for supersonic spy flights over their territory.

veillance of communications transmissions are listening posts that use extremely sensitive antennae. Two representatives of this form of espionage are the famous Government Communications Headquarters (GCHQ) at Cheltenham and the mysterious US National Security Agency. The cryptanalysis and encryption done by such organisations has played a vital role in modern warfare since World War I. To monitor Soviet compliance with arms treaties, a US intercept station at Kabkan in Iran listened to Soviet missile tests and space launches for the telemetry signals sent back to earth, signals that provide data such as speed and trajectory of a missile or rocket. The station was closed as a result of the 1979 Iranian revolution but a new facility is to be provided in China.

Procuring intelligence

On-the-ground surveillance is just as important, however; satellite and signals intelligence supplement it. It has been reported that the US conducted an intelligence operation involving satellites and listening posts to determine the calibre of the T72's tank gun; and the operation failed. The British sent in a team of spies that broke into a Soviet tank depot in East Germany; the gun was measured and a copy of the tank manual was stolen. Meanwhile a French military attache in Moscow expressed interest in the tank to his Soviet liaison; he received a guided tour of the tank and a free dinner.

It does not follow, of course, that the accumulation of knowledge and its storage in the formidable array of data banks now available, inevitably leads to decisive action or the implementation of what seems to be the sensible policy. It now seems staggering, for example, that Western intelligence agencies did not

particular sort; but it is usually wide coverage over an expansive area, that is, exterior intelligence: what is going on on the outside, not the inside. The United States Air Force has conducted satellite intelligence since 1961 and the Soviet Union since 1963. Improvements over the last 25 years have really been qualitative. By 1968 satellite cameras were able to pick out aircraft on runways or vehicles on roads and even to discern information about them. But knowledge of this kind has severe limits – satellite photographs such as that of the Soviet carrier under construction at Nikolayev on the Black Sea which were published in 1984 show broad details, but the inferences of analysts are necessary for specific features.

Complementing the satellites by providing sur-

share with King Idris of Libya their knowledge of the impending military coup about to be mounted by Colonel Gaddafi. This was a monumental misjudgement which no amount of additional information could rectify – the Gaddafi regime has now become an international centre for terrorist activities. But as a former British intelligence agent candidly admitted, 'The intelligence world is not answerable to secretaries of state. It is accountable to nobody – not the prime minister, not parliament, not the courts. An intelligence department decides what information politicians should be given and they're rarely, if ever, given the full facts.' The 1984 controversy over the clandestine CIA mining of Nicaraguan harbours which has caused the Reagan administration grave embarrassment, is yet futher confirmation of this fact of intelligence life.

Turning traitor

Futher embarrassment can be caused by the revelation of a 'mole' or double agent in an intelligence organisation. This can be an effective source of intelligence for the side with the mole in place, particularly if he gains for himself a position of importance. The Geoffrey Prime scandal highlights these features. Prime was recruited by the KGB in 1968 while a sergeant in the RAF; he supplied secret documents and information about the monitoring of Soviet communications. Then Prime got a job in the Joint Tech-

Below: An artist's impression of a US Navstar I military navigation satellite, flying at some 20,200 km (12,500 miles) above the earth. Below left: A satellite photograph of a Soviet aircraft carrier (Nato code-name *Kremlin*) under construction in the Black Sea port of Nikolayev. The photograph shows the power of modern satellite intelligence.

nical Language Service of GCHQ where he listened to communications between Warsaw Pact embassies; and he kept his Soviet contacts informed about the methods used in surveillance of these. As Prime rose through the service, he was able to pass more and more sensitive information to his contacts; he would have remained a valuable Soviet intelligence asset had his paedophilia not brought him to the attention of the police.

Technological improvements in intelligence gathering cannot replace the older methods. But they have had a decisive influence on the way that states look at one another and weigh up the potential threat. It is quite possible that the continuous collection of information from outer space and the storage of vast masses of data on computers, with rapid access by the organs of state of either superpower, might well provoke resentment from those states who cannot

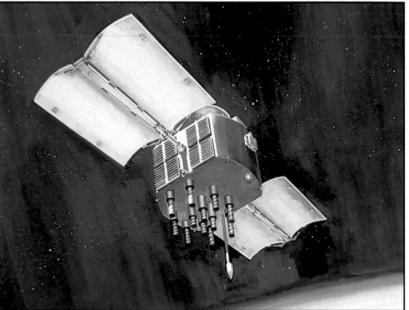

retaliate in kind; that the middle-ranking states, like France, will become irritated by American attempts to observe their nuclear tests from space. This may well be so. The real value of these methods is that they reduce uncertainty. Satellite and communications surveillance has considerably reduced the possibility that government agencies will in the future be thrown into a frenzy of uncertainty and confusion by imagined missile and bomber 'gaps', as in the late 1950s. An opponent's intentions can be more accurately gauged from space, the skies and radio frequencies, than from more patchy sources. An important check on any Soviet temptation to risk some kind of pre-emptive conventional strike in Europe is the knowledge that Nato would acquire advance knowledge of this intention and clear evidence of any unusual troop build-ups.

The function of intelligence in the 1980s is increasingly to cement rather than disrupt the existing superpower balance. The more each superpower knows about its rival the easier it will become to gauge efforts to shift that balance. Arms control agreements can now be more easily verified by use of intelligence from satellites. The exchange of information between East and West, whether witting or unwitting, demonstrates its greatest value in keeping the peace.

Brian Holden Reid

The Saab
Viggen

Design work on the Saab 'System 37' began in the early 1960s with the ambitious aim (partly to reduce costs) of producing a single basic aircraft which could carry out fighter, attack and reconnaissance roles. The Swedish government signed a development contract with the Saab-Scania company in October 1962 and the first prototype Saab 37, named Viggen (Thunderbolt), made its maiden flight on 8 February 1967. Early production effort concentrated on the all-weather attack and two-seat training versions, with deliveries of the AJ37 attack aircraft beginning in 1971. In all, five distinct variants of the Viggen have been built, including the SK37 two-seat trainer, the SF37 reconnaissance aircraft and the SH37 maritime reconnaissance and attack aircraft, which were all based on the AJ37. The all-weather interceptor version, designated JA37, required more extensive modification of the basic design and in effect represents a second-generation Viggen. It was the last of the variants to appear, making its first flight in November 1977, and entered service with the Swedish Air Force two years later.

The Viggen's most unusual design feature – unique among the world's warplanes at the time of its entry into service – is the canard foreplanes mounted ahead of the delta wing. This arrangement not only makes the Viggen a highly manoeuvrable aircraft at all speeds, but also contributes to its excellent short take-off and landing characteristics. The Swedish Air Force is well aware that its permanent airfields will be priority targets for an attacker in time of war and in consequence places great emphasis on the ability of its aircraft to operate from damaged runways and from temporary airfield sites such as suitable lengths of roadway. In this respect the Viggen is well suited to Swedish operational requirements, being able to take off and land within a distance of only 500m (550yd). Another feature of the aircraft that has been dictated by the Swedish Air

Force's unique operating methods is the folding vertical fin, which provides the necessary height clearance for the aircraft to be accommodated in underground hangars. Yet perhaps the most notable feature of all in the Viggen programme is that Sweden – a nation with a population of only some eight million – has the necessary design skills and manufacturing capacity to produce a combat aircraft which will stand comparison with the most advanced of its kind in the world.

The AJ37 Viggen is powered by a single Volvo Flygmotor RM8A turbofan, which is a development of the American Pratt & Whitney JT8D-22 civil airliner powerplant fitted with a Swedish-designed afterburner. It produces a maximum thrust of 11,800kg (26,000lb) with afterburning, giving the AJ37 a maximum speed of Mach 2 at high altitude. A Saab-Scania CK-37 miniaturised digital computer deals with many of the routine tasks of navigation, fuel management and calculation of weapons' delivery parameters, so that the pilot's workload is

Previous page: A Saab JA37 Viggen, fully armed with British Sky Flash and Rb24 Sidewinder (Swedish licence-produced US AIM-9L) missiles. Above: Two AJ37 Viggens demonstrate their short take-off capability.

Below: A Viggen on a road in Sweden. The Swedish Air Force required the Viggen to be capable of taking off from lengths of road 500m (550yd) long.

Left: An AJ37 equipped with rocket pods streaks across a frozen inlet. Below: Armed with bomblets and carrying a drop tank, an AJ37 makes a diving attack. Bottom: A 'finger-four' formation of Viggens banks to make a turn. Deliveries of the AJ37 Viggen began in June 1971, and a total of 100 models were produced. The AJ37 can carry rocket pods, cannon pods, air-to-surface and air-to-air missiles, depending on mission requirements.

reduced to a considerable degree. The computer is fed with information from the Viggen's search and fire control radar, and also Doppler and radio navigation equipment; after processing this mass of raw material, it relays the essential data to the pilot by projecting it onto his head-up display. Therefore the Viggen's computer essentially takes the place of the second crew member carried by most all-weather attack aircraft. Its weapons' load, mounted on seven underwing and fuselage stores pylons, can be made up of varying combinations of bombs, unguided rockets, air-to-surface missiles and pod-mounted 30mm Aden cannon. In addition the JA37 can be armed with Rb28 Falcon and Rb24 Sidewinder infra-red guided air-to-air missiles to give it a secondary fighter capability. Its main air-to-surface missile armament comprises the locally-produced Rb04E anti-shipping missile, or the more versatile Rb05.

The SK37 operational conversion trainer is essentially similar to the AJ37 and retains the armament capacity, although without the avionics, of the AJ37. The instructor pilot's cockpit is positioned above and behind that of his pupil and occupies a position taken up by fuel in the single seater. For this reason the SK37 is invariably fitted with an auxiliary fuel tank on the fuselage centreline stores station and a larger tail fin compensates for the increase in fuselage area resulting from the installation of a second cockpit. The modifications necessary to produce the SH37 maritime reconnaissance and attack version of the Viggen are less conspicuous. The radar has been modified for overwater surveillance, while long-range day and night reconnaissance cameras are carried in pods beneath the fuselage. The SF37 reconnaissance Viggen also carries night cameras and illumination equipment in under-fuselage pods, but the nose radar of other versions is replaced by two high altitude cameras, an infra-red camera and four low altitude cameras. Both reconnaissance versions can carry ECM (electronic counter-measure) pods and Sidewinder air-to-air missiles for self-defence.

Production of the first-generation Viggens ended in February 1980 with the delivery of the 180th aircraft, an SF37, to the Swedish Air Force. By that time the first of the second-generation JA37 all-weather interceptors was already in service, with 149 of this version on order. Although in outward appearance the JA37 differs little from its predecessor the AJ37 attack aircraft (except that it has the larger tail fin of the SK37), its airframe, powerplant and

Left: Two AJ37 Viggens from F7 Wing of the Swedish Air Force fly over the Swedish coastline; the Viggen also equips the F6 Wing. Below left: An SK37 operational trainer with a centreline auxiliary fuel tank; this tank was made necessary by the addition of the instructor's seat, which reduced the amount of space available for fuel, and also required enlargement of the fin.

Above: The JA37 interceptor model of the Viggen in an experimental low-visibility paint scheme.

avionics have all been modified for the interception mission. The JA37's RM8B turbofan produces 10 per cent more thrust than the earlier RM8A, while consuming little more fuel. The aircraft's structure has been strengthened both to cope with a take-off weight increased by nearly one tonne and to permit greater 'G' loadings during air combat manoeuvres. Yet the most radical changes have been to the aircraft's avionics systems, which are for the most part entirely new. The radar is a multi-mode sensor produced by the Swedish L.M. Ericsson company, which is capable of detecting high-speed targets flying at low level and can carry out interceptions in heavy ECM jamming conditions without the help of ground radar control. A new central computer, with five times the capacity of that fitted to the AJ37, automatically processes much of the data necessary for a successful interception. Essential information is conveyed to the pilot by means of a head-up display for close-in combat, or on a head-down display for all-weather interception, while a tactical display presents him with an overall picture of the combat situation. Although the JA37 can operate autonomously, communication with ground control is highly desirable and the aircraft is fitted with two UHF/VHF radio sets, each of which can handle both voice communication and data link.

The JA37's main armament comprises a pair of British Aerospace Sky Flash medium-range air-to-air missiles carried on the inboard underwing attachment points. For close-range combat the JA37 car-

Right: The maritime reconnaissance version of the Viggen, the SH37. It is carrying a camera on a pylon under the air intake.
Below right: This rear-view of the JA37 shows the outlets for the thrust-reverser; the thrust-reverser cuts in when the nose touches the ground, enabling the Viggen to make a short landing, even in severe weather conditions of snow and ice.

ries a pair of AIM-9L Sidewinder air-to-air missiles on the outboard underwing pylons and a further pair can be mounted beneath the fuselage. This version of the infra-red homing Sidewinder can be launched at virtually all angles off its target, unlike earlier AIM-9s which had to be fired from near the 'six o'clock' position. In addition to its missile armament the interceptor Viggen is fitted with an integral Oerlikon KCA 30mm cannon, which has a rate-of-fire of 1350 rounds per minute and a higher muzzle velocity than the Aden cannon of similar calibre.

Even with a heavy weapons load the JA37 retains the excellent manoeuvrability of earlier models of the Viggen and like them can operate from dispersed sites. Its reaction time is very fast and a Viggen can be scrambled from ground alert in less than a minute and reach an altitude of 10,000m (32,000ft) in under two minutes. Rapid turn-around between sorties is also achieved, with a seven-man ground crew requiring about 10 minutes to re-arm and refuel the aircraft. Ease of maintenance is another feature of the Viggen, with only 10 maintenance man-hours required per flight hour, and much of the servicing is carried out by conscripts with only limited technical training. From the pilot's viewpoint too the Viggen is an undemanding aircraft, as it is easy to fly because many of its systems are automatically managed by computers. Such qualities will ensure that the Viggen family continue to perform effectively as attack, reconnaissance and interceptor aircraft until well into the 1990s.

Left: As well as cameras mounted in its nose, this SF37 has a pod containing a night camera on the fuselage pylon.

JA37 Viggen

Type Air defence interceptor with secondary attack capability

Dimensions Span 10.6m (34ft 9in); length 16.4m (53ft 9in); height 5.9m (19ft 4in)

Weight Take-off with standard armament 17,000kg (37,500lb)

Powerplant One 12,750kg (28,110lb) thrust Volvo Flygmotor RM8B turbofan with afterburner

Performance Maximum speed above 11,000m (36,000ft) Mach 2.1, or 2195km/h (1365 mph); climb from sea level to 11,000m (32,000ft) 1.5 minutes

Range Tactical radius 1000km (620 miles); typical patrol endurance two hours

Ceiling Over 18,000m (60,000ft)

Armament One 30mm Oerlikon KCA cannon, plus up to four AIM-9L Sidewinder and two Sky Flash air-to-air missiles

Top: A JA37 Viggen with British Aerospace Sky Flash missiles on the wing pylons. The bulge on the underside contains the Oerlikon KCA 30mm cannon. Above right: Five Viggens of the F15 Wing operating in the snow.

Right: The Viggen family, from left to right: the AJ37, the SK37, the SH37, the SF37 and the JA37.

The path of violence

Terrorism in the 1980s

During the 1970s a rising tide of international terrorism, centred on European revolutionary movements and various Palestinian groups, was checked by the effective implementation of counter-terrorist techniques by the authorities. Terrorist acts did not cease, however, continuing in a more sporadic, fragmentary form into the 1980s.

Movements such as the Irish Republican Army (IRA), the Palestine Liberation Organisation (PLO) and the Basque separatist group Euskadi Ta Askatasun (ETA), which had become strongly established during the 1970s, continued to be active. Their aim of national independence struck a genuine chord within the clearly defined ethnic communities among which they operated. This element of popular support meant that they represented a political problem which could not simply be policed or eliminated by the formidable array of security counter-measures developed to combat them. The IRA hunger strike campaign of 1981, which was skilfully exploited and

Above: A police dog-handler surveys the Grand Hotel in Brighton, shortly after the IRA bomb attempt to kill the leadership of the British Conservative Party during its annual conference in October 1984. The words of the IRA press statement which claimed responsibility for the explosion chillingly exposed the logic of terrorism: 'We have only got to be lucky once; you have got to be lucky always.' Right: The attempted assassination of Pope John Paul II in 1981 showed the intense vulnerability of public figures.

consolidated by the election of Bobby Sands and subsequently Gerry Adams to the Westminster Parliament, indicated the degree to which the Republican paramilitaries in Northern Ireland, for all their inability to win majority support for their campaign of violence, were still able to play upon the nationalist sentiments and traditions of the Catholic community.

In spite of the success of the British security forces in combating terrorism in Northern Ireland through improved intelligence work, the use of 'supergrass' informers, and greater cooperation with the authorities in the Republic of Ireland, both the IRA and the Irish National Liberation Army (INLA) remained formidable threats to security, both in Ulster and in mainland Britain. The IRA, for example, retained an ability to operate active service units on the mainland, striking at 'soft' targets, such as in the December 1983 Harrods bombing, and at the well defended heart of the British political system with the Brighton bombing of October 1984, the purpose of which was to assassinate as many senior members of the British government as possible during the Conservative Party conference.

In Spain, in spite of a number of major political concessions by the government to demands for greater autonomy by the population of the Basque region, ETA separatists maintained their campaign of violence aimed at achieving the establishment of an independent Basque homeland. Economic targets were attacked, at least where their owners neglected to pay protection money, and the terrorists mounted an assassination campaign against police and army officers. ETA hoped to provoke a backlash from the still deeply conservative Spanish Army establishment which would discredit the Spanish government's strategy of solving the Basque problem within the context of a united democratic Spain, and rally Basque support behind their demands.

In the Federal Republic of Germany, the left-wing terrorists of the Red Army Fraction (RAF) continued to pursue a similar aim. Regarding liberal democracy as simply a mask to conceal the essentially repressive, fascist character of capitalism, they hoped to make the state discard that mask by forcing it to adopt increasingly comprehensive and authoritarian security measures for its own defence. Sensitivity towards Germany's Nazi past was exploited as a

weapon in the terrorist armoury. The most spectacular RAF attack during the 1980s was carried out on 15 September 1981 when a group of terrorists concealed on a hill high above a road in Heidelberg hit the car of US General Frederick Kroesner, commander of US forces in Europe, with an RPG-7 rocket. The incident indicated the degree to which the RAF was able to maintain its network of activists and supporters despite the extremely vigorous security measures of the West German authorities, including the centralised computerisation of intelligence records and the extensive infiltration of the left-wing scene within which the RAF recruited its supporters. Nevertheless, with the capture of Christian Klar on 16 November 1982, the first generation of RAF terrorist leaders had been eliminated. Either dead or in prison, they made way for a new, equally dangerous generation of young terrorists, many of whom were organised in autonomous groups known as Revolutionary Cells, which have proved much more difficult to infiltrate. Their bombings of US military targets in West Germany accompanied the growth of protests against the stationing of American cruise and Pershing II missiles in Europe.

Innocent victims

The bombing of the Munich Oktoberfest on 26 September 1980 heralded a new development on the terrorist scene in West Germany, however. The bomb, which killed 12 innocent visitors to the famous beer festival, was planted by a member of a well-known West German neo-Nazi group, the Wehrsportsgruppe Hoffmann, who himself died in the explosion. The group was banned following the Munich attack, and its leader, Karl-Heinz Hoffmann, was subsequently charged with the murder of a Jewish publisher in December 1980, but it continued to exist underground.

Similar patterns of continuing sporadic terrorist acts by both left and right-wing groups were found in Italy and France. The worst single massacre of the whole period in Europe was the bombing of Bologna

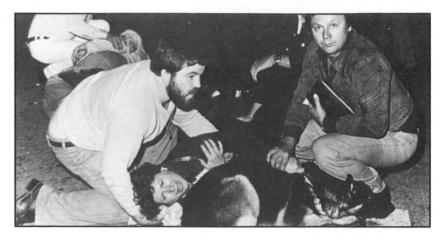

railway station by an Italian fascist organisation in 1980, and the Red Brigades were still able to mount operations such as the kidnap of US General Dozier in December 1981, although their activities were much reduced from the level of the 1970s. In France, as well as right-wing attacks especially concentrated on Jewish targets, there was a resurgence of terrorism by the famous 'Carlos' (Ilich Ramirez Sanchez), who was apparently responsible for the bombing of Marseilles railway station in December 1983.

The former allies of Carlos, the Palestinians, had abandoned the spectacular terrorist attacks which brought them to international prominence during the early 1970s, but they continued to employ terror, either in order to inflict damage upon an otherwise well-defended Israel, or to eliminate rivals and enemies within the Palestinian movement itself. One terrorist attack, the attempted assassination of the Israeli ambassador to London in June 1982, provided the pretext for Israel's invasion of the Lebanon, which in turn led to the withdrawal of the PLO from Beirut. The dispersion of the PLO's forces throughout the Arab world made it even more vulnerable to manipulation by rival Arab governments who employed Palestinian terrorists, such as the PLO

Above: German rescue workers tend to victims of a neo-Nazi bomb outrage which killed 12 during the 1980 Oktoberfest in Munich. During the early 1980s, extreme right-wing terrorists were active in West Germany, Italy, Spain and Turkey, and there was evidence of the development of an international network of neo-fascist groups.

Below: Ten of the Provisional IRA prisoners who escaped from the Maze prison during a mass break-out in September 1983. Both the IRA and the INLA remained dangerous threats to security both in Northern Ireland and on the British mainland.
Below right: Republican graffiti celebrating the Maze escape.

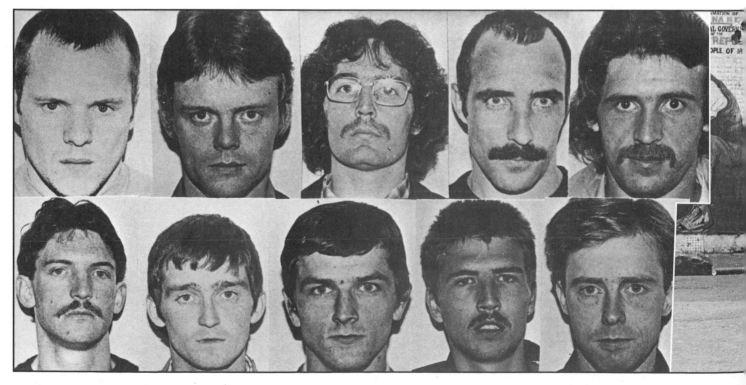

renegade Abu Nidal who transferred his services from Iraq to Syria after the opening of the Gulf War, in their continued and bloody feuds.

The most disturbing development in Middle East terrorism, however, was the suicide attacks by Islamic fundamentalists on US and French targets in Beirut. In attacks by vehicles packed with explosives and driven by fanatical terrorists, who were widely believed to be Shi'ite supporters of the Ayatollah Khomeini, the US embassy in Beirut was destroyed in April 1983, and the headquarters of both the US Marine and French parachute contingents in Beirut were blown up with the loss of 318 lives in a simultaneous operation on 23 October 1983. This massacre illustrated the vulnerability of even well-guarded targets to determined terrorist attackers prepared to sacrifice their own lives, and the White House itself was defended by anti-truck bomb barriers in the aftermath of the Beirut incident. The impossibility of guaranteeing total security was graphically displayed, however, by the almost carbon-copy bombing of the temporary US embassy building in the heart of Christian East Beirut in September 1984.

State-supported terrorism

The most insidious element of the new wave of Middle East terrorism was the suspected involvement of the Iranian government, allegedly pursuing its war against the United States by means of Lebanese surrogates. The presence of large Shi'ite communities throughout the Middle East, many of whose members were sympathetic to the fundamentalist regime in Tehran, created a potential terrorist problem which went far beyond the borders of Lebanon.

The most well documented example of state sponsorship of terrorist actions has been that of Libya, however. Not only has the government of Colonel Muammar Gaddafi supported Palestinian terrorist groups, using them in its own battle against PLO moderates and rival Arab governments, but

Libyan nationals, including diplomats, have been directly involved in a number of incidents of terrorist violence throughout Western Europe. The most notorious example of Libyan terrorism was the murder of WPC Yvonne Fletcher by a gunman firing from the Libyan People's Bureau in London's St James's Square in April 1984. The subsequent siege of the People's Bureau by British police ended with its evacuation and the return to Tripoli of the Bureau's staff, among whom was the still unidentified assassin. Later reports emanating from Libya indicated that Colonel Gaddafi may have executed the gunmen as punishment for an unauthorised action which severely damaged Anglo-Libyan relations. Nevertheless, it is clear that Libyan diplomatic facilities in a number of countries have been used as bases for terrorist campaigns mounted by teams of Libyan assassins whose task was to eliminate exiled critics of the Gaddafi regime.

The attempted assassination of Pope John Paul II by the right-wing Turkish terrorist Mohammed Ali Agca on 13 May 1981 led to further speculation about state involvement, this time by the Bulgarian secret service acting, it was alleged, on behalf of the Soviet KGB, which wished to remove a Polish pope who was offering open support and encouragement to the Solidarity free trade union movement in his homeland. Most of the evidence for these allegations came from Agca himself. His story of Bulgarian backing changed several times under interrogation, and it has since been thought to have been largely discredited. Nevertheless, the possibility that a major power was resorting to terrorism as a tool of state policy had disturbing implications for the future character of international relations.

Ironically enough, in spite of the repeated denunciation of state-backed international terrorism by President Reagan, it was revealed in October 1984 that the US-backed Nicaraguan Contras had been issued with a CIA-published handbook on sabotage and terrorism. One man's terrorist may still be another man's freedom-fighter. **J.S. Common**

Below: Police marksmen of Scotland Yard's C11 unit arriving at the scene of the siege of the Libyan People's Bureau in St James's Square, London, in April 1984. The growth of a serious terrorist threat during the 1970s led many countries to develop specially trained and equipped units to combat the new problem. In Britain, the army's SAS and police units such as the Anti-Terrorist Squad (C13) and C11 comprised the highly-skilled front line of the fight against terrorism, of which another aspect was the great increase in the number of police officers issued regularly with firearms.

With hindsight, the Iranian embassy in London offered a vulnerable terrorist target in the spring of 1980. In the wake of the Islamic revolution of January 1979, the Iranian diplomatic service had been purged from top to bottom, and career diplomats had been replaced by young, inexperienced supporters of the Ayatollah Khomeini. Security inside the embassy in Princes Gate on the southern edge of Hyde Park was non-existent, and the safety of the building depended totally upon the armed officer of Scotland Yard's Diplomatic Protection Group (DPG), who stood guard in the embassy doorway.

On the morning of Wednesday, 30 April 1980, the officer on duty was 41 year-old PC Trevor Lock. At 1130 hours, PC Lock was enjoying a cup of coffee just inside the entrance to the building, when three young men stormed through the embassy doors. Lock was overpowered, but managed to send an alarm signal to the Information Room at Scotland Yard. As members of the DPG rushed from surrounding embassies and their nearby headquarters in Walton Street, units of the Special Patrol Group, and officers of the Anti-Terrorist Squad (C13), the Technical Support Branch of Scotland Yard (C7), and police marksmen of C11 were informed of the seizure of the embassy and were soon taking up positions in the police cordon which rapidly sealed off the building in Princes Gate from the outside world. By mid-afternoon, experts of the army's Bomb Squad were also on the scene, as were the first shadowy representatives of the elite 22nd Special Air Service Regiment (22 SAS), which is automatically notified of all such terrorist incidents.

Inside the embassy, the assault group of three terrorists, along with three other gunmen who had entered the building unnoticed and unopposed shortly before the attack, had taken 26 hostages, including 16 Iranian embassy staff, two BBC journalists, Sim Harris and Chris Cramer, and Mustapha Karkouti, a Syrian journalist. The hostages were herded together in a small office on the first floor. Astonishingly, the gunmen failed to search PC Lock who still had his revolver concealed beneath his uniform jacket.

At 1435 hours, the gunmen released their first statement to the police over the field telephone which had been passed into the embassy. Describing themselves as the 'Group of the Martyr', they announced that their aim was autonomy for the predominantly Arab Iranian province of Khuzestan – an oil-rich region on the Gulf. They demanded the release of 91 Arab prisoners being held by the Iranian authorities by midday on Thursday, 1 May, and threatened to blow up the embassy if their demands were not met. They also asked for mediation by Arab ambassadors. Later in the afternoon, after releasing an Iranian hostage, the terrorists telephoned the BBC's World Service to publicise their demands, but throughout the next three days, as they listened with increasing frustration to radio news bulletins, their proposal for mediation by the Arab ambassadors remained secret at the request of the top-level government committee which had been assembled to exercise overall control of the siege operation. This committee, known as COBRA (cabinet office briefing room), and chaired by Home Secretary William Whitelaw, was in close and direct contact with the prime minister, Margaret Thatcher. The Scotland Yard officer directly in charge of siege operations at Princes Gate was

Storming the embassy

The SAS and the Princes Gate siege

Deputy Assistant Commissioner John Dellow, under whom a team of four police negotiators (later expanded to six) worked throughout the siege.

As the midday deadline approached on the morning of 1 May, tension mounted inside the embassy. One of the gunmen fired a shot into the ceiling, but their leader, whom they called Oan, but who adopted the code-name Salim in his contacts with the police, remained cool. A cultivated man in his late 20s, Oan continued to negotiate with the police, allowing the release of Chris Cramer, who had developed severe stomach pains, and agreeing to an extension of the deadline. At 1730 hours the police sent in the first meal the occupants of the embassy had eaten since the beginning of the siege.

Further signs of the development of a rapport between the gunmen and the police negotiators came during the evening of 1 May. At 2100 hours the gunmen gave the police a list of their hostages, and half an hour later PC Lock was allowed to speak through the window to officers on the pavement

Left: Two SAS men moving into position for the assault on the Iranian embassy in Princes Gate, London on 5 May 1980. Protected by gas-masks and flack-jackets, and armed with Heckler & Koch MP5A2 sub-machine guns, the SAS team burst into the embassy from several points, blasting in windows with frame charges and following up with stun grenades hurled into the building to neutralise terrorist opposition. Five terrorists were killed and one taken prisoner, and one hostage was killed by terrorist gunfire during the rescue operation.

Below: Covered by a police marksman, the body of Iranian press attache Abbas Lavasani is carried away after being dumped by the terrorists outside the embassy on the sixth day of the siege. The murder decided the government to send in the SAS. Below right: A terrorist collects food from the steps of the embassy. Police negotiators maintained contact with the terrorists throughout the siege, in an attempt to win their confidence and safeguard the lives of the hostages.

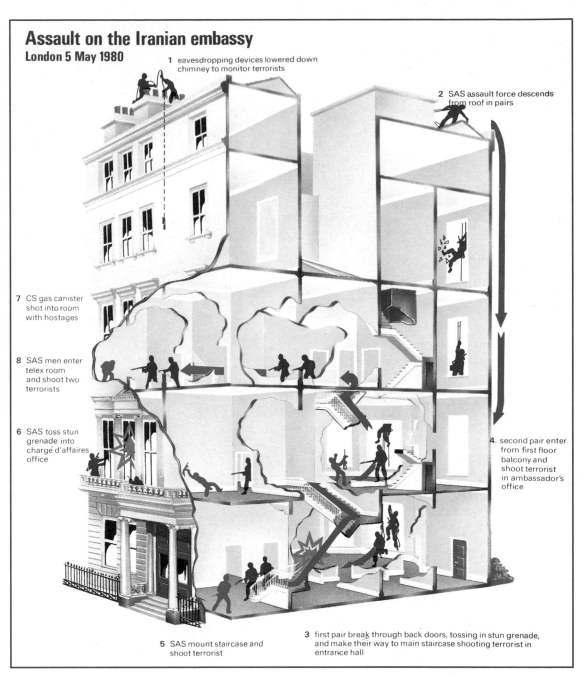

Assault on the Iranian embassy
London 5 May 1980

1 eavesdropping devices lowered down chimney to monitor terrorists

2 SAS assault force descends from roof in pairs

7 CS gas canister shot into room with hostages

8 SAS men enter telex room and shoot two terrorists

6 SAS toss stun grenade into chargé d'affaires office

4. second pair enter from first floor balcony and shoot terrorist in ambassador's office

5 SAS mount staircase and shoot terrorist

3 first pair break through back doors, tossing in stun grenade, and make their way to main staircase shooting terrorist in entrance hall

outside. The mood among the gunmen was pessimistic, however – they may have been experiencing depression following the climactic excitement of the previous two days and the failure of their operation to achieve swift success. Their main hope now was mediation by Arab ambassadors who might be able to win them a safe conduct out of Britain and publicity for their cause. They quietly dropped the demand for the release of prisoners in Iran. COBRA had decided to oppose ambassadorial intervention, however, reasoning that there should be no sign of weakness.

Friday morning began with the gunmen, disturbed by strange noises which they had heard coming from the walls of the embassy, blocking the stairs between the third and fourth floors with furniture and office equipment. PC Lock tried to reassure them that the noises were nothing more than mice, but the cause was in fact the installation of cameras and bugging devices through the walls of the adjoining buildings. During the late evening, compressors and road-drills were started up in nearby Ennismore Gardens to mask some of the noisier activities of Scotland Yard's C7 and of the SAS.

The following day, the police were forced to take an initiative on the question of the Arab ambassadors by the obvious fury of the gunmen at the continued failure of the BBC to mention this demand. Tony Crabb, a senior BBC executive, was called to Princes Gate to take a statement from Oan, and the gunmen were persuaded to agree to the release of one of their hostages as soon as the statement was broadcast. The crisis took a potentially deadly turn later in the day, however, when the terrorists heard a report on Radio Tehran that the British government was seeking permission from the Iranian authorities to storm the London embassy. At 1900 hours, the gunmen threatened to begin shooting hostages unless their statement was broadcast. The threat induced a state bordering on hysteria among the hostages, but Karkouti persuaded Oan to release a pregnant Iranian hostage, 21 year-old Hiyech Sanei Kanji. Shortly after 2100 hours, Oan, Karkouti and Harris heard the terrorists' statement broadcast on a Capital Radio news bulletin. In the sudden release of tension they hugged each other, and a further hostage was freed.

By the morning of Sunday 4 May, the fifth day of the siege, it was becoming clear that the strategy of negotiation was reaching its limit. Powerless to influence government strategy, the police negotiators began to lose the confidence of the gunmen whose frustration was expressed in a raging argument with some of the Iranian hostages over the Ayatollah Khomeini, whom the gunmen had criticised. One of the hostages, Abbas Lavasani, the embassy's 29 year-old press officer and a fanatical supporter of Khomeini's Islamic revolution, was almost shot by Faisal, Oan's second-in-command, as he attempted physically to assault him in the heat of the argument. During the evening Karkouti, who was suffering severely from a stomach infection, was released. Inside the embassy, the strange disturbing noises from the walls continued into the night.

On the morning of the sixth day of the siege, Bank Holiday Monday, 5 May, Oan began to display signs of the strain under which constant responsibility for the terrorist operation must have placed him. As his

Above: An armed officer of Scotland Yard's C7 Technical Support Branch lowers a microphone into the chimney of the Iranian embassy. The police and SAS were able to construct a detailed picture of the situation inside the embassy through the use of highly sophisticated surveillance devices, including microphones and video cameras. Below left: Two SAS men, faces concealed by balaclavas, cover the front of the embassy with Browning 9mm pistols.

Below: Hostage Sim Harris, a BBC journalist, escapes to safety and the protection of armed police officers moments after the SAS had burst into the embassy. Inside the smoke-filled embassy, the SAS assault team raced to secure the safety of the other hostages.

strength diminished, the atmosphere inside the embassy deteriorated, and tension grew. At 1100 hours, Lock relayed a message to the police outside that the terrorists would begin to shoot a hostage every 30 minutes if there continued to be no news of the arrival of an Arab ambassador. The police were able to persuade the gunmen to wait for the midday BBC news bulletin, but its wording was vague and unencouraging. As the police continued to play for time, the terrorists tied up Lavasani, who had earlier volunteered to die. At 1331 hours, the other hostages and the police outside heard three shots. Oan told the hostages that Lavasani had been killed.

Now that the gunmen had begun to murder the hostages, the storming of the embassy was only a matter of time. The gunmen seemed to adopt a fatalistic attitude, accepting that events were totally beyond their control. They again announced that they would kill hostages if they received no news of the arrival of an Arab ambassador. At 1850 hours three more shots were heard from inside the embassy and the body of Lavasani was pushed out of the embassy door into the street. It is uncertain whether Lavasani had been killed earlier, or immediately before. The police were also uncertain whether one or two hostages were now dead, and the incident finally persuaded COBRA, after consultation with the prime minister, to order an assault on the embassy by the SAS. As the SAS team began to take up its final positions, the police negotiators re-established contact with the gunmen in an attempt to fix the position of Oan beside the telephone, and in order to create a false sense of security among the terrorists. The police offered safe-conduct and a plane out of the country, and as details were being settled, at 1923 hours, the SAS smashed into the embassy.

Dressed in black, and wearing balaclavas and gas-masks, the SAS men, armed with Heckler & Koch MP5A2 sub-machine guns and Browning High Power 9mm pistols, entered the building literally from all sides. As two SAS men stormed in through the front first-floor window which they had blasted in with frame charges, eight more abseiled down from the roof. One of the SAS men became caught in his rope, which prevented frame charges being used on the rear windows. The men simply crashed their way in, making immediately for the telex room where their surveillance had revealed some of the hostages were being held. A third group of SAS smashed through the wall of the adjoining building from which they had removed the bricks, leaving only a thin plaster partition.

A hail of SAS bullets

The embassy was now on fire, and the first hostage to emerge from the smoke was Sim Harris, who crawled out onto the first floor balcony and made his way carefully to the balcony of the next building. Meanwhile, PC Lock, who had been with Oan when the assault began, saw the terrorist leader raise his gun to fire at an SAS man who appeared at the window. Leaping forward, he grappled with the gunman who fell in a hail of SAS bullets.

As the SAS team raced through the burning, smoke-filled building towards the telex room on the second floor where the male hostages were being held, the terrorist on guard there opened fire on the Iranian hostages huddled together in the centre of the room. Ali Akbar Samadzadeh, a student working temporarily in the embassy press office, was killed and two others wounded. Another terrorist ran into the room, and as he did so the shooting stopped. What happened next remains unclear, but one hostage alleged later that the gunmen surrendered their weapons to the hostages, who threw them down into the street. Another hostage later told journalists that the gunmen had shouted 'Tasleem, tasleem' ('we surrender'). Nevertheless, when the SAS burst into the room, they found smoke, confusion and a group of people scattered around the floor, two of whom were terrorists. Amid shouts of 'We're hostages', the SAS asked 'Which ones are the terrorists?'. Then, according to Muhammad Hashir Faruqi, the hostages identified the gunmen, who were ordered to stand up by the SAS men, and as they did so, were immediately shot.

The terrorist who had been guarding the women prisoners was more fortunate. He threw away his gun and tried to hide among his captives, but, identified by the SAS, he was searched and dragged outside, where he was taken into custody by police officers. The fifth gunman died on the ground floor and the sixth on the first floor, both shot by SAS men entering from the rear of the building.

The hostages were hastily evacuated to the street outside, where they had their hands tied and were taken away for interrogation and identification. As the police moved in to take control, the SAS men were driven off under motor-cycle escort in a pair of Avis vans to their base in St John's Wood, near Regent's Park. **J. S. Common**

Invaders in the paradise islands

Mercenary activities in the Indian Ocean

In 1978 and 1981 respectively, two notorious mercenary leaders, the Frenchman Bob Denard and the Englishman 'Mad Mike' Hoare – a former British Army officer – both led coup attempts in the Indian Ocean, with very different results. These were, at least in appearance, isolated acts, involving only mercenaries and the tiny forces of two archipelagos, the Comoros and the Seychelles. Yet there was a measure of strategic significance to both attempts, for in both cases the mercenaries set out to overthrow left-wing regimes, and in both archipelagos what was at stake in the long term was control of two superb natural harbours, at Mayotte in the Comoros and at Victoria in the Seychelles.

The strategic importance of the tiny four-island Comoros archipelago has always been considerable. It controls the northern entrance to the 'Mozambique Channel', the stretch of water lying between the east coast of Africa and the large island of Madagascar. For centuries, till the coming of the French, the islands were basically nests of pirates and slave traders, ruled by 'the Battling Sultans'. In the 19th century, the French first seized Mayotte, third in size of the four islands, whose natural harbour is so fine that all the three fleets now patrolling the Indian Ocean – the French, the American, and the Russian – could easily lie at anchor together inside it. The other three islands soon also passed under French control.

By the 1970s, with the tide of decolonisation having carried away most of the former French Empire, it was clear that some arrangement for independence was needed even for such small-fry as the Comoros. The French were most keen, however, to maintain their presence in Mayotte, to be used as a Foreign Legion base as well as for its harbour. While the French prevaricated, the Comoros Government Council declared total unilateral independence. Taken by surprise, the French allowed the independence of three of the islands, but simply stayed in Mayotte, whose inhabitants in any case had no desire to join the newly independent state.

The government of the three independent islands soon shifted leftwards. Ahmed Abdullah, the leader of the old conservative families who became president at independence, was deposed in August 1975 by Ali Soilih, a bright young politician who had been the true power behind the move to independence. Ali Soilih decided on shock tactics, Maoist principles of government, nationalising the spice plantations, and sweeping aside all the traditional Islamic practices.

Meanwhile, exiled representatives of the old families, led by Ahmed Abdullah, looked around for a saviour who would rid their islands of this new regime. Bob Denard had won fame as a mercenary leader 10 years earlier in the Congo. Since then, he had based himself in Gabon, attached to President Omar Bongo's presidential guard, a haven of former Foreign Legionnaires, and had attempted a number of mercenary ventures in West Africa. On 16 January 1977 he and 90 'technicians' (60 white and 30 black, hired for half a million dollars) had landed at dawn on Sunday morning on the near-deserted airport of Cotonou, capital of the Marxist West African state of Benin, in an attempt to overthrow the government of President Mathieu Kerekou. But Kerekou had not

Above: Mercenary leader Bob Denard, veteran of the Congo and former bodyguard of the president of Gabon, who led the May 1978 coup which overthrew President Ali Soilih of the Comoros and brought back to power his predecessor, Ahmed Abdullah (below).

Right: Deposed President Ali Soilih under armed guard, shortly before he was shot 'while trying to escape'. After the death of Soilih, the Comoros became a mercenary paradise, and for a time Denard held the post of minister of defence in the islands' government, although international pressures later forced the mercenaries to adopt a lower profile.

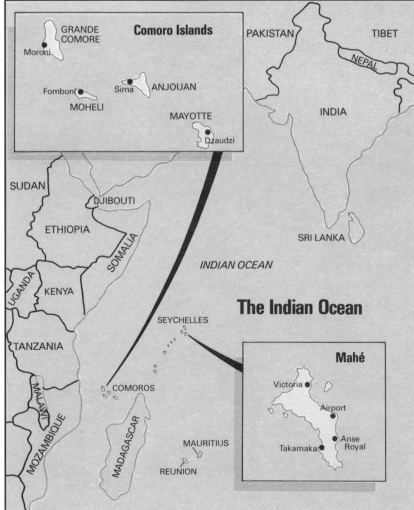

been sleeping in the Presidential Palace, which Denard's mercenaries assaulted an hour after landing; and two hours later his force had re-embarked, having failed in its mission. Despite this, Denard was the choice a year later to lead a similar assault against President Ali Soilih.

This time Denard decided that he would go in with white mercenaries alone, not by air at dawn but by sea at night. He and 50 mercenaries – very probably the same men he had used for the failed Cotonou attempt the year before – landed at 0100 hours on the night of 13/14 May 1978 on Itsandra beach outside the capital of the Comoros, Moroni. They had accomplices and guides on the island who led them through the darkness to the Presidential Palace. This time the president was there: indeed, according to one version he was found in bed with two girls. In the brief scuffle that followed one mercenary was wounded and one presidential bodyguard killed. By 0400 hours the coup had been successful and Ahmed Abdullah was preparing to fly in. A few days later it was announced that Ali Soilih had, according to the time-honoured formula, been shot 'while trying to escape'.

Denard stayed on to become minister of defence in Abdullah's new government, to convert to Islam – he took the name of Said Mustapha M'hadju – and, with his 50 mercenaries, to run the new presidential guard and take over a set of flourishing import-export agencies trading with South Africa. The Comoros became a mercenary paradise, though their presence got more discreet with time.

The only thing that does not ring true in Denard's 'authorised' account of the coup is the story that the 'mother-ship' of the mercenaries was bought in Brittany and had spent 35 days sailing round the Cape before arriving in the waters of Moroni and launching its Zodiac landing craft upon Itsandra beach. It seems far more likely that Denard and his commando set out from the neighbouring island of Mayotte, with at least the complicity of the French military and naval authorities there. Mayotte remains firmly under French control.

North of the Comoros, far deeper into the Indian Ocean, lies the very large archipelago of the Seychelles. But most of its islands are uninhabited; and the total population, at 65,000, is only one-fifth of that of the Comoros, and is concentrated largely on the main island, Mahé. In 1814 France ceded the Seychelles to Britain and for another century and a half the islands slumbered, almost untouched by modern civilisation. Then in 1971 an airport opened on Mahé, near the capital, Victoria, and the great tourist and development boom of the 1970s followed, under the guidance of the young chief minister, James Mancham. On 29 June 1976 the Seychelles were granted independence and Mancham became the islands' first president. A year later he was in London for the Commonwealth Conference when, in the early hours of 5 June, he heard that he had been deposed in a coup led by his own prime minister, Albert René.

Creating an army

There was no army at all on the Seychelles. René's supporters had simply seized the only weapons on the island, in the police armoury at Montfleury, and taken over the government in an almost bloodless coup. But to defend 'the revolution' against a counter-coup, René had to create an army – a small army, numbering only 600 men, but large in proportion to the population of the islands. Furthermore, he invited the Tanzanians to send a military force (variously estimated at 50 to 150 men) to back him up and serve as a presidential bodyguard. The people of the Seychelles approved in the main of René's social reforms, but most loathed the one-party state René imposed, and the army and the alien Swahili-speaking Tanzanians. Many of the middle classes went into exile – to Australia, to Britain, to France and, in the case of a large proportion of the white-skinned upper classes, to South Africa. Plots to overthrow René and restore President Mancham began to proliferate.

'Mad Mike' Hoare had been living outside Durban in Natal since his famous mercenary exploits in the Congo in 1964 and 1965. His various attempts to launch a new mercenary venture – in Biafra, in Angola, in the Gulf Emirates – had come to nothing. He had yachted around the Seychelles – yachting was his passion – as a young man and he considered the islands to be a true paradise. He put himself in touch with the Seychellois exiles and offered to lead a mercenary coup that would overthrow René and his regime. Perhaps he had never forgotten his rivalry with Denard in the Congo, and Denard's success in the Comoros was the real stimulus to 'Mad Mike's' desire – he was aged over 60 – for a comeback. It still took him three years of planning to pull the various strands of his proposed coup together; at long last, in the summer of 1981, his plans were nearing completion.

He obtained weapons from South African Military Intelligence; in early October they delivered a lorry-load of arms and ammunition (East European, captured in Angola) to Hoare's home, The Old Vicarage, in the Natal hills. He hired men from three sources: 'old hands' – not many of them – who had served with him in the Congo; ex-Rhodesian soldiers who had

Above: Mike Hoare supervises the construction of a bridge during his heyday as a mercenary leader in the Congo during the early 1960s. Hoare attempted to emulate his rival Denard by mounting a coup in the Seychelles in November 1981, but the adventure ended in fiasco. Hoare escaped back to South Africa with the bulk of his men, but was arrested for hijacking. Left: Hoare during his trial in 1982.

Left: Some of the weapons which Hoare's men tried to smuggle through customs at the Seychelles' Mahé airport. Detected by a customs officer, the mercenaries attempted to fight their way out. Right: The airliner on which the mercenaries had arrived, damaged during the fighting.

crossed the Limpopo and settled in Durban when Robert Mugabe, their enemy, took power in what then became Zimbabwe; and Afrikaner-speaking part-time members (used to sudden summons for 'special operations') of the South African Defence Force's Recce Commandos. The 'new government' headed by Mancham he arranged to have standing by in Kenya, ready to fly in to Mahé International Airport when the success signal was given – to be followed by one planeload of Kenyan troops and another of Kenyan police, to 'restore order' if the Tanzanians should attempt to intervene.

The ingenious operational plan was for Hoare and his 50 men to fly in as tourists on a package deal, stay for several days in one of the many luxury hotels frequented mainly by South Africans, and then, when all were familiarised with the layout of the islands, to launch a coup at midday. Three assault groups were to be formed: one would seize the radio station and play a tape by Mancham announcing René's overthrow and his imminent return; the second would seize the airport and the army barracks at its southern end, 'neutralising' the Tanzanians in their afternoon siesta; the third would arrest the whole government at State House in Victoria at their weekly meeting. Once the coup was successful, the mercenaries would hand over to the incoming exiles, return to their hotels for a week's sunbathing, and then go back as innocent tourists to South Africa to collect their reward: £5000 each man, twice as much for the officers.

Smuggling in weapons

The only difficulty was how to get the arms into the Seychelles. Schemes for using an ocean-going yacht had to be abandoned on grounds of expense. Hoare decided they could be smuggled in – an AK-47 plus 60 rounds per man – in the false bottom of travelling grips. He tested the system. He sent an advance party in with three grips – all got through; a second party of two; a third party of three. Never once were their grips examined. With eight mercenaries and eight weapons already on the island he decided to go ahead with the main venture.

At dusk on 25 November 1981, a Royal Air Swazi flight carrying 44 members of a beer-drinking club, the Ancient Order of Frothblowers, touched down at Mahé airport. Hoare and over 40 of his men came striding cheerily through customs where minibuses were waiting to take them to the Reef Hotel. But one mercenary, Beck, went through the 'Something to Declare' channel. The false bottom was spotted by an astute young customs officer. When the police sergeant from the airport guardroom attempted to detain all the 'Frothblowers', they swiftly assembled their weapons and seized the airport. But it was now dark, the element of surprise had been lost, and the plan had obviously failed. In sporadic skirmishes around the airport one mercenary, Johan Fritz, and one Seychellois lieutenant, David Antat, were killed. At midnight Hoare and his men seized an incoming Air India flight and diverted it back to Durban – leaving seven mercenaries in the Seychelles. They were caught, subsequently tried, and four were sentenced to death, although later they were pardoned and released. Less lucky, Hoare, abandoned by the South African government which had at least tacitly backed the coup, was jailed in Natal for the hijacking of the Air India jet – and is due to remain there until 1992.

Anthony Mockler

Above right: Seychelles President James Mancham (centre) reviewing troops with Egyptian leader Anwar Sadat. Mancham was overthrown in June 1977 in a coup mounted by Albert René. Right: René, whose reforms were popular, but whose one-party state and reliance upon Tanzanian military backing provoked increasing opposition.

The Tamil Tigers

Guerrilla war in Sri Lanka

Sri Lanka (known as Ceylon until 1972) achieved independence from Britain in 1948. The 1948 constitution was modelled upon the Westminster Parliament, and was thought to provide guarantees of the civil rights and cultural identity of the predominantly Hindu Tamil minority community. As in Northern Ireland, however, the dominant majority community, in this case the largely Buddhist Sinhalese, was able to manipulate what was formally a model parliamentary democracy through gerrymandering of elections and its inbuilt parliamentary majority in order to deprive the minority of effective political representation.

Tamils and Sinhalese had both inhabited the island of Sri Lanka for over 2000 years before the arrival of the British in the 18th century, but with the development of large-scale tea plantations during the 1840s, Tamil plantation workers were also imported from India. Their status remained uncertain in 1948, which was also the year of Indian independence. The first post-independence Sri Lankan government introduced an act in 1948 which deprived approximately one million Tamils of Indian origin of Sri Lankan citizenship, and a further act in 1949 which excluded them from participation in elections. During the 1950s, Sinhalese gradually became the single official language, a status which was recognised by the Official Language Act of 1956. This step was accompanied by widespread anti-Tamil riots, which recurred with increased ferocity in May 1958, leading to the introduction of the country's first state of emergency.

The assassination of Prime Minister Solomon Bandaranaike in September 1959 led to the dissolu-

tion of parliament, and in the subsequent general election his wife, Sirima Bandaranaike, became head of government. During her two periods of administration, from 1960 to 1964 and from 1970 to 1977, official policy continued to favour the Sinhalese language, leading to discrimination against Tamils in higher education and the civil service, the main channels of social and economic advancement. Bandaranaike's defeat of the United National Party (UNP) in the 1970 general election at the head of a left-wing United Front led by her own Sri Lanka Freedom Party (SLFP), coincided with the onset of a severe crisis in the Sri Lankan economy with mounting unemployment and food prices resulting from a drastic fall in the world market price of the country's main exports, tea, rubber and coconut. A serious insurgency waged by the predominantly Sinhalese Janatha Vimukti Peramuna (JVP) in 1971 led to the introduction of a nationwide state of emergency which lasted until 1977.

In May 1972, a new constitution transformed Sri Lanka into a republic, and in the same month a number of Tamil opposition groups joined together to establish the Tamil United Front (TUF) which called for linguistic and religious equality. By September 1973, the TUF had moved to a more radical position, proposing for the first time the creation of an independent Tamil state. Young Tamils in particular were angered by what they saw as mounting government attempts to impose Sinhalese cultural and political domination, and it was they who were most deeply affected by the barriers which were being erected to Tamil entry to universities and government service. The first sign that some Tamils might be moving beyond the non-violent tactics of the TUF came in June 1973, when a Sri Lankan naval patrol intercepted a boat-load of 48,000 Indian-manufactured detonators. Young Tamil militants, calling themselves 'Tigers', spearheaded a radicalisation of the TUF leading to its transformation into the Tamil United Liberation Front (TULF) on 17 May 1976, which was pledged more firmly to the creation of a separate Tamil state, to be known as Tamil Eelam.

The break-up of the left-wing coalition govern-

Above: Armoured cars of the Sri Lankan Army patrol the streets of the largely Tamil city of Jaffna in the north of the island during the violence which accompanied the district elections of June 1981. By the late 1970s, Tamil separatists had begun to resort to open violence to achieve their aim of a separate state of Tamil Eelam. Above left: Tamil Tiger leader Prabhakaran in the jungle of the northern province of Jaffna. The Tamil Tigers were the most militant of the Tamil separatists, and were responsible for a number of attacks on police officers and police outposts.

Left: Sirima Bandaranaike (left), under whose SLFP governments discrimination against Tamils and the Tamil language fuelled separatist agitation, and President Junius Jayawardene (right), whose UNP defeated Bandaranaike in the July 1977 general elections. Jayawardene cracked down firmly on the militant Tamils, sending in the army to impose central control upon the mainly Tamil provinces in the north and east of Sri Lanka. Right: Sri Lankan troops patrol the capital, Colombo, shortly after the violent anti-Tamil riots which shook the country in July 1983.

ment, and the virtual electoral annihilation of the SLFP and its former allies in the July 1977 general election which returned a UNP government under Junius Jayawardene, left the TULF as the largest single opposition party. This apparent strengthening of Tamil separatism provoked violent anti-Tamil riots in which approximately 125 people were killed. Over 40,000 Tamils, mostly tea plantation workers, were forced from their homes, and fled to the safety of refugee camps. The governing UNP and the opposition SLFP both accused each other of responsibility for the disturbances. The TULF renewed its call for a separate Tamil state, but the UNP insisted that the unity of the Sri Lankan state must be maintained.

In October 1977, the Jayawardene government used its massive parliamentary majority to adopt a constitutional amendment which introduced a French-style presidential system, and on 4 February 1978, Prime Minister Jayawardene was sworn in as president. This represented a substantial increase in central authority and was opposed by the TULF. But whereas sections of the TULF leadership were prepared to compromise with the UNP government, the younger Tamil militants began to adopt more radical tactics.

On 7 April 1978, four policemen, one of whom was allegedly responsible for the torture of a number of young Tamil detainees, were killed in an ambush near Mannar by a group calling itself the Liberation Tigers of Tamil Eelam, and on 6 May, a police inspector was assassinated in Jaffna. President Jayawardene reacted by sending in the armed forces to maintain order in the predominantly Tamil north and east of Sri Lanka, in what virtually amounted to a military occupation of a hostile country. Parliament

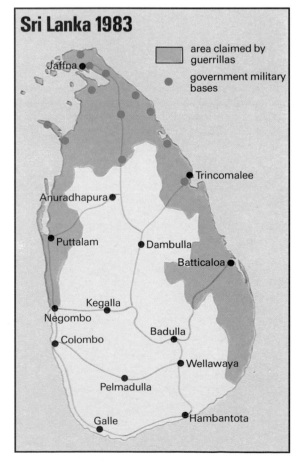

Sri Lanka 1983

area claimed by guerrillas

government military bases

Jaffna

Trincomalee

Anuradhapura

Puttalam

Dambulla

Batticaloa

Kegalla

Negombo

Badulla

Colombo

Wellawaya

Pelmadulla

Galle

Hambantota

voted the president special powers to proscribe subversive organisations, and the Liberation Tigers were banned on 19 May.

Despite the efforts of the security forces, the Liberation Tigers became increasingly active, being responsible for the murder of 14 police officers during the period up to July 1979, as well as for the destruction of Sri Lanka's one airliner in a sabotage attack on Katunayake airport on 7 September 1978. The failure to contain the mounting insurgency with the already considerable powers available to the government led to the passing of a Prevention of Terrorism Act by parliament on 19 July 1979, which increased penalties for terrorist offences as well as police powers of arrest and detention. Four battalions of troops were despatched to the Jaffna area in order to carry out President Jayawardene's instruction to 'wipe out the terrorists'. Nevertheless, attacks by separatist guerrillas on police stations and patrols continued and provided the rebels with a source of arms and ammunition.

Police on the rampage

During the campaign leading up to the June 1981 district council elections, a UNP candidate was shot dead by Liberation Tigers at an election meeting on 24 May, and the shooting of three police officers at a Jaffna election rally on 31 May led to the introduction of a dusk-to-dawn curfew throughout the whole area. During the following week, police rampaged through Jaffna, looting, burning houses and killing innocent Tamils. A state of emergency was declared in Sri Lanka's Northern Province on 2 June, and was extended to the whole country from 4-9 June.

The Sinhalese population reacted violently to the increase in Tamil terrorist activity, and during August 1981 there were anti-Tamil disturbances in many parts of the country. Again, the communal riots led to a hardening of the ethnic divide as large numbers of Tamils living in predominantly Sinhalese areas fled to the largely Tamil provinces of the north and east.

The most serious Sinhalese attacks upon the Tamil community followed an ambush on 23 July in Jaffna, in which a bomb thrown at an army truck by Tamil guerrillas killed 13 soldiers. Anti-Tamil riots broke out in Colombo on 24 July, with serious incidents in a

number of Tamil areas the following day. Government troops were alleged to have participated in attacks on Tamils, and on 25 July, 35 Tamil prisoners were murdered by Sinhalese fellow inmates of the Welikada maximum security prison in Colombo.

The official death toll of the 1983 massacres had reached 384 by 12 August, and the violence indicated the degree to which normal relations between the two Sri Lankan communities had broken down. It was therefore natural that support for the militant separatism of the Liberation Tigers should have greatly increased, both among Sri Lankan Tamils and among the large Tamil communities in southern India and Malaysia. The overseas Tamils were an important source of financial support for the separatist insurgents, who, although poorly equipped with a collection of Sten guns, captured SLRs and Lee Enfield 303s in 1982, by 1983 were reported to be operating in large areas of the Tamil provinces, well armed with modern automatic weapons. The tacit support of the Indian central government and of the state government of Tamil Nadu in southern India was an important factor in sustaining the Tamil separatist movement. With the arrival of boatloads of Tamil guerrillas from the Indian mainland in December 1984, fighting reached a new peak. The Sri Lankan government was losing control of many areas of the country and the continued existence of Sri Lanka as a unitary state was threatened.　　**J. S. Common**

Above: The body of a Tamil victim of the July 1983 riots burns in the streets of Colombo. The majority Sinhalese community reacted violently to any suggestion of concessions to the Tamils. Below: Tamil shops, looted and burned by Sinhalese rioters.

Key Weapons

Heavy Machine Guns

Heavy machine guns are defined as automatic weapons with a calibre of 12·7mm or over and under 20mm. Within this calibre range there are surprisingly few weapons to consider, but these few are important and have been produced in large numbers.

The heavy machine gun was a product of the experience of World War I. Two situations had been encountered during the war where rifle calibre ammunition proved unsatisfactory: a large amount of it was necessary to shoot down an observation balloon and it narrowly failed to penetrate the thin armour of contemporary tanks. Experiments were made with larger calibre rounds to overcome these difficulties and, after the end of the war, John M. Browning attempted to scale up his 0·3in water-cooled gun to take some 11mm French ammunition. This proved unsatisfactory, but the Winchester Company, working from a German 13mm anti-tank rifle cartridge, provided Browning with a more suitable cartridge for a heavy machine gun. By 1921 the Browning 0·5in heavy machine gun was ready for service. In the 1930s a version with an air-cooled barrel appeared: the M2. The M2 with a heavy barrel became the standard type; it served successfully not only throughout World War II, but on into the 1980s. It is still produced in a number of centres in the United States and by Fabrique Nationale (FN) in Belgium.

The reasons for its success are not hard to discover. The round fired by the Browning M2 is still one of the most powerful available to the foot soldier. It can penetrate the light armour of such vehicles as armoured cars and armoured personnel carriers, and this capability has been enhanced in recent years by the introduction of specialised anti-armour ammunition in several forms. Some are tungsten-cored projectiles that provide the gun with more punch, while recently numerous saboted fin-stabilised kinetic energy rounds have been produced in order to increase the M2's armour penetration. All M2s use a belt feed system for their ammunition. Once the belt feed is inserted into the weapon the first round is fed into the receiver by a pull on the cocking handle; another pull cocks the weapon and it is ready to fire, usually by

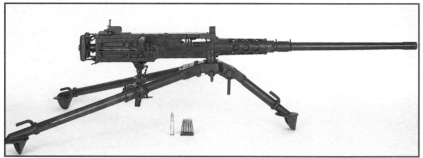

Previous page: Afghan guerrillas demonstrate to their comrades how to fire an M1938/46 DShKM 12·7mm heavy machine gun on a tripod mounting. The wheels are for the trolley on which the gun may be placed; it was a feature common to Russian machine guns of World Wars I and II. Left: The spade grip and trigger of the M2 Browning 0·5in heavy machine gun. The bolt latch release between the two prongs of the trigger is depressed and this shows that the gun is ready to fire. Below: The M2 Browning, which has had a long and varied service life with a fine record for reliability.

Browning 0.5 cal M2 machine gun

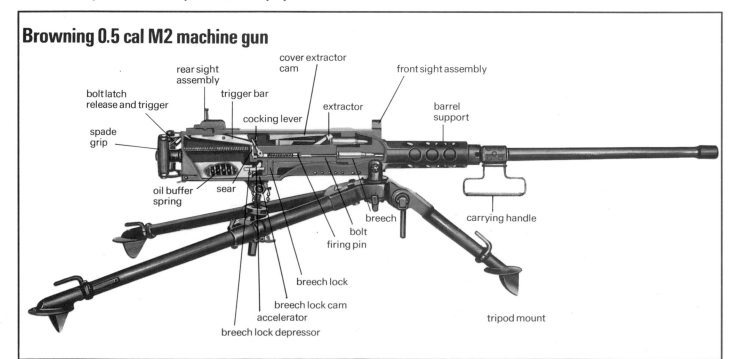

rear sight assembly
cover extractor cam
front sight assembly
bolt latch release and trigger
trigger bar
extractor
barrel support
spade grip
cocking lever
oil buffer spring
sear
breech
carrying handle
bolt
firing pin
breech lock
breech lock cam
accelerator
breech lock depressor
tripod mount

using a spade grip with a thumb trigger.

The M2 couples its striking power with only limited mobility, however, for the M2 is a heavy weapon. In its basic form the machine gun alone weighs 39·1 kg (86lb), and that does not include the heavy tripod or other forms of mounting used. The recoil forces produced by firing large and powerful cartridges have to be absorbed by making the receiver and its associated components very strong and therefore heavy. Some of the recoil forces are absorbed by the use of a heavy buffer (originally an oil buffer was used) that enables the gun to fire at a cyclic rate of between 450 and 600 rounds a minute. The barrel has to be heavy to absorb some of the heat produced by the passage of the projectiles. The barrel can be changed if it gets too hot; unfortunately this normally involves some complex adjustments to the cartridge 'head space' (the degree to which the barrel can be inserted into the receiver in order fully to enclose the cartridge as it is fired – too much and the firing pin will not strike the cartridge base, too little and the cartridge will protrude from the chamber and jam).

The M2 is still in use with the American armed forces and many other nations continue to retain it in their inventories. It was employed as an anti-aircraft gun by the British Army during the Falklands campaign. Many tanks in service carry an M2 on the turret roof for use in the anti-infantry role and there is now a specialised co-axial version for mounting alongside the main gun of a tank. The Israeli Defence Forces make great use of tank and armoured personnel carrier-mounted Browning M2s.

Since the M2 is still in production, many manufacturers find it very well worth their while to produce spare parts, special mountings and ammunition of all kinds for the weapon. The M2 appears to have a long life ahead but in the 1980s the US forces began to look for something lighter. Predictably, some designers have attempted to produce specially lightened versions with all manner of weight-savings such as aluminium components, light barrels with muzzle brakes, and so on. But while this path may have its attractions, an entirely new design has appeared.

Top: An M-55 anti-aircraft machine gun mount with four Browning 0·5in heavy machine guns belonging to Battery B, 25th US Anti-aircraft Artillery Battalion during a field exercise at Kaiserslautern, West Germany. The mounting's cost of $9957 is displayed for the troops' information. Above: Guerrillas in El Salvador practise assembling a Browning M2. The tripod mount weighs about 18kg (40lb) in addition to the gun's weight of 39·1kg (86lb). Right: An M2 Browning of the Gambian Army; the Browning is in service with a variety of the world's armies.

Left: A tank-mounted DShKM M1938/46 gun belonging to the Syrian Army. The Soviet Army and those of its allies make great use of the turret machine gun for the purpose of anti-aircraft defence; the threat of anti-tank helicopters emphasises the need for such weapons. Right: A pair of KPV 14·5mm heavy machine guns on an anti-aircraft mounting in the back of a Land Rover. The heavy machine gun can be used to provide an effective yet inexpensive defence against aeroplanes and helicopters. Below: The experimental GPHMG (general pupose heavy machine gun), also known as the Dover Devil, being test-fired by a Marine officer.

The new design, still in the development stage, is a US Army project for a GPHMG (general purpose heavy machine gun), known colloquially as the 'Dover Devil', after the location of its development agency in Dover, New Jersey. It is an odd-looking weapon but it has several very modern features. One is that by simply changing the barrel and some feed components it can fire either 0·5in or 20mm ammunition. Another is that it has an ammunition dual-feed system that at a press of a lever can enable the weapon to fire either ball or armour-piercing ammunition; the two types of ammunition feed are fed from opposite sides of the weapon. The Dover Devil has about half the number of components of the M2 and it is much lighter (29·5kg – 64lb as opposed to 39·1kg – 86lb) and easier to produce. Thus whatever advantages the lightened M2s may offer, in the long term the Dover Devil seems the more attractive proposition.

Away from the United States, few other heavy machine-gun designs remain in service. Only in the Soviet Union did a pre-war design survive World War II to remain in use into the 1980s. This design is the 12·7mm Degtyarev M1938 DShK, that first appeared in 1938, with its postwar variant, the M1938/46. These two models differ mainly in the type of

Above: A member of the Alianza Revolucionaria Democrática (ARDE – a movement opposed to the Sandinista government of Nicaragua) armed with an M1938/46 DShKM 12·7mm machine gun. The cartridges of the DShKM are 108mm (4·25in) long and can penetrate up to 20mm (0·8in) of armour. Left: A North Vietnamese DShKM machine gun equipped for anti-aircraft duties; US Army trials have demonstrated that the DShKM firing at a helicopter 500m (547yd) away has a 10 per cent chance of shooting it down. Right: An M55 quad 0·5in machine gun mount on the back of a US Marines 2·5 ton truck in Vietnam.

Browning M2	M1938/46 DShK	KPV
Calibre 0·5in	**Calibre** 12·7mm	**Calibre** 14·5mm
Length 165·3cm (65in)	**Length** 155·8cm (61in)	**Length** 200·6cm (79in)
Weight 39·1kg (86lb)	**Weight** 35·7kg (77lb)	**Weight** 49·1kg (108lb)
Operation Short recoil	**Operation** Gas automatic	**Operation** Gas assisted short recoil
Feed system Belt	**Feed system** Belt	**Feed system** Belt
Rate of fire 450-600rpm	**Rate of fire** 575rpm	**Rate of fire** 600rpm
Muzzle velocity 853mps (2799fps)	**Muzzle velocity** 860mps (2821fps)	**Muzzle velocity** 1000mps (3281fps)

ammunition feed, as the M1938 DShK uses a form of rotary feed and displays a prominent drum-type feed cover on top of the receiver, while the M1938/46 uses a more conventional feed. Both weapons are gas-operated but fire a different 12·7mm cartridge to that of the similar calibre Browning M2. The performance of the Soviet weapon is generally similar to that of its American equivalent but in detailed design the two differ considerably.

Both forms of the Degtyarev heavy machine gun display typical Soviet design trends. The barrel is ribbed to aid cooling. The gun itself, at 35·7kg (77lb), is slightly lighter than the Browning M2, but the usual form of mounting is very heavy. This mounting is a descendant of the old Soviet 7·62mm Model 1910 Maxim and comprises large wheels, an optional shield and a seat for the gunner. While this enables the weapon to be towed behind a light vehicle, it is still a heavy load to lug around a battlefield which is probably why both models of this weapon are now gradually being phased out of Warsaw Pact service. This is not happening elsewhere, especially in the Far East where both models are still used in large numbers. The Chinese have contributed to this by producing their own copy of the M1938/46, known as the Type 54. This version was extensively used as an anti-aircraft gun during the Vietnam War and it is still a popular weapon in the area. Many Middle East states also use the DShK and more are found in the service of insurgents and pro-Soviet government forces in Africa.

The other Soviet heavy machine gun is the 14·5mm KPV. This first appeared shortly after World War II; it was designed at the outset for ease of manufacture and thus makes great use of stamped components, simple welds and rivets. The KPV fires a cartridge originally intended for use in the PTRD-41 and PTRS-41 anti-tank rifles but subsequently developed into a high-explosive round, in addition to the original armour-piercing. Overall the KPV is a simple weapon that is well-suited to installation in light armoured vehicles; the design has also been produced in several forms as an anti-aircraft weapon, usually mounted in multiples of up to four guns. Ammunition is fed into the weapon in short belt lengths of 10 rounds that can be joined together.

Perhaps the best-known versions of the KPV are used in the ZPU series. These come in three models: the ZPU-1 (one gun), the ZPU-2 (two guns) and the ZPU-4 (four guns). These anti-aircraft guns are mounted on simple towed carriages, and in Vietnam US helicopter pilots regarded them as their most dangerous opponent. They are now mainly used by Third World nations; the Chinese have produced a copy of the ZPU-4 known as the Type 56 and supplies many to smaller countries.

The preference for larger calibre automatic weapons in the 1980s appears to herald the end of the heavy machine-gun's service life. New cannon designs of 20mm calibre or larger are being produced that are as light or lighter than existing heavy machine guns. In the immediate future the heavy machine gun will certainly remain in service, however, and will no doubt still be firing away somewhere well into the next century. Its centenary will be a triumph of armaments' design that few weapons can claim.

Below: A ZPU-4 anti-aircraft gun consists of four KPV 14·5mm heavy machine guns. The weight of the whole mounting is 1810kg (3990lb) when firing; the maximum range is 5000m (16,404ft) but the effective range is only 1400m (4593ft). The ZPU-4 has fought in Korea, Indochina, the Middle East and Africa. It is in service with many countries; this example is in Angola with the forces of the Marxist Movimento Popular de Libertação de Angola (MPLA).

Right: A ZGU-1 belonging to pro-Syrian Lebanese Ba'athist militia in the Beqaa Valley. The ZGU-1 is a ZPU designed for service in mountainous terrain, and uses the KPV machine-gun barrel. Its cartridge is 114mm (4·5in) in length and can penetrate up to 32mm (1·3in) of armour. BTR-60PB and BRDM-2 scout cars carry a KPV machine gun for their dual-purpose armament. The KPV is a robust example of Soviet weapons' engineering, with excellent protection against dust and dirt for the firing mechanism. The DShK and the KPV, when firing in the anti-aircraft role, use green tracer; this presents an excellent show but is not very effective.

The Ayatollah's republic

Iran under Khomeini

In the weeks following the victorious January 1979 Islamic revolution in Iran, over 200 Iranian generals were purged or retired, and many senior officers died before firing squads, while both the Shah's Imperial Guard, which had played a major role in the previous winter's bloody confrontations with unarmed demonstrators, and the Javidan (Immortals) Brigade were disbanded. Responsibility for local security was taken over by neighbourhood committees of Khomeini supporters, and on 5 March 1979 Khomeini ordered the formation of an Islamic Revolutionary Guard Corps as a counter-balance to the suspect regular armed forces.

The government of the new Islamic Republic announced that the Revolutionary Guards, commonly known as Pasdaran, would combine the functions of the army, the police and the mosque, and that their duty would be to 'spread Iran's Islamic revolution throughout the world'. The Pasdaran were directly responsible to the Revolutionary Council presided over by the Ayatollah Khomeini and were composed of volunteers, largely from the urban lower-middle class and poor who were the new regime's most fervent supporters. Most of these volunteers were literate, and many had completed a high-school education, but Islamic purity was prized far beyond technical expertise or professionalism.

Training was originally the responsibility of officers seconded from the regular army, and seems at first to have been rather rudimentary. The regular officers were soon replaced by Palestinian-trained Pasdaran and a number of Palestinian instructors, however, and training became more formalised. Recruits were given a six-month intensive course of instruction in basic infantry techniques, and great emphasis was placed upon the detailed study of Islamic texts.

At first, veterans of the left-wing Islamic Mujahidin and Marxist Fedayeen guerrilla groups, which had played a crucial role during the pre-revolutionary resistance to the Shah and in the February 1979 battles against the Shah's army, were welcomed into the ranks of the Pasdaran. The anti-Shah coalition rapidly disintegrated, however, and the conservative Islamic fundamentalist supporters of Khomeini became increasingly dominant, particularly within the Revolutionary Guard, from which the members of the guerrilla organisations were purged during the summer of 1979.

The militant conservatism of the Khomeini regime also led to the rapid disillusionment of Iran's ethnic minorities, whose hopes of achieving the autonomy for which they had fought the Shah came into violent conflict with the new government's insistence upon maintaining a strongly centralised Iranian state under the control of the traditionally dominant majority Persians. As early as April 1979, the Pasdaran were involved in heavy fighting in the northern province of Azerbaijan, where Turkoman

Top: Iranian Revolutionary Guards trample the US flag underfoot as they march off to the war against Iraq. The Revolutionary Guards (Pasdaran) have provided the backbone of Iran's military forces since the outbreak of the Gulf War in September 1980. Above: Leading Iranian fundamentalist clergyman, Ayatollah Mohammed Beheshti, the head of the country's Revolutionary Tribunals, speaks at a press conference shortly before his death in a terrorist bomb attack in August 1981.

advocates of greater local autonomy had seized control of the provincial capital, Tabriz. The fighting ended with the suppression of the local revolt, but reports indicated that the Pasdaran had displayed a serious lack of training and discipline.

The ethnic minorities were further alienated by the adoption of a new constitution in December 1979. The Kurds in the northeast protested at its failure to satisfy their demand for greater regional autonomy, while the Baluchis, in the southeast region bordering on Pakistan, who are predominantly Sunni Muslims, objected to the special position given to the Shi'ite sect of Islam, of which Khomeini was the Iranian head. In Kurdistan, opposition erupted into rebellion, and by March 1980 an estimated 40,000 Pasdaran, supported by units of the regular army, were committed to a war against guerrillas of the Kurdish Democratic Party of Iran (KDPI) and the Marxist Komaleh. Revolutionary Guards also provided the firing squads which carried out the stream of death sentences passed on Kurdish rebels by Revolutionary Tribunals.

Under the new constitution, ultimate power was in the hands of the Velayat Faghih, or religious leader, a position occupied for life by the Ayatollah Khomeini. The Velayat Faghih was supreme commander of the armed forces, and appointed both the joint chiefs of staff and the commander of the Revolutionary Guard. He also appointed four of the seven-member National Defence Council, upon whose recommendation he nominated the senior commanders of the armed forces.

The first president to be elected under the December 1979 constitution was Abolhasan Bani-Sadr, who took office in February 1980 with the strong backing of Khomeini. Both Khomeini and Bani-Sadr seemed to agree that the Iranian Islamic revolution would only ultimately be successful if it was exported to Iran's neighbours, while Khomeini often gave the impression that its mission was to conquer the world. But Bani-Sadr's support came essentially from the educated urban middle-class, and he represented their hopes of a more secular, pluralistic society. With the outbreak of the war with Iraq in September 1980, Bani-Sadr's influence began to wane, and the nationalist and religious hysteria created by the war helped increase the influence of the Islamic Republican Party (IRP), which was

Above: Fanatical supporters of the Ayatollah Khomeini carry out the public execution of victims of the Revolutionary Tribunals. The new Islamic regime suppressed all rivals to power, including its former allies. National minorities such as the Kurds and left-wing groups such as the Mujahidin guerrillas and the Communist Tudeh Party were all brutally suppressed. Left: Abolhasan Bani-Sadr (second from right), shown in conference with Pasdaran and army officers during a visit to the Gulf War front line, also fell foul of the Islamic traditionalists. Iranian president from February 1980, he was forced to flee the country in July 1981. Left: Revolutionary Guards march chanting from prayer in a mosque. The religious and patriotic fervour of the ordinary Iranian fighting man has been a vital factor in Tehran's war effort, allowing the otherwise inexplicable use of suicidal human-wave attacks on Iraqi positions. Right: An Iranian boy-soldier, ready to fight and die for the Ayatollah Khomeini. Children as young as 12 years of age are recruited to serve at the front. Convinced that death in battle is a passport to paradise, they are sent to clear the minefields for the Pasdaran.

dominated by the Muslim clergy. The IRP called for the country's whole strength to be thrown into what it proclaimed to be a holy war (jihad) against the infidel President Saddam Hussein of Iraq.

On 27 May 1981, Bani-Sadr was strongly criticised by Khomeini, and on 22 June was dismissed as president for allegedly favouring officers of suspect loyalties, as well as for differences with Khomeini over the handling of the US embassy hostage crisis. In danger of arrest and execution, on 29 July Bani-Sadr escaped to exile in France in an Iranian Air Force jet flown by a senior officer, and on 2 August he issued an appeal to the Iranian armed forces to overthrow the Khomeini regime.

In Paris, Bani-Sadr formed an alliance with the now persecuted and underground Mujahidin, whose terrorist experience was shown on 30 August, when a bomb destroyed the Tehran headquarters of the IRP, killing Mohammed Ali Radjai, who had replaced Bani-Sadr as president on 24 July, Prime Minister Hojatolislam Bahonar, 10 other ministers and 20 members of the Iranian parliament (Majlis). Fearing that the attack was the signal for a military coup, Pasdaran units surrounded army and air force bases in Tehran. The purges which followed this incident were particularly severe in the air force, which was suspected of sympathies with Bani-Sadr, after whose escape it was virtually grounded. On 2 October 1981, Hojatolislam Khamenei was elected as Iran's third president, marking a further step towards the total domination of the Islamic clergy.

The most important factor in Iranian politics remained the war with Iraq. The Ayatollah Khomeini and his fundamentalist supporters in the IRP had never claimed to offer the Iranian people anything other than Islamic purity and a permanent struggle against the enemies of Islam and Iran. The Gulf War not only provided an opportunity to attempt the overthrow of the Ba'athist regime of

President Saddam Hussein in Iraq and, potentially, for spreading Iran's Islamic revolution throughout the Middle East, but also strengthened the Khomeini regime internally by allowing it to mobilise the passions of, on the one hand, Iranian nationalism, and on the other, Shi'ite traditions of fanaticism.

The appeal to Iranian nationalism was particularly important in order to ensure the loyalty of the regular armed forces, which had not only been severely disorganised by the confusion and purges of the revolution, but had also been dangerously weakened by the US embargo on deliveries of arms, ammunition and spare parts as a result of the hostage crisis during 1980. Although the Revolutionary Guards had been built up in order to provide a balance to the still suspect armed forces, Islamic fervour could not substitute for technical skill and professionalism in the high-technology air force and navy.

Children at the front

The ground war remained the most important theatre of operations, however, and here the main brunt of the bitter and costly fighting was borne by the Revolutionary Guards, numbering some 250,000 by 1984, and by the Baseej militia. The latter was a volunteer force numbering some 100,000, composed largely either of the very old or the very young. Indeed, on 20 March 1982, the Ayatollah Khomeini announced that as a 'special concession', boys between the ages of 12 and 18 would be allowed to fight at the front. Receiving as little as one week's training, the Baseej were repeatedly thrown into human-wave attacks against well-defended Iraqi positions, while there were many reports of children being used to clear minefields.

Iranian casualties have been enormous, and by November 1984 it was estimated that between 150,000 and 300,000 had died in the war against Iraq. The regular army, which had largely been held in reserve, and which retained responsibility for heavy artillery and armoured operations, became increasingly critical of the wasteful human-wave tactics advocated by the mullahs and employed by the Pasdaran and Baseej. It was reported that their unwillingness to become involved in such suicidal attacks was a major reason for the continual postponement of the massive Iranian offensive which had been prepared for the spring of 1984.

Differences within the Iranian leadership may also have been a factor in delaying a further offensive, and there was much speculation as to the course which this internal conflict might take. It was known that the Iranian President Khamenei had offered his resignation as he felt unable to ask the people for further sacrifices in order to sustain the war effort. Though the war has cost Iran dearly, that country has a distinct economic advantage over Iraq. Iranian oil revenues continue to more than cover the cost of the war, and though basic foodstuffs are rationed, there have been no shortages.

Iran's reserves of manpower are far from exhausted, and it now appears that the stability of the Khomeini regime is intimately linked to its continued ability to maintain the spirit of fanatical self-sacrifice, with martyred troops promised the key to paradise. The mullahs may therefore be prepared to accept a continued bloody stalemate at the front in order to be able to preserve their own power at home.

Robin Corbett

Operation Babylon

The Israeli attack on Iraq's nuclear reactor

On 30 September 1980 two Phantom jets streaked in low over the Iraqi countryside to deliver an attack on the brand-new nuclear reactor at Osirak near Baghdad. The Gulf War between Iraq and Iran was just eight days old and Iranian raids were still commonplace; the attack was greeted with the usual wailing of sirens and a rattle of anti-aircraft fire. None of this dissuaded the Phantoms which pressed home their strike and, according to eyewitnesses, scored a direct hit on the reactor building, but damage was slight. Within hours the Middle East's rumour machine was in action, pointing out that the Israelis possessed Phantom jets just as the Iranians did and that the Israelis had long been bitter enemies of the Iraqi nuclear industry. In no time at all the Israelis had been credited with the raid on very slender grounds.

The truth behind this raid may never be known. Some eyewitnesses made confident claims that the mysterious aircraft had been seen heading back in the direction of Iran, and in any case it did not seem credible that the Israelis had sent two underarmed and unprotected aircraft over 1900km (1200 miles) of hostile territory to undertake a slapdash job. On the other hand it did not seem typical of the Iranian Air Force to mount such a discriminating strike and, having done so, not to return soon to finish the job. Whoever was responsible it was the Israelis who learnt the necessary lessons from the raid and it was they who mounted one of the most precise air actions in history to destroy the reactor eight months later.

The first signs that Israel had taken notice of the failed strike of 30 September can be recognised only in hindsight. An assistant to the science counsellor at the Israeli embassy in Washington arranged for a meeting with structural specialists of the American Nuclear Regulatory Commission in mid-October. The contact was comparatively informal and was arranged directly with the commission rather than through the State Department, which would have been more normal but also more calculated to alert the Americans. The meeting was ostensibly to discuss ways of defending nuclear installations from aerial bombardment. An internal memo from a commission officer, dated 15 October 1980, states that the Israelis clearly defined the threat that they wanted assessed: 'A 1000kg (2200lb) charge which penetrates concrete barriers and detonates after penetration'; and the memo adds: 'Because of lack of any real interest in underground siting as a protective measure against sabotage, it was unclear whether the Israelis were interested in defending their own plants or destroying someone else's.' Perhaps it was not coincidence that the eventual Operation Babylon – as the raid on the reactor was called – was carried out with 1000kg (2200lb) bombs set to penetrate concrete and detonate afterwards.

It had long been clear that the Israelis were prepared to use violent means to prevent the Iraqis acquiring a nuclear capability. In their opinion any Iraqi nuclear energy programme would lead to eventual weapons production, ultimately threatening a nuclear strike against Israel. Iraqi President Saddam Hussein had made statements suggesting a desire for nuclear weapons, but Iraq's nuclear power programme would proceed under the surveillance of the International Atomic Energy Agency (IAEA), responsible for preventing the diversion of such peaceful nuclear programmes to military ends. The Israelis did not trust the IAEA controls, however, and their traditional belief that attack is the best form of defence made it inevitable that they would do all in their power to frustrate the Iraqi nuclear programme.

The Iraqis had chosen the French as their partners in the nuclear energy enterprise. The French were eager for exports to oil-rich Iraq, but even so they were as careful as possible; they agreed to play their part only because Iraq had signed the nuclear non-proliferation treaty and assented to the inspections of the IAEA.

If the French were doubtful, the Israelis were not. To them the risk of an Iraqi nuclear weapon was simply too great to be borne. Long before the reactor building had neared completion or any nuclear material had reached Iraq, Mossad, the Israeli secret service, had resorted to terrorist acts in France. In April 1979, carefully placed explosives damaged the electronic equipment of the two nuclear reactors destined for Iraq as they lay in the warehouses of Les Constructions Navales et Industrielles at La Seyne. Then, in June 1980, Egyptian Professor Yahia El Meshad was murdered in the Hotel Meridien, Paris. The professor was a leading nuclear scientist under contract to Iraq.

Despite every effort on the Israeli's part, however,

Top: An Israeli F-16. Eight of these aircraft took part in the Israeli bombing attack on the Osirak nuclear reactor in Iraq on 7 June 1981. Known as Operation Babylon, the raid knocked out the reactor, which Israel claimed was being used to develop an Iraqi nuclear weapon. Above: Israeli Air Force chief, Major-General David Ivry, at a press conference following the Osirak raid. The operation won massive approval from the Israeli electorate, and helped Prime Minister Menachem Begin win the June 1981 general election, but provoked doubts elsewhere as to the validity of the Israeli concept of self-defence.

progress at the Osirak site went ahead. Besides the French construction of the nuclear reactor, the Iraqis had negotiated a contract with an Italian firm to build a 'hot' laboratory nearby. The purpose of the laboratory was to make industrial and medical nuclear products, but it would also serve to give the Iraqis a great deal of scientific knowledge in the nuclear field. Israeli suspicion was further increased by this display of Iraqi interest in acquiring technical proficiency in handling nuclear material. The time was fast approaching when it would be too late to take action: once the reactor became operational, the low-level radioactivity of the uranium fuel would be transformed into a number of hazardous fission products including plutonium. When this happened any attack on the plant would release potentially lethal radioactivity in large quantities, and Osirak was only 24km (15 miles) from the populous city of Baghdad. The consequent human catastrophe would make such a raid politically disastrous for the Israelis. If they were to strike, it would have to be before the plant started up, and the date for that was estimated to be July or September 1981.

A tough target

As the Israelis planned their attack, the Iraqis were by no means unaware that a danger to the Osirak plant existed. Defences around the site were substantial. There were earthwork barriers to missile attack, artificial 'anthills' covered in anti-aircraft guns, and an array of mobile surface-to-air missiles. There was also a tented camp of soldiers ready to meet any commando raid. Ostensibly the target was a very tough one, but the Israelis had every confidence in their ability to destroy it.

For a start they counted on the most prized of all military advantages – surprise. In the early stages of the Iran-Iraq war the air-raid sirens had constantly sounded the alert but, as the conflict entered a period of stalemate, the sirens fell silent after 5 March 1981. The missile and gun crews were not at peak readiness and, in any case, they had enjoyed a lamentable record against the Iranian Air Force. Modern gun and missile systems simply are not as deadly as their makers claim (as both British and Argentinians

discovered in the Falklands War), besides which the Israelis were expert in electronic counter-measures to baffle radar or confuse missile guidance systems. According to General Ivry, the Israeli Air Force chief, months of preparation went into planning the systems needed to enable the aircraft to survive.

The attack was set for 7 June 1981, late on a Sunday afternoon. The Israelis believed that the shift changes worked on the Osirak site meant that there would be few foreign technicians in the danger area at the time; they had no wish for the diplomatic fall-out that would follow the deaths of a substantial number of French or Italian citizens. The eight designated F-16s took off with an umbrella of F-15 interceptors to deal with any hostile fighter patrols and streaked off on the ground-hugging 960km (600 mile) outward leg of their journey.

The details of the mission remain in many ways unclear. To keep the advantage of surprise the attacking aircraft would need to reach their target without being detected by the radars of Jordan, Saudi Arabia or Iraq. To do this they needed to undertake the entire outward leg of their mission at very low level to duck under the radar screen. Their probable route lay over the waist of Jordan south of Amman, the empty northwest corner of Saudi Arabia and then the desert quarter of Iraq. Such a long low-level flight would encounter a serious fuel problem, however.

Above: An Israeli Air Force F-15, several of which took part in the Osirak mission as a defensive umbrella for the attacking F-16s. The Israeli aircraft flew in low over the Saudi and Iraqi desert, possibly tricking the Saudis by using Jordanian call-signs.

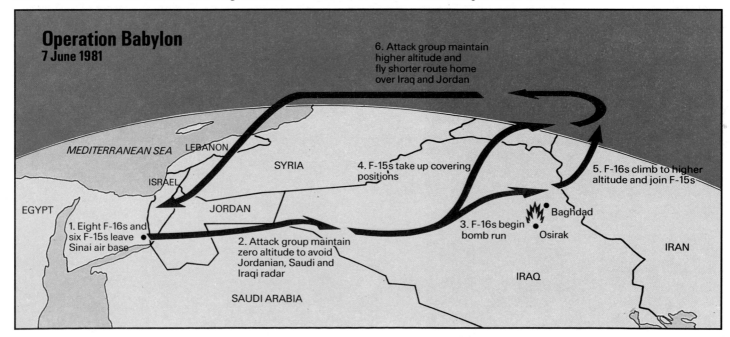

Operation Babylon
7 June 1981

6. Attack group maintain higher altitude and fly shorter route home over Iraq and Jordan

MEDITERRANEAN SEA

LEBANON

SYRIA

4. F-15s take up covering positions

5. F-16s climb to higher altitude and join F-15s

ISRAEL

EGYPT

JORDAN

1. Eight F-16s and six F-15s leave Sinai air base

2. Attack group maintain zero altitude to avoid Jordanian, Saudi and Iraqi radar

3. F-16s begin bomb run

Baghdad

Osirak

IRAN

IRAQ

SAUDI ARABIA

Osirak was just within the range of Israel's F-15s and F-16s, but only if they flew at high altitude to conserve fuel. A low-level attack would mean that the aircraft would either carry drop tanks or need refuelling. If they used drop tanks this would severely reduce their load-carrying capacity and therefore the number of bombs they could deliver at the target. Nevertheless, General Ivry hinted strongly at a post-raid press conference that this was the method they adopted – evidently mid-air refuelling at low altitude was too complex to be feasible.

Another problem about the flight was the role of American AWACS aircraft being operated by the USAF on behalf of Saudi Arabia. With their downward-looking radar, the AWACS aircraft were designed to spot low-flying intruders into Saudi airspace. Various explanations have been offered as to why they failed to spoil the Israeli's surprise. According to one version, only a single AWACS aircraft was aloft at the time and it was patrolling Saudi Arabia's northeast frontier to watch for incursions by Iranian aircraft, so the Israeli planes were too far distant to register on its radar screens. In another version, the Israelis successfully imitated Jordanian call signs and frequencies, confusing the AWACS observers as to their identity. It has also been suggested, however, that given the close relationship between Israel and the United States, the USAF may have cooperated with the attackers, either by turning a blind eye or even by actually guiding the Israelis onto their distant target.

Whatever the truth, the aircraft were not detected, and the whole mission went with that uncanny precision which is the hallmark of Israeli special operations. The eight F-16s burst upon the surprised Iraqi defences in two formations of four. The defenders managed to fire off a few rounds from anti-aircraft guns but failed to bring their missiles into action or to scramble interceptors. The guns were ineffective and all 16 bombs appeared to one eyewitness to be accurate 'to a metre'. This accuracy convinced many experts that American laser-guided 'smart' bombs were used. The Israelis denied this: General Ivry claimed that the phenomenal accuracy of his bombers was achieved by months of practice on a specially built reproduction of the Iraqi plant.

Strike on film

After the strike, the circling Israeli aircraft were able to take video film of the reactor's walls collapsing before gaining altitude to make their way back to their base across Jordan. At height they could save fuel and increase speed, so that when they were picked up by Jordanian radar they would be uncatchable. Indeed, the Jordanians wisely did not bother to scramble their own slower, less modern aircraft when the Israeli raiders were finally spotted.

The results of the action were all the Israelis could have hoped for. The reactor had been destroyed and it would need between three and five years to bring it back to its nearly operational state again. Levels of radioactivity released by the destruction were very low and posed no threat of mass casualties in the immediate area or nearby Baghdad – indeed, the greatest hazard amid the rubble was a single Israeli bomb which had failed to explode. All the Israeli aircraft returned safely; three people – one a French technician – had been killed at Osirak. Operation Babylon had been an almost surgically precise action crowned with success. **P. J. Banyard**

Above: Egyptian nuclear physicist, Professor Yahia El Meshad, who was murdered in his Paris hotel room in June 1980. His death was linked to his participation in the Iraqi nuclear project, and Israel claimed that it was a major setback for the alleged Iraqi plan to develop a nuclear weapon.

Below: USAF AWACS, such as this aircraft, were stationed in Saudi Arabia to monitor the Gulf War. Their ability to detect aircraft over a wide area was a potential threat to the security of the Israeli bombing mission, though the US later claimed that they were operating in a different sector at the time of the raid.

Fighting to a standstill

The continuing war between Iran and Iraq, 1983-84

The war between Iran and Iraq – known as the Gulf War – which had begun in September 1980, had by 1983 settled into a prolonged stalemate. The failure of the initial Iraqi offensives to achieve any decisive objectives had allowed the Iranians to reorganise and seize the initiative during 1982, but the Iranian offensives of that year only succeeded in recovering small areas of territory, at the cost of very high casualties.

On 7 February 1983, to mark the fourth anniversary of the Islamic Republic, a new Iranian offensive began in an area 64km (40 miles) east of Al Amarah, an important staging post on the Baghdad-Basra road. There was swampland immediately east of Al Amarah but nearer the border this turned into flat desert terrain. The area was defended by the Iraqi Fourth Army under the command of Major-General Hisham Sabah al-Fadhri. In the flat desert area, exposed tracks linked strongpoints ringed by head-high earthworks in which artillery and tanks (used as artillery) were deployed. The Iraqis had also dug deep ditches to act as tank traps. In this terrain, large, tracked earth-moving vehicles were as important as the tank.

Force levels and casualties were difficult to assess in the week-long fighting, which took place mainly around the Fakkeh-Bostan border area. The pattern of the offensive is relatively clear. Waves of lightly-armed Revolutionary Guards attacked Iraqi positions at night and, despite suffering heavy casualties, were able to push across the border into Iraq. In the first phase of the fighting, darkness and surprise gave the Iranians the advantage. Subsequently, Iraqi firepower and control of the air contained the Iranian

advance, for, in the second phase of the offensive, beginning on 10 February and again mounted at night, the Iranian forces were held just inside the Iraqi border where a spearhead was trapped by Iraqi artillery and helicopter gunships. The fighting was fierce, even if the published casualty figures need to be taken with a pinch of salt. Iraqi communiques said that Iran lost 7000 dead in the first 24 hours of fighting, 2500 in the first day of the second phase, and 16,000 altogether in the week-long fighting. Both sides gave exaggerated numbers of prisoners, but 1000 Iranians were paraded through Baghdad after the fighting had subsided.

It seems clear that the areas where the Iranian forces could mount sustained offensives were diminishing as Iraq's defensive line was augmented, for the push against Al Amarah was followed by a new Iranian offensive in July in the far northern Kurdish border areas. This new northern front was unlike the mix of desert and marsh in the south: it was rugged mountain terrain cut by deep valleys and populated on both sides of the border by Kurdish tribes which opposed their respective governments. From the beginning of the war the Iraqi government had supplied arms to dissident Iranian Kurds, and the cutting of these supply lines was probably an objective of Iran's July offensive. Early reports suggested that the offensive began on the initiative of local Revolutionary Guard commanders who were responsible for security in the Kurdish areas of Iran.

The Iranian offensive began with a push from Piranshahr and Iranian troops quickly surrounded Haj Omran, a small Iraqi border garrison post. The fighting in this area devolved into a fragmentary

Above: An Iraqi soldier moves forward through a burning village during the Iranian offensive in the spring of 1984. Though initially successful in capturing Majnoon Island, the Iranian Revolutionary Guards were decimated in their exposed positions by Iraqi helicopter gunships.

struggle for peaks and strategic heights until, in the last few weeks of September, fighting spread out on a long front. Although the offensive was originally described as a push on Kirkuk, the centre of Iraq's oil-producing and refining area, the mountain ranges, gorges and valleys made this an unlikely objective. The Iranian goals were probably more limited: cutting supplies to the Iranian Kurdish movement and putting Marivan and Baneh out of reach of Iraqi artillery. The launching of an offensive in the far northern border illustrated how Iran could mobilise manpower to probe Iraq's defences anywhere from Basra to Kurdistan; but the fighting also showed that Iraq could mount a tenacious defence of its own territory.

In September 1983 another Iranian offensive began north of Marivan along a 150km (93-mile) front; fighting flared up again in October with Iranian claims that they had taken two Iraqi garrison towns and had advanced 16km (10 miles) into Iraq in a long finger of land stretching northward from Dezh Shahpur. On 24 October, Iranian troops advanced on Penjwin, after taking the surrounding heights, announcing that they had crushed five Iraqi counter-offensives, destroying more than 100 tanks and armoured personnel carriers. Although distant from the major Arab cities, the area was sensitive for Iraq since it contained the major oil centre of Kirkuk and, more importantly, had had a history of Kurdish nationalist rebellion against Iraqi central governments. The fighting in this northern sector continued until late November. It was clear that the fighting was ferocious and substantial numbers of troops were involved. The commander of Iraq's First Army described the offensive as involving seven divisions of Revolutionary Guards, the 28th and 30th regular army divisions, the 2nd Brigade of the 21st infantry division, two commando batallions and an armoured force. In the initial stages, the Iranians infiltrated at night, and at dawn the Iraqi Air Force responded, using jets and helicopter gunships. By 20 November, the fierce fighting seemed finished, both sides settling into artillery exchanges.

In a new phase of the war, the Iranian government shifted to a propaganda battle over the use of poison gas. Photographs of soldiers with abscesses, blisters and black and purple flaking skin were exhibited in Tehran at an international medical conference. The Tehran authorities gave dates and places: 9 and 19 November at Penjwin. Independent experts remarked on the 'probable' use of nitrogen mustard gas.

Throughout the period of fighting in the northern sector, the Iraqi high command exploited its superior airpower. In winter 1983 Iraq took delivery of five Super-Etendard strike aircraft equipped with Exocet missiles and 30 Iraqi pilots had undergone 14 weeks training in France. However, Iraqi threats and attempts to hit Kharg Island, Iran's major terminal, and thereby stop Iranian oil exports, were met with the terse Iranian response that if Iranian oil did not leave the Gulf, then no one's oil would leave the Gulf through the Strait of Hormuz. As it happened, Iraqi attacks on Kharg Island in this period were unsuccessful, in part because of Iranian defences and in part because of inaccurate Iraqi bombing. A broadened involvement did result, however: the United States, committed to keeping the Strait of Hormuz open, moved another naval battle group,

including the aircraft carrier *Ranger*, into the Indian Ocean.

Iraq countered Iranian pressure in the north by missile attacks on Iranian towns in the central sector. On 30 September, Iraq launched missile attacks on Dezful and Andimeshk, killing 56 and injuring 250; attacks on Dezful and Masjed Soleyman followed on 23 October and on 26 October Iraq gave the Japanese government formal warning of intent to bomb the Japanese-constructed multimillion-dollar petrochemical plant at Bandar Khomeyni. Probably more accurate when specifying Iranian casualties than when estimating Iraqi ones, Iranian communiques stated that in October, Iraqi air raids and bombardments had killed 3700 civilians and wounded 16,200. Since Iraq had withdrawn from Iranian territory, the only military initiatives it could take were attacks on Iranian towns, oil installations and shipping which carried Iranian oil. Iraq's better furbished air force and missiles were used as a threat against any further Iranian land offensives.

Attacks on shipping

At the end of November 1983, *Antigone*, a Greek-registered ship, was hit close to Kharg Island. It seems that an Exocet missile was used for the first time but failed to explode on impact. The crew members had evacuated the ship and were about 500 metres away when the explosion took place and the ship broke in half. Iraq's attacks on tankers carrying Iranian oil were paralleled by missile attacks on Iranian cities as broader punitive measures. Terrorist bombings of the US and French embassies in Kuwait, an ally of Iraq, brought retaliatory Iraqi missile attacks on six Iranian cities: Ahvaz, Andimeshk, Dezful and Ramhormoz (between 80-120km – 50-75 miles within Iran), Behbehan (220km – 135 miles) and Nahavand (200km – 125 miles).

As the 1983-84 winter retreated, reports of an imminent Iranian offensive began to appear. On 2 February 1984, the Iraq government countered by announcing that, after 6 February, Dezful, Shush, Andimeshk, Ahwaz, Kermanshah, Ilam and Abadan would be hit. The effects of civilian casualties from Iraqi shelling and missile attacks brought a

Below: These World War I-type Iraqi defensive positions, against which massive Iranian human-wave attacks have repeatedly been hurled, transform the desert into a deadly moonscape of trenches and dug-outs. Despite Iranian numerical superiority, Iraq has the advantage of better supplies of equipment and well-constructed defences.

Above: Iranian troops drag a wounded comrade to safety during house-to-house fighting in Dezful. The ability of both sides to blunt each other's offensives either from prepared positions or in the ruins of shattered cities helped transform the Iran-Iraq conflict into a bloody war of attrition.

Above: Trapped in an anti-tank ditch, a T55 lies abandoned on the battlefield. Since the early days of the Iraq offensive of September 1980, tanks have played only a minor role in the Gulf War, and the courage and determination of the ordinary infantryman has been more important than high-technology equipment.

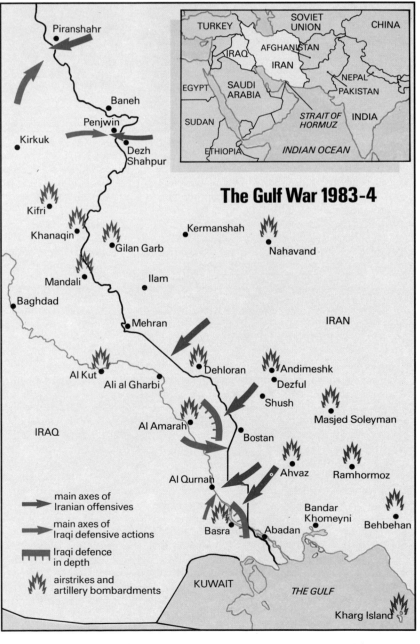

The Gulf War 1983-4

Piranshahr

Baneh

Penjwin

Kirkuk

Dezh Shahpur

Kifri

Khanaqin

Kermanshah

Gilan Garb

Nahavand

Mandali

Ilam

Baghdad

Mehran

IRAN

Al Kut

Dehloran

Andimeshk

Ali al Gharbi

Dezful

Shush

Masjed Soleyman

IRAQ

Al Amarah

Bostan

Ahvaz

Ramhormoz

Al Qurnah

Bandar Khomeyni

Behbehan

Basra

Abadan

→ main axes of Iranian offensives

→ main axes of Iraqi defensive actions

⊢ Iraqi defence in depth

✶ airstrikes and artillery bombardments

KUWAIT

THE GULF

Kharg Island

Inset map: TURKEY, SOVIET UNION, CHINA, IRAQ, AFGHANISTAN, IRAN, EGYPT, SAUDI ARABIA, NEPAL, PAKISTAN, SUDAN, STRAIT OF HORMUZ, INDIA, ETHIOPIA, INDIAN OCEAN

reversal of Iranian policy which had avoided Iraqi civilian targets. After 4600 civilians had died and 22,000 had been injured by Iraqi attacks, Iran responded by announcing an intention to shell Mandali, Khanaqin and Basra. Both sides then proceeded to attack each other's towns.

This air and missile offensive was followed by yet another Iranian ground offensive in the central sector. After shelling Al Kut and Al Amarah on 16 February, Iranian troops moved forward on 17 February. Iranian planes attacked Ali al Gharbi and a three-hour battle took place between Mehran and Dehloran. On 22 February, Iran launched a two-pronged offensive along a 105km (65-mile) front from Chilat.

The area of fighting was flat but very marshy land. The Iranian choice of this area for a new offensive was based on the possibility of a gap between the Iraqi Fourth Army defending Al Amarah and the Third Army defending Basra. The marsh area also was not so deeply fortified and reed beds provided greater cover than the flat desert terrain. Iran used pontoons, track-laying equipment, motorised canoes and small ferryboats to move across the Hawizah marsh to Al Qurnah where the Iranian forces were stopped some 9km (6 miles) from the town. In the advance the Iranian forces took Majnoon Island, a few kilometres east of Al Qurnah. The island itself had no particular strategic significance; although it is an oil-bearing area, the oilfields were undeveloped. Iraq was not able to cut off Iranian reinforcements which came in by boat after dark when Iraqi helicopter gunships were unable to operate.

The 'daily harvest'

According to the no doubt partial account by the Iraqi Third Army commander, Major-General Mahir Abd al-Rashid, the Majnoon Island area became a 'fish trap' and in the process of the fighting Iranian soldiers were 'daily harvested' by the helicopter gunships which were able to operate at will. According to the Iraqi commander, because of the marshy terrain, the Iranians were effectively isolated. They had no artillery support, only mortars.

No independent accounts of the fighting in this area exist but Iraqi television film shot in the marsh area to the east and southeast of Al Qurnah showed hundreds of corpses along the sides of dykes surrounded by reedy lakes. The Iranians had clearly been defenceless as they left their boats. On 4 March Iraq announced that Iran had suffered 50,000 casualties since the 22 February offensive.

Subsequent to the offensive against Al Qurnah and Ali al Gharbi, on 29 February the Iranians undertook an offensive south of the marshes to the east of Basra, involving three infantry divisions supported by tanks. The depth of the Iraqi defensive line easily blunted the offensive. Independent accounts of the Iraqi positions near Basra described them as comprising minefields, forward infantry units backed by T55 and new T72 tanks, artillery in support with inexhaustible ammunition, and more tanks and Soviet Mil Mi-24 helicopter gunships in the date palms. Such defences in the southern sector protecting Basra must have been an important influence in forcing Iran to attack in the more difficult terrain of the Hawizah marshland.

There were further reports of an impending Ira-

nian offensive at the beginning of April, but no offensive took place. In the event, the war shifted southward. In January Iraq had begun attacks on Iranian shipping, and in April the 'tanker war' began in earnest. On 18 April *Rover Star* was hit, on 25 April, *Safina al-Arab*, a Saudi-owned tanker, and on 7 May *Alahood*. On 13 May the Iranian Air Force hit the *Umm Qasbah*, a 55,000-tonne tanker sailing between Kuwait and Bahrain. The Iranian strategy was to hit oil tankers approaching or leaving the ports of the Arab Gulf states which provided Iraq with finance for its war. The attacks continued throughout May and June and a further expansion of external involvement took place on 5 June when Saudi Arabian F-15s, aided by US-manned AWACS aircraft, shot down an Iranian F-4 Phantom which had entered Saudi air space. Oddly, there was no Iranian retaliation.

At the same time, artillery duels and air bombardments resumed in both north and south. Iran shelled Basra, Khanaqin and Mandali and the Iranian Air Force went into action bombing Kifri and Jalola. Iraq responded by bombing Baneh, Gilan Garb, Dehloran and Dezful. The course of the war did not change, only the numbers of civilian casualties increased.

By the summer of 1984 the Iraq-Iran war had reached a complete stalemate. Iraq had proved unable to defeat the Iranian armed forces, to maintain control of the territory it occupied in 1980, or to prevent Iran from shipping oil. Iraq had been able to contain Iranian offensives in Iraqi territory through its firepower and the construction of heavily mined and fortified front lines in the central and southern sectors. The defensive line in the south was enhanced in July 1984 when Iraqi engineers, using giant

Above: Iranian assault teams in the Hawizah marshes. After this offensive in February 1984, human-wave tactics, which had been so wasteful of Iranian lives (below) were apparently dropped, probably on the insistence of the regular army, whose support was vital to breach the strong Iraqi defences. Below right: A young Iranian boy trains determinedly to take his place at the front.

pumps, flooded vast tracts of desert, forming a lake 24km (15 miles) long and ranging from 1-3km (a half to 3 miles) wide. In the mountainous north and east of Al Amarah where defensive lines were more difficult to construct, Iraqi artillery and airpower were able to contain Iranian offensives.

By 1984 Iran had achieved far greater coordination between Revolutionary Guard commanders, the Baseej and the regular army, but was still handicapped by the lack of artillery and particularly air support in battle. Spare parts for the US-supplied air force were difficult to come by because of the US boycott, although there were reports that Israel sold Iran 250 tyres for the F-4 Phantoms. In June 1984, US intelligence sources estimated that Iran had 25 operational Phantoms out of a pre-war 166 and between 5 and 10 F-14s out of a pre-war 150. Iranian politics since 1979 had affected the air force as much as the army. Captain Hamid Zirak-Bash, a liaison officer between the air force commanders and the commanders of the army and Revolutionary Guards who defected, told *The Times* that the best fighter pilots had been executed, jailed or dismissed and that morale was low among the remainder because of mistrust. Pilots were spied on to see if they prayed; they were searched before take-off for indications of an intention to defect and flight plans were supplied only at the last minute before take-off. Another defecting officer, Lieutenant Reza Asadi, said that all fighter-bombers were based deep in Iran and required refuelling in the air.

Despite greater firepower and air superiority, Iraq has been unable to destroy Iran's war capacity. Over the four years of war, Iraq's response to Iran's regular spring and autumn counter-offensives has been to increase the scope of the fighting by using poison gas, shelling towns and in 1984 attacking Iran-bound shipping. Between March and September 1984 Iraq hit 26 ships in the Gulf.

As the fourth anniversary of the start of the war approached, both sides were bogged down along a 640km (400 mile) front with nothing more to show for four years of fighting than an Iranian occupation of a few kilometres of territory in marshy and mountainous areas and casualties on an enormous scale. It has been said that Iran has lost between 150,000 and 300,000 and Iraq between 75,000 and 150,000 dead.

David Pool

The arms bazaar

The Gulf War provided a bonanza for arms dealers of all sorts. While one private Armenian dealer made a fortune by buying captured Iranian equipment from Iraq and selling it back to Iran, the superpowers have also been heavily involved. Iran, whose main sources of military equipment under the Shah were France, the USSR, Italy, Britain, and above all the United States, experienced particularly severe problems in maintaining the combat-readiness of its advanced weapons systems.

Although Washington placed an embargo upon arms sales to Iran, either by US companies or foreign licensees, Tehran was able to keep a small proportion of its F-4, F-5 and F-14 fighter aircraft in the air with spares and munitions bought from South Africa, Taiwan, Argentina, Britain and Israel. As such sales are extremely carefully monitored by the US, they were probably approved by Washington.

Israel, in particular, supplied vital spares for Tehran's US-built equipment, and Israeli Boeing-747s reportedly flew regularly over Lebanon and Syria on their way to Iran, loaded with military supplies. It has also been suggested that Israeli technicians have taken over the maintenance of Iran's US-built fighters. Israel's interest in preserving a strong Iran as a counterbalance to its much nearer Arab enemies has produced one of the Middle East's more bizarre alliances.

Equally interesting has been the scale of support which Iran has received from Peking. China and Iran signed a $1·3 billion agreement in April 1983 for the supply of Chinese military equipment, including F-6 and F-7 fighters (the Chinese versions of the Soviet MiG-19 and MiG-21), T59 tanks, 130mm artillery and smallarms. Delivery was to take place over three years, and Iran agreed to provide China with examples of the latest Soviet-built equipment captured from Iraq. Most of these Chinese supplies were channelled through North Korea, where Iranian pilots reportedly received training, and there were up to 300 North Korean military instructors and technicians in Iran. China also supplied large quantities of arms to Iraq, apparently with the aim of earning foreign exchange with which to help finance its own ambitious programme of military modernisation.

After a cooling of relations between Iraq and the Soviet Union during the early stages of the Gulf War, Moscow renewed arms deliveries to Baghdad in June 1982 after the suppression of the Communist Tudeh Party in Iran, providing the bulk of Iraq's armour and smallarms, as well as fighter aircraft, helicopter gunships, surface-to-air and surface-to-surface missiles, and reports indicated that Moscow had delivered 15 long-range SS-12 missiles. France has been another major source of supplies to Iraq.

The United States also swung its support behind Iraq, particularly after the series of Iranian-inspired terrorist attacks upon US Marines in Lebanon, and it therefore appears that although Iran has been able to find sufficient quantities of equipment to sustain its war effort, and remains far superior to Iraq in terms of manpower, the Iraqis had by 1984 established a lead in modern weapons of all kinds, allowing them to repel the increasingly futile Iranian human-wave offensives.

The tanker war

The Iran-Iraq confrontation at sea

Throughout the postwar era, the dominant power in the Gulf has always been one of the Western nations, either Britain or the United States. Iran, as a client of both of these countries until 1979, and the only nation in the area with a long coastline and more than one port capable of sustaining naval shipping, has always been the paramount indigenous naval force.

Iraq, after the 1958 revolution, adopted a nationalist stance and drew closer to the Soviet Union. In an attempt to provide a counterweight to Iranian naval power, expansion of the Iraqi Navy was planned, but there was an immediate practical difficulty: the coast of Iraq was only 58km (36 miles) long, much of it mudflats and shallows. The Iraqis had a naval base at Basra, built by the British, but its proximity to the Iranian border placed it in an insecure position. Under the terms of the Iraqi-USSR Friendship Treaty of 1972, a loan of $150 million was granted to Iraq for the construction of a naval base at Umm Qasr on the border with Kuwait.

Main picture: The Saudi-owned oil tanker *Al Ahood* aflame; it was attacked on 7 May 1984 and afterwards burned for over two weeks. Left: Firefighters attempt to put out the blaze on the *Al Ahood*. Below left: The hulk of the *Al Ahood*. Gulf oil is of some importance to the world economy, but it is all-important to Iran, since it provides the main means of finance for the war effort; Iraq's aerial attacks seriously threatened Iran's ability to wage war.

As well as a naval base, Iraq also acquired a navy from the Soviet Union. At the time of the 1958 revolution, the Iraqi Navy consisted of a royal yacht and a few aged gunboats, but in 1959 12 P-6 motor torpedo boats were bought from the Soviet Union. Further expansion was achieved between 1972 and 1976 with the addition of six Osa I and eight Osa II-class missile boats equipped with SS-N-2 Styx surface-to-surface missiles, and two T-43-class ocean-going minesweepers; all of these were delivered by the Soviet Union. Between 1977-79, Iraq also received four Polish-built Polnocny-class tank landing craft. For a country with a small coastline, Iraq had established a respectable little navy.

Iran, which possessed the largest navy in the Gulf throughout the postwar era, began a programme of naval expansion in the early 1960s by ordering four corvettes from the United States. This was followed by the four Saam-class frigates built by Vosper Thorneycroft and armed with surface-to-surface and surface-to-air missiles. These were supplemented by ex-World War II US and British destroyers in the late 1960s and early 1970s. In the mid-1970s, Iran began placing orders for the latest examples of fighting ships, such as La Combattante fast attack craft from France, Spruance-class destroyers and Tango-class submarines from the United States, and Type 209 submarines and F-122 frigates from West Germany. Only the La Combattante-class boats had been delivered by the time of the Iranian 1979 revolution, but the Iranian Navy was still the predominant naval force among the Gulf States.

The emergence of the revolutionary regime, however, destroyed the navy both materially and morally. Iran was soon alienated from the United States, its major source of war material and expertise. Many senior officers fled, and others were

killed. The command of the navy fell to an officer holding only the rank of captain. The flow of supplies was halted. Inevitably, the navy was forced to generate spares from its own vessels, cannibalising equipment and pooling crews from semi-operational units in order to maintain a few vessels such as frigates, fast attack craft and hovercraft. A greater problem was posed by the inability to procure ammunition: the entire stock of missiles for the nine fast attack craft amounted to only six Harpoons.

The Iraqi invasion in September 1980 appears to have caught the Iranians completely by surprise, even though there had been a series of border incidents over the previous months. The Iranian light naval forces along the Shatt al Arab were wiped out by the Iraqi offensive, but the intended lightning campaign ground to a halt in the streets of Khorramshahr, where bitter fighting absorbed all the Iraqi capacity for offensive action. Although Khorramshahr fell, the failure to capture Abadan and the determined response of Iran ensured that the war would continue until one side was exhausted.

The naval fighting in these early stages remains obscure; both sides have imposed a severe censorship on their losses and seem prone to exaggeration in their claims. In the only major naval battle reported, which occurred in November 1980, Iraq claimed to have sunk three Iranian vessels, and Iran claimed 11 Iraqi ships. The loss of one of the Iraqi Polnocny-class tank landing craft in the action is generally accepted by naval analysts, which suggests the possibility that Iraq may have attempted a landing of forces near Abadan, and that the assault force was intercepted by an Iranian flotilla. The effect of this battle was to exhaust Iraqi naval offensive capabilities, giving the Iranians control of their coastal shipping routes.

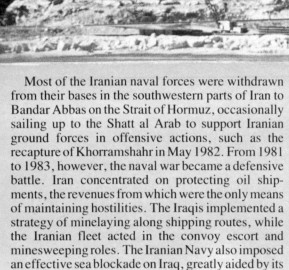

Most of the Iranian naval forces were withdrawn from their bases in the southwestern parts of Iran to Bandar Abbas on the Strait of Hormuz, occasionally sailing up to the Shatt al Arab to support Iranian ground forces in offensive actions, such as the recapture of Khorramshahr in May 1982. From 1981 to 1983, however, the naval war became a defensive battle. Iran concentrated on protecting oil shipments, the revenues from which were the only means of maintaining hostilities. The Iraqis implemented a strategy of minelaying along shipping routes, while the Iranian fleet acted in the convoy escort and minesweeping roles. The Iranian Navy also imposed an effective sea blockade on Iraq, greatly aided by its geographical position.

In late 1983, however, the Iranians lost control of their shipping routes, as the Iraqis acquired new equipment. The arrival of French and Soviet air-to-surface missiles meant that Iraq was able to challenge the Iranian fleet from the air. At first, raids were launched on the Iranian port facilities of Bushire and Bandar Khomeyni, but these proved to be the trial run for a new campaign against Iranian shipping.

Sinking Iranian ships

On 2 January 1984, the Iraqis launched a naval and air attack on an Iranian convoy sailing towards Bandar Khomeyni. It seems to have been very successful as five Iranian ships were sunk and an Iranian helicopter gunship shot down; the Iraqis lost two aeroplanes. In February 1984, another attack was made and another five ships were claimed sunk. These attacks occurred regularly at monthly intervals; they were accompanied by opportunistic attacks on any unescorted shipping in the Iraqi military exclusion zone.

The Iranian response was to wage a reprisal campaign against the members of the Saudi Arabian-organised Gulf Cooperation Council (which included Bahrain, Kuwait, Oman, Qatar, Saudi Arabia and the United Arab Emirates), who were believed to be paying for the Iraqi war effort. On 13 May a Kuwaiti tanker, the *Umm Qasbah*, was strafed by Iranian aircraft, and on 24 May a Liberian tanker in Saudi territorial waters was also attacked. The Saudi Arabian government reacted angrily to this

and lodged an official complaint with Iran.

The Iranians moderated their attacks as a result of this and as a consequence of the shooting down of an Iranian F-4 Phantom by Saudi F-15s (assisted by a US Airborne Warning and Control – AWACS – aeroplane) on 5 June. Iran attacked a Kuwaiti ship and another Liberian vessel in June; Iraq stepped up its attacks throughout the summer of 1984, raiding convoys and using helicopters to make Exocet attacks against Iran's oil terminal on Kharg Island. During this summer campaign an incident may have pointed out a new direction in the war. On 23 August, Iraq claimed to have attacked a large naval target; salvage tugs from Bahrain came out but only found a small Iranian supply boat that was quickly towed away. The next day, the Iranians claimed to have a counter to the Exocet, possibly indicating that some kind of radiation reflector was mounted in the supply boat, creating a false target to mislead the missile's guidance system.

The conduct of the naval fighting in the Gulf War has been marked by the inability of either side to maintain an effective fleet. On the Iranian side, shattered discipline and the difficulty of acquiring spare parts for the fleet have hampered operational performance. On the Iraqi side, lack of a naval tradition meant that their inexperienced and comparatively small fleet was totally outclassed by whatever forces the Iranians managed to put to sea, as demonstrated by the naval battle of November 1980. The Iraqis have turned to airpower, an arena where they are stronger, to break the Iranian control of the sea, with much damage inflicted but, as far as was possible to tell in mid-1984, no appreciable effect on Iranian military capabilities. The large number of warships under construction for Iraq in the shipyards of Europe may yet alter this situation.

Alexander McNair-Wilson

Above: The Iranian oil installations on Kharg Island, which have been subjected to a number of Iraqi attacks. However, none of these seem to have hampered Iran's ability to ship oil. Indeed, in late November 1984, Kharg Island once again began shipping oil out at maximum capacity; the Iraqis at the same time resumed attacks on Gulf shipping. Inset: Iraqi soldiers with a Soviet-supplied ZU-23 anti-aircraft gun on the Shatt al Arab. The Iraqi Navy has not challenged Iranian control of Iraq's Gulf littoral, but a new battle-fleet was under construction for the Iraqis in European shipyards in late 1984, threatening Iranian dominance in the Gulf.

Key Weapons

Fast Attack Craft

In enclosed waters such as the Baltic, the Mediterranean and the Red Sea, or on long, island-studded coastlines such as are found in the Adriatic, Aegean and China Seas, navies which deploy MTBs (motor torpedo boats) and MGBs (motor gunboats) have traditionally been able to create conditions which place larger and more powerful enemy warships at a serious disadvantage. Since 1945 the performance of these fast attack craft has been improved by the development of compact lightweight gas-turbine and diesel power units as well as electronic target detection, acquisition and fire-control equipment. Similarly, the arrival of anti-ship guided weapons has led to the development of a third type of vessel, the missile boat, and to the installation of defensive ECM (electronic counter-measures). By comparison with the vessels manned by the coastal forces of most nations during World War II, therefore, the modern fast attack craft is an extremely sophisticated and expensive piece of equipment, yet in relation to the soaring cost of larger warships it offers excellent value for money and poses a very serious threat to a potential enemy.

Since the mid-1960s, the hydrofoil has been replacing the conventional planing hull of fast attack craft. Although it is expensive, the hydrofoil has an important advantage in that it provides greater stability for the boat. At speed, the planing hull rises out of the water causing it to slam into the crests of the waves; in rough water, with waves reaching a height of 1·22m (4ft), the hull is liable to break up. The hydrofoil, by contrast, will push the hull entirely out of the water by aerodynamic lift as the submerged foils move through the water stream like wings. Combined with a self-stabilising mechanism to reduce pitch and roll, the hydrofoil will give a stable and fast weapons platform, capable of operations in heavy seas of up to 3·96m (13ft), and very economical in its fuel consumption.

The world's largest user of fast attack craft is the People's Republic of China. The majority are the Shanghai class of MGBs, numbering 310 in 1984. Many different variants in armament have been produced, but the two most common have either one twin 57mm gun mounting or two twin 37mm mountings, together with two twin 25mm cannon mountings. The Shanghais, displacing 150 tonnes, are driven by four diesel engines producing 28 knots. Chinese Shanghai-class attack craft have been exported as far afield as Albania, Romania, Bangladesh, Pakistan and Vietnam.

The Shanghai class is being progressively replaced by the Hai Dau-class missile boats and the Huchuan-class torpedo hydrofoils. The Hai Daus are armed with Chinese versions of the Soviet SS-N-2 Styx SSM (surface-to-surface missile) and their engines are believed to be gas turbines. The Huchuan class entered service in 1966, and was one of the first operational hydrofoil classes in the world; its diesel engines drive three shafts to a maximum speed of 54 knots. The Huchuans' armament consists of two 533mm (21in) torpedo tubes and two twin 14·5mm heavy machine-gun mountings.

The Soviet Navy also maintains a very large fleet of fast attack craft. Its early postwar designs, the P-6, P-8 and P-10 classes, were 75-tonne MTBs armed with two 21-inch torpedo tubes and twin 25mm cannon mountings fore and aft, although in some cases ASW (anti-submarine warfare) weapons or

Page 2123: A Dutch Willemoes missile boat fires a Harpoon. Based on the Swedish Spica design, these boats are powerfully armed with missiles, torpedoes and a dual-purpose gun. Top left: The Hai Dau class is a Chinese version of the Soviet Osa I design; one change is the replacement of the 30mm cannon mountings by 25mm ones. Centre left: The P6 class, although retired from Soviet service, is operated by many Third World navies; this example is a Cuban vessel. Bottom left: One of the four Osa II boats operated by the Finnish Navy. Right: A Soviet Osa I in the Baltic, with its missile bins open. Soviet-supplied Osas have fought in the 1971 Indo-Pakistan War, the 1973 Yom Kippur War and the Iran-Iraq War. Below right: The Shershen class is similar to the Osa class, but with torpedo tubes in place of the missiles.

mines were substituted for torpedo tubes. The P-6s were diesel powered and had a maximum speed of 43 knots, but the P-8s and P-10s were driven by gas turbine engines and were two knots faster. It is estimated that well over 500 P-class attack craft were built, but none remain in service with the Soviet Navy today. On the other hand, some 200 have been exported to Russia's clients and a further 100 have been converted into Komar-class missile boats. These are armed with two Styx SSM launchers and one twin 25mm cannon mounting and can travel at 40 knots.

The small size of the P-class hull proved unsatisfactory in that the boats were too small for operations in any sea heavier than a moderate swell. The replacement for the Komars, the Osa I class, introduced in 1961, displaced 200 tonnes, which made them much better sea boats capable of maintaining a speed of 38 knots in all save the most severe operational conditions. They are armed with four SS-N-2 Styx launchers, plus two 30mm cannon mountings fore and aft. The Osa II class appeared in 1966, equipped with the improved SS-N-2B missile in tube, as opposed to box, launchers. Some Osa IIs carry quadruple SA-N-5 SAM (surface-to-air missile) launchers and appear to act as flotilla air defence boats. The Osas are powered by three high performance diesel engines with a top speed of 40 knots. The Osa hull was also used for a new generation of MTBs, the Shershen class, of which approximately 100 were built between 1962 and 1974. The Shershens' principal armament consists of four 533mm (21in) torpedo tubes; they are powered by three diesels, like the Osas, but because they are lighter (180 tonnes) they achieve a 47 knot top speed.

Together, the Shershens and the Osas operate in coastal force flotillas, but the numbers of the two classes are declining steadily as the Soviet Navy turns towards hydrofoils for its fast attack craft.

The first Soviet hydrofoil to enter service was the 70-tonne Pchela class which appeared in the early 1960s, and is armed with four 23mm cannon and depth-charges. When foilborne, the Pchelas can achieve 50 knots. The larger (190-tonne) Turya-class torpedo hydrofoils, based on the Osa hull, are believed to have entered service in 1971 and, although they are capable of attacking surface vessels, seem to have been designed with ASW duties in mind. Their armament consists of four acoustic-homing torpedoes, twin 25mm cannon forward and twin 57mm guns aft. Of identical parentage to the Turyas are the Matka-class missile boats, first seen in 1978. These are armed with two SS-N-2C Styx missiles which have a range of 74 km (46 miles) and either infra-red or active-radar homing; secondary armament consists of either one 76mm gun or one radar-controlled Gatling-type machine gun. The Turyas and Matkas can achieve 40 knots when foilborne.

With a displacement of 770 tonnes the Nanuchka-class missile corvettes hardly fit the description of light attack craft, nor is their maximum speed of 32 knots compatible with any of the classes mentioned above. When the first of the Nanuchkas appeared in 1969 it therefore posed something of an enigma. The type is suitable for the task of flotilla leader and its two triple SS-N-9 launchers have a range of 110km (68 miles), providing an impressive addition to the firepower already available: three versions of the Nanuchka are known to exist with different permutations of secondary armament including SA-N-4 SAMs, single or twin 57mm guns, single 76mm guns and Gatling machine guns. It has also been suggested that the Russians were fully aware of the ECM deficiencies of their fast attack craft before these were revealed during the Yom Kippur War, and that the Nanuchkas could provide an answer.

Above: The Swedish Spica class were among the first warships to be propelled by gas-turbine engines. This particular boat, the *Halmstad,* is of the Spica II group which have a more up-to-date fire-control system than Spica Is. Left: The Greek vessel *Antiploiarhos Laskos,* a member of the French-built Combattante III class; these are equipped with MM38 missiles and 76mm dual-purpose guns. Below: An Egyptian Komar-class missile boat fires an SS-N-2 Styx during an exercise in 1966. It was an Egyptian Komar that sank the Israeli destroyer *Eilat* in 1967.

The navy which has consistently obtained the best results from its fast attack craft is that of Israel, which was dramatically restructured following the loss of the destroyer *Eilat* to SS-N-2 Styx missiles in 1967. The 250-tonne Saar-class missile boats were built to a German design at Cherbourg between 1967 and 1969 and carry a variety of weapon systems including Gabriel short-range (23km – 14 miles) and Harpoon intermediate range (80km – 50 miles) missiles, nine 76mm or 40mm guns and anti-submarine torpedoes. The Reshef class, displacing 450 tonnes, are similarly armed but were built indigenously from 1973 onwards. They are intended for longer missions than the Saars, as are the Alia class, which carry a Bell 206 helicopter for target-spotting and over-horizon missile guidance, as well as the usual armament. The Saars have a maximum speed of 40 knots, the Reshefs and Alias 32 knots.

Most Western navies do not envisage a role for fast attack craft in any future war with the Warsaw Pact, and consequently their numbers have declined. Those navies that operate in the Baltic are the exception to this. The West German Navy operates

three types of fast attack craft armed with missiles: the Type 143, the Type 143B and the Type 148. All are armed with four MM38 Exocet SSMs and one or two 76mm dual-purpose guns in single mountings. Sweden operates three types of Spica-class fast attack craft. The first two variants both displaced 215 tonnes, but the newest model, which also goes under the name Stockholm class, is heavier (320 tonnes) and is designed to act as a flotilla leader. The Spica Is and IIs are armed with a 57mm single mounting and six 533mm (21in) torpedo tubes, but two or four of the tubes will be replaced in 1985 with four or eight Bofors RbS 15 SSMs. The *Stockholm* is armed with a 57mm gun, a 40mm gun, two torpedo tubes and eight SSMs; the class will also have ASW equipment.

Such is the competitive nature of the Western international arms market that today a fast attack craft's hull, power units, missiles, armament and electronic systems can all be manufactured in different countries and assembled by the builder to suit his customer's demands. A typical example of this is provided by the French-built La Combattante class, which has been purchased in various forms by the navies of Greece, Iran, Libya and Malaysia. Similarly, the six Ramadan-class missile boats, purchased by the Egyptian Navy from the British Vosper Thornycroft yard to make good its losses during the

1973 war, are armed with the Franco-Italian Otomat SSM, the Italian Oto-Melara 76mm dual-purpose gun and twin Breda 40mm AA mounting, and are equipped with Marconi Sapphire radar fire-control systems and Decca-Racal Cutlass ECM. The Ramadans displace 312 tonnes, are powered by four MTU diesels producing a maximum speed of 40 knots, and have a complement of 40.

Only two Nato navies have developed hydrofoil fast attack craft, those of the United States and Italy. The American Pegasus-class missile hydrofoils were intended to replace the Asheville patrol gunboats which were progressively sold or phased out following the Vietnam War. The 240-tonne Pegasus craft can achieve 48 knots when foilborne and are armed with eight Harpoon SSMs in two quadruple launchers, and one 76mm gun. Although a total of 30 was planned, this was cut back to six because of cost overruns. They are based in Florida as the US Navy is reluctant to deploy them abroad. The Italian Navy, on the other hand, plans an active role for the seven vessels of its 62·5-tonne Sparviero-class missile hydrofoils. These are powered by a Rolls Royce Proteus engine driving a water jet when foilborne and otherwise by a conventional diesel engine, and are capable of 52 knots. They are armed with two Otomat 2 SSMs and one 76mm gun.

Above left: An Israeli Reshef-class missile boat armed with Gabriel missiles aft and Harpoons amidships. Above: The South African Navy also has Reshef missile boats, built under licence at Durban and armed with Skerpioen missiles (South African Gabriels).

Below left: The *Grifone*, a hydrofoil of the Italian Sparviero class. Below: The USS *Aquila*, fourth of the Pegasus-class vessels. Both of these boats had their origins in a failed plan to build a standard Nato hydrofoil; the US and Italian Navies used the experience gained in this project to build their own.

New weapons, new strategies

The Nato alliance in the 1980s

The North Atlantic Treaty Organisation (Nato) faced a number of crucial issues during the 1980s which posed fundamental questions about its strategy, tactical doctrine and role in the world beyond the area covered by the 1949 North Atlantic Treaty. That these issues were discussed in an atmosphere of apparent crisis was due to the dominance within the public debate of the problems raised by the Nato programme for the deployment of US cruise and Pershing II missiles in Western Europe.

The background to this proposed deployment, agreed in 1979, was from the beginning complex. On the one hand, it was presented as a routine modernisation of the US ground-based nuclear capability in Europe, represented by the Pershing I missile, which the Pentagon had marked down for replacement as early as October 1971. The Pershing I, carrying a nuclear warhead and with a maximum range of 740km (460 miles), had been classed as a medium-range missile, and was incapable of reaching targets in the Soviet Union from its bases in West Germany. The new ground-launched cruise missiles (GLCMs) and Pershing IIs were both capable of striking targets deep inside the Soviet Union, and the Pershing II in particular, with its 1700km (1050 mile) range and short flight time seemed to the Soviets to represent an escalation to what was in effect a strategic nuclear weapon, capable of use in a potential first strike against the Soviet homeland.

The issue was complicated, however, by the fact that the Soviet Union was itself engaged in a process of modernising its medium-range nuclear missiles during the mid-1970s. The replacement of obsolescent SS-4 and SS-5 missiles by mobile, multiple-warhead SS-20s from approximately 1976 onwards, raised fears in Western Europe that the Soviet Union was establishing a clear superiority in nuclear weapons in the European theatre which would lead to

a decisive shift in the military balance in Europe in favour of the Soviet Union; theoretically, the Soviet Union would be in a position to use its superiority in both conventional and theatre nuclear weapons to blackmail the West European Nato members and prise them away from their American ally. This fear was most clearly expressed by West German Chancellor Helmut Schmidt in a speech to the London-based International Institute for Strategic Studies on 28 October 1977. The speech initiated a debate in Nato which had momentous consequences: on 12 December 1979, Nato agreed to what became known as the 'twin-track' policy of pursuing arms control talks with the Soviet Union in order to achieve a withdrawal of the SS-20s, while at the same time proceeding with plans to station 108 Pershing II missiles and 464 GLCMs in Western Europe from 1983 onwards.

Above: A US Pershing II missile being launched from its mobile transporter during tests in the United States. With a maximum range of 1700km (1050 miles), the Pershing II was capable of hitting targets deep inside the Soviet Union from launching sites in West Germany, provoking criticism that it could be a potentially destabilising first-strike weapon. The December 1979 Nato decision to station Pershing IIs and GLCMs in Western Europe led to a storm of protest that shook several governments.

Left: Helmut Schmidt, Social Democratic Chancellor of West Germany from 1974 to 1982. By drawing attention to the growing threat to West European security posed by the Soviet Union's SS-20 missiles, Schmidt became labelled as the father of the 1979 Nato 'twin-track' decision to deploy US cruise and Pershing II missiles in Europe. His defence of that policy contributed to the fall of his government in October 1982. Christian Democrat Helmut Kohl (right) succeeded Schmidt as chancellor, and was able to carry out the stationing of the first GLCMs in December 1983. Far left: French President François Mitterrand, whose government's fear of West German instability led France to move closer to the United States.

The 'twin-track' policy came after a number of controversies that had occurred under the administration of US President Jimmy Carter, such as the decision first to manufacture and then to shelve the enhanced radiation weapon (the so-called neutron bomb), which had provoked enormous opposition in Western Europe. But if the indecisiveness of President Carter created unease both among supporters and opponents of Nato policy in Western Europe, the election of President Ronald Reagan in November 1980, coming as it did at a time when East-West relations were rapidly heading for a new Cold War, fuelled fears that superpower rivalries and conflicts might lead to greater tension, or even war, which President Reagan at one stage even suggested might be restricted to Europe.

The arms-control element of the 1979 'twin-track' decision seemed at first to be largely ignored by the new American administration; repeated references to the need to rebuild US military strength suggested that the modernisation of theatre nuclear weapons would be pushed through as part of an overall policy of attempting to attain military superiority over the Soviet Union. Such, at least, was the fear of the rapidly growing peace movement which was active throughout Western Europe, particularly in West Germany and Great Britain, both of which were to provide bases for the new US missiles. In West Germany the peace movement was closely identified with a well-established and powerful ecology lobby, which opposed not only nuclear weapons, but also the peaceful use of atomic energy. This alliance of peace and ecology activists, which found political expression with the emergence of the opposition Green Party, undermined support for Chancellor Helmut Schmidt, who was closely identified with the Nato 'twin-track' policy.

By the winter of 1981-82, large-scale demonstrations throughout West Germany were raising fears among Bonn's Nato allies that the Schmidt government might not be strong enough to carry out the stationing of cruise and Pershing II, particularly as

Above: Spanish troops, wearing a helmet modelled on the pre-1945 German type, march through Madrid during a military parade. The loyalty of the armed forces to the post-Franco democratic Spanish regime was open to question, and Spanish entry to Nato was suggested partly as a means to divert them from their interventionist political role.

Left: Women peace-protesters form a human chain around the cruise missile base at Greenham Common in southern England. During the 1980s, criticism of Nato strategies was not confined to fringe groups, but was also expressed by leading politicians, who questioned the wisdom of the new missile deployments and military doctrines such as the American AirLand Battle concept.

Nato/Warsaw Pact balance of forces 1984

Nato forces

United States
Total armed forces: 2,135,900 personnel
Strategic nuclear forces: 592 SLBMs, 1037 ICBMs and 356 combat aircraft
Army: 780,800; reserves 929,766; equipment: 12,023 tanks, 625 aircraft and 9000 helicopters
Navy: 564,800; reserves 115,000; equipment: 4 cruise missiles and 95 attack submarines, and 206 principal surface combat vessels
Air Force: 594,500; reserves 182,700; equipment: some 3700 combat aircraft
Marine Corps: 196,600; reserves 43,900; equipment: 550 tanks, 436 combat aircraft and 102 helicopters

Belgium
Total armed forces: 93,607 personnel
Army: 65,102; reserves 160,000; equipment: 449 tanks, 5 aircraft and 62 helicopters
Navy: 4557; reserves 4500; equipment: 4 frigates
Air Force: 20,948; reserves 14,000; equipment: 147 combat aircraft

Canada
Total armed forces (unified in 1968): 82,858 personnel
Mobile Command: some 16,000; reserves 16,000; equipment: 114 tanks
Maritime Command: some 8700; reserves 3250; equipment: 3 submarines and 20 destroyers
Air Command: 23,000; reserves 950; equipment: 160 combat aircraft and 32 helicopters
Remainder of forces not assigned to specific command

Denmark
Total armed forces: 31,400 personnel
Army: 18,100; reserves 125,400; equipment: 256 tanks, 16 aircraft and 12 helicopters
Navy: 5900; reserves 3800; equipment: 5 submarines and 10 frigates
Air Force: 7400; reserves 9400; equipment: 96 combat aircraft

France
Total armed forces: 474,938 personnel (including 3588 central staff)
Strategic nuclear forces: 16 SLBMs, 18 IRBMs and 28 Mirage IVA bombers
Army: 304,500; reserves 305,000; equipment: 1602 tanks, 70 aircraft and 659 helicopters
Navy: 67,700; reserves 30,000; equipment: 17 attack submarines and 48 major surface combat vessels
Air Force: 99,150; reserves 58,000; equipment: 492 combat aircraft and 111 helicopters
(France withdrew from Nato's integrated military structure in 1966)

West Germany
Total armed forces: 495,000 personnel
Army: 335,600; equipment: 4227 tanks and 697 helicopters
Navy: 36,200; equipment: 24 submarines, 7 destroyers, 8 frigates
Air Force: 106,000; equipment: 486 combat aircraft
Reserves (all services): 750,000

Greece
Total armed forces: 178,000 personnel
Army: 135,000; reserves some 350,000; equipment: 2237 tanks and 155 helicopters

Navy: 19,500; reserves about 24,000; equipment: 10 submarines, 14 destroyers and 7 frigates
Air Force: 23,500; reserves about 30,000; equipment: 303 combat aircraft

Italy
Total armed forces: 375,100 personnel
Army: 260,000; reserves 550,000; equipment: 1770 tanks, 105 aircraft and 371 helicopters
Navy: 44,500; reserves 221,000; equipment: 10 submarines, 22 major surface combat vessels and 93 combat helicopters

Luxembourg
Total armed forces: 720 personnel

Netherlands
Total armed forces: 103,267 personnel
Army: 64,664; reserves 145,000; equipment: 1004 tanks and 97 helicopters
Navy: 16,867; reserves about 20,000; equipment: 6 submarines, 2 destroyers and 16 frigates
Air Force: 16,810; reserves 6000; equipment: some 174 combat aircraft

Norway
Total armed forces: 36,785 personnel
Army: 19,500; reserves 165,000; equipment: 170 tanks
Navy: 7500; reserves 25,000; equipment: 14 submarines and 5 frigates
Air Force: 9500; reserves 25,000; equipment: 114 combat aircraft

Portugal
Total armed forces: 63,500 personnel
Army: 39,000; equipment: 59 tanks
Navy: 15,000; equipment: 3 submarines and 17 frigates
Air Force: 9500; equipment: 74 combat aircraft
Reserves (all services): 169,000

Spain
Total armed forces: 330,000 personnel
Army: 240,000; equipment: 940 tanks and 157 helicopters
Navy: 57,000; equipment: 8 submarines and 23 major surface combat vessels
Air Force: 56,000; equipment: some 458 combat aircraft
Reserves (all services): 1,085,000
(Spain was not committed to Nato's integrated military structure by 1984)

Turkey
Total armed forces: 602,000 personnel
Army: 500,000; reserves 700,000; equipment: 3532 tanks and 236 helicopters
Navy: 46,000; reserves 70,000; equipment: 16 submarines, 15 major surface combat vessels and 18 combat aircraft
Air Force: 56,000; reserves 66,000; equipment: some 458 combat aircraft

United Kingdom
Total armed forces: 325,909 personnel
Strategic nuclear forces: 4 SSBNs each with 16 Polaris A3 missiles
Army: 161,539; reserves 219,642; equipment: 1241 tanks and 314 helicopters
Navy: 71,281; reserves 34,928; equipment: 28 attack submarines, 57 major surface combat vessels, 26 combat aircraft and 177 combat helicopters
Air Force: 93,089; reserves 23,893; equipment: some 620 combat aircraft

opposition to this policy was growing within Schmidt's own Social Democratic Party (SPD). There was much talk of the possibility of West Germany adopting a neutralist position, and it was suggested that West Germany might come to an arrangement with the Soviet Union, by which it would abandon its commitment to Nato in return for reunification with East Germany. Such speculation, combined with Schmidt's barely concealed contempt for the policies of the Reagan administration, led to a marked cooling in relations between Bonn and Washington; leading figures within President Reagan's Republican Party made no secret of their desire to see the Schmidt government replaced by the Christian Democrats, who could be counted upon to carry out the deployment of the US missiles.

Fears of West German instability also prompted the socialist government of President François Mitterand in France to move closer to the United States after almost two decades of French isolation within Nato. The French press was full of discussion of the apparent re-emergence of the 'German problem', and the hitherto firm Bonn-Paris axis was threatened with collapse as the situation in West Germany came to a head. In October 1982, however, Schmidt's coalition government collapsed and he was replaced

Warsaw Pact forces

Soviet Union

Total armed forces: 5,115,000 personnel (including 1,500,000 command and support troops)
Strategic nuclear forces: 981 SLBMs in 79 SSBNs, 1398 ICBMs (Strategic Rocket Forces, 412,000 men) and 143 long-range bombers
National Air Defence Troops: 370,000; equipment: some 4000 aircraft
Army; 1,840,000; reserves 3,500,000; equipment: some 51,000 tanks and some 4100 helicopters
Navy: 490,000; reserves 840,000; equipment: 67 cruise missile submarines, 201 attack submarines and 293 principal surface combatants
Air Force: 400,000; reserves 400,000; equipment: some 3260 combat aircraft

Bulgaria

Total armed forces: 147,300 personnel
Army: 105,000; reserves 150,000; equipment: 1500 tanks
Navy: 8500; reserves 25,000; equipment: 2 submarines and 2 frigates
Air Force: 33,800; reserves 20,000; equipment: some 188 combat aircraft

Czechoslovakia

Total armed forces: 207,250 personnel
Army: 148,000; reserves 200,000; equipment: 3500 tanks
Air Force: 59,250; reserves 30,000; equipment: 439 combat aircraft

East Germany

Total armed forces: 172,000 personnel
Army: 120,000; reserves 330,000; equipment: about 1500 tanks
Navy: 14,000; reserves 25,000; equipment: 2 frigates
Air Force: 38,000; reserves 30,000; equipment: 359 combat aircaft

Hungary

Total armed forces: 105,000 personnel
Army: 84,000; equipment: some 1230 tanks
Air Force: 21,000; equipment: 145 combat aircraft
Reserves (all services): 143,000

Poland

Total armed forces: 323,250 personnel
Army: 210,000; equipment: 3450 tanks
Navy: 22,000; equipment: 3 submarines and 1 destroyer
Air Force: 91,250; equipment: 625 combat aircraft
Reserves (all services): 500,000

Romania

Total armed forces: 189,500 personnel
Army: 150,000; reserves over 500,000; equipment: some 1230 tanks
Navy: 7500; reserves 20,000; equipment: 1 frigate
Air Force: 32,000; reserves 45,000; equipment: 318 combat aircraft

as chancellor by Christian Democrat leader Helmut Kohl. The accession to power of the Kohl government in Germany and the re-election of the Thatcher government in Britain in June 1983 dispelled doubts about the immediate future of Nato and the deployment of the first cruise missiles went ahead as planned in December 1983. But the crisis over cruise and Pershing II had revealed a more fundamental issue which continued to trouble the alliance. The degree of opposition within the Nato alliance to the stationing of the new weapons came not only from the extreme left and the extra-parliamentary peace movement, but also spread to some of the socialist

and social democratic parties of Western Europe, without whose support the traditional consensus on defence policy which had sustained the unity of Nato since 1949 would collapse.

The Belgian and Dutch governments were forced in June 1984 to suspend their decisions to station 48 GLCMs in each of their countries. The Dutch government sought to pacify the anti-cruise movement, which had even spread to the ranks of the ruling Christian Democrats, by promising not to sanction the deployment of the US missiles if the Soviet Union unilaterally cut the number of its own SS-20s.

Top: A British Ferret scout car precedes a Centurion tank, fitted with mine-clearing plough, through the streets of a small West German town during Exercise Lionheart.
Centre: West German Panzergrenadiers lie in ambush for enemy tanks, armed with a Milan anti-tank guided missile, during exercises in Germany.
Above: A US Army AH-1S attack helicopter.

The essence of the crisis seemed to be that growing numbers of people in the West European Nato countries perceived the rising East-West tension as a result of rivalries between the USSR and the USA, most of which had their causes outside Europe. Clinging to the benefits of detente, which had been constructed upon a mutual recognition with the Warsaw Pact of the need for stability in Europe in order to preserve world peace, many West Europeans thought that Nato's reliance upon nuclear weapons to counter-balance Warsaw Pact conventional superiority was leading, with the introduction of potential first-strike weapons such as Pershing II, to a situation where nuclear war, rather than being the ultimate peacekeeping deterrent, was becoming an increasingly probable threat.

Official Nato tactical doctrine remained welded to the principles of forward defence and flexible response. Forward defence had been adopted as Nato policy in 1972 because West European countries, and most notably West Germany, could not contemplate surrendering territory to a Soviet advance or having a war fought on their territory. Flexible response, first adopted in 1967, posited a rising scale of Nato reaction to attack, from conventional defence through the use of battlefield and then tactical nuclear weapons up to a full strategic nuclear exchange. It was held to maintain deterrence while at the same time removing the need for an immediate strategic nuclear response to a conventional attack.

In the 1980s, however, new tactical thinking grew up alongside these well-established principles. In 1983 the US armed forces adopted a new tactical doctrine, commonly known as AirLand Battle. This doctrine, though not that of Nato as a whole, would nevertheless be that which guided US forces in any major conflict in which they might be involved, including in the European theatre, whose Nato commander is traditionally an American officer.

Raising the nuclear threshold

The AirLand Battle doctrine was an attempt to adapt to the military possibilities created by modern high technology weapons systems, and to the future promise of emerging technology (ET). Proponents of the new weapons claimed that they offered a possibility of considerably raising the nuclear threshold by providing the West with an effective sub-nuclear war-fighting capability which would compensate for the Warsaw Pact's numerical advantage. By adapting recent advances in electronic communications technology to military command, control and communications systems, Western forces would be able to strike far into the rear of any Warsaw Pact advance into Western Europe, destroying rear echelon formations and disrupting the enemy's vital logistical support system. Intelligence on enemy movements would be gained from unmanned drones (RPVs), satellites and AWACS aircraft, which would look down into territory occupied by Warsaw Pact troops. Supplied to computerised control systems, this information would allow precision-guided weapons to be launched against targets far behind the advancing Warsaw Pact formations. Forward enemy armoured formations would also be vulnerable to new weapons, such as armour-piercing

Main picture: A drone, or remotely-piloted vehicle (RPV), being prepared for use during Nato exercises in West Germany during the autumn of 1984. RPVs would play a vital role in any modern war in central Europe, providing intelligence of enemy movements and allowing powerful and accurate strikes against targets deep behind his front line. Below left: An M1 Abrams tank of the US Army's 1st Tiger Brigade during Exercise Lionheart in West Germany, September 1984. The offensive capability of armoured vehicles has been increasingly questioned with the development of high-technology anti-tank weapons, carried by infantry or tank-killer helicopters. Below right: Belgian paras land from a West German Sikorsky CH-53G Sea Stallion during exercise Roaring Lion, September 1984.

munitions activated by electronic sensors, either scattered across the path of advancing enemy units or delivered from aircraft.

The disadvantages of this new doctrine were that, firstly, the new technology was costly, both to procure and to maintain, and its reliability under combat conditions was open to question. Further, precisely because AirLand Battle sought to raise the nuclear threshold, it might render an East-West military conflict, which no one could guarantee would be limited to the conventional level, more rather than less likely.

The accession of Spain to the North Atlantic Treaty on 30 May 1982 marked the first expansion of the alliance since the mid-1950s, and occasioned new discussion as to the character and role of Nato. Within Spain, membership of the alliance was often presented as a means to preserve both internal and external security, as the Nato commitment of Spain's armed forces would provide them with a new, non-political role, and reduce the possibility of a right-wing military coup. The entry of Spain into the Nato alliance also added new fuel to the strategic and tactical debate, as some strategists suggested that the value of Spanish membership would be in adding depth to Nato's defence, and that Spain might provide a last bastion into which Nato forces could retreat if faced by a Warsaw Pact invasion. Such theories further convinced many observers, again particularly in West Germany, that forward defence and flexible response were being eroded.

US pressure for the West European Nato governments to accept a greater responsibility for military operations outside the Nato area, for example in the Indian Ocean or the Gulf, created further divisions within the alliance. While Britain and France had retained an out-of-area intervention capability, they and the other West European Nato members generally resisted involvement in what were widely perceived to be operations essentially in pursuit of American interests.

Sharing the military burden

Growing demands within the US for the European NATO members to accept a greater share of the financial and military burden of the defence of Western Europe, also posed a threat to alliance unity. An increasingly influential section of American opinion called for a withdrawal of US ground forces from Europe if the Europeans did not take a greater responsibility for their own defence. In fact, the bulk of conventional forces in Western Europe was provided by the European Nato partners, who had little sympathy for the assertion that they were sheltering behind the protection of the United States.

The main task facing Nato by the mid-1980s was the formation of a new consensus, which would ensure public support for Nato strategy and preserve alliance unity into the 21st century. Shifting perceptions of the United States prompted suggestions that the European members of Nato should have a more independent voice within the alliance, but attempts to resurrect the moribund West European Union, or to construct some alternative forum for West European opinion seemed fated to flounder.

Robin Corbett

The doomsday arsenal

World nuclear forces in the 1980s

At the beginning of the 1960s, only three countries held nuclear weapons (the United States, the Soviet Union and the United Kingdom); by the beginning of the 1980s this exclusive club had increased by two (France and China) and a further three nations were suspected of being in possession of nuclear weapons (India, South Africa and Israel). By the end of the decade, further countries (Argentina, Brazil, Pakistan) were widely expected to have tested a nuclear device.

The strategic nuclear arsenals of the superpowers were composed of three elements known in the United States as the 'strategic triad' – manned strategic bombers, land-based intercontinental ballistic missiles (ICBMs) and submarine-launched ballistic missiles (SLBMs). Their nuclear arsenals also comprised shorter-ranged ballistic and cruise missiles, tactical bombers and battlefield nuclear weapons.

At the heart of the United States' nuclear forces in the 1980s is the Minuteman missile, which is deployed in two models: the Minuteman II which carries a single warhead of one or two megatons and the Minuteman III which carries three multiple independently-targetable re-entry vehicles (MIRVs) of 335 kilotons; the missiles are located in hardened silos (made of concrete reinforced with steel), scattered through six states of the United States. The Minuteman remains an effective missile despite its lengthy service life – Minuteman I first entered service in 1962 – and the introduction of the Mk12A warhead system on the Minuteman III in 1979 gave the United States an excellent first-strike weapon for use against Soviet ICBM silos.

A new missile, the MGM-118A Peacekeeper, which was originally known as the MX (missile experimental), is to be deployed alongside Minuteman by the end of the 1980s. The Peacekeeper can carry 12 warheads of twice the accuracy of those carried by the Minuteman, although limited to 10 by the terms of the SALT II agreement. Indecision on the method of deployment led to delays in the funding of the project but the missile will certainly enter service during the second Reagan administration. The main justification provided for the alloca-

Right: The test launch of a Trident missile from the US submarine *Francis Scott Key* off Cape Canaveral. The multi-warheaded Trident represented a huge increase in the power of both the British and US nuclear arsenals. Below: A long-range Soviet Tu-26 Backfire bomber, carrying an AS-4 Kitchen air-to-surface missile. Below centre: B-52G bombers of the US Strategic Air Command, re-equipped to carry air-launched AGM-86B cruise missiles. Below right: The most modern US strategic bomber, the Rockwell B-1A.

tion of funds to the Peacekeeper programme was its ability to carry penetration aids to overcome any future ballistic missile defence measures adopted by the Soviets.

The second part of the US strategic triad is provided by Poseidon and Trident SLBMs. The Poseidon is a design evolution from the earlier Polaris missile and first entered service in 1971. A Poseidon missile can carry between eight and 14 40-kiloton MIRVs in the Mk3 system, but their accuracy is only about half that of the Minuteman's MIRVs. The Trident is intended to replace the Poseidon and two models are to be in service by the end of the 1980s. The Trident I C4 is a development of the Poseidon. The most important change is the provision of a mid-course correction device that improves accuracy; this involves the use of a stellar sensor which takes at least one star sighting during flight and compares it with a star map held in its on-board computer which then makes any necessary adjustments to the trajectory. Also, the Trident I is capable of carrying 100-kiloton warheads in place of the Poseidon's 40 kilotons. The Trident II D5 has an increased range compared to the Trident I – 12,000km (7500 miles) as against 7000km (4350 miles) – and an increased payload. A Trident II missile can carry at least 14 150-kiloton warheads and probably as many as 17 (SALT II placed a limit of 14 on the number of warheads carried by SLBMs). It also offers the option of carrying eight 350-kiloton warheads using the Mk12A MIRV system; this option would enable the Trident force to be accurate enough for the purposes of first-strike counterforce employment against ICBM silos.

The manned bomber rounds out the US strategic nuclear force. Since the mid-1950s the mainstay of this arm has been variants of the Boeing B-52 Stratofortress. The last two models which are intended to serve out the 20th century are the B-52G and the B-52H, some carrying a bomb-load of 47,603kg (105,000lb) and some air-launched cruise missiles (ALCMs). Resurrected by the Reagan administration in 1981 after the programme had been cancelled by President Carter in 1977, the B-1 bomber – originally intended to replace the B-52 but now intended to supplement it – will provide a low-altitude manned bomber designed with high-technology features to reduce its radar image. The bomb-load is increased to 52,160kg (115,000lb) with an alternative load of 22 ALCMs.

The varieties of cruise missiles that will have entered service through the 1980s were originally thought to provide an answer to the threat posed by high-performance interceptors and surface-to-air missiles (SAMs) to the US strategic bomber force. Cruise was intended to fly beneath the enemy air-defence radar system and, by means of its sophisticated guidance, steer very accurately onto target. The Carter administration saw the cruise missile as an inexpensive yet versatile replacement for an outdated manned bomber force. The Reagan administration preferred to have bombers and cruise missiles, with cruise given a role as a medium or intermediate range (2500km – 1553 miles) weapon. With versions that can be launched from the ground, in the air or at sea, the cruise missile combines all the elements of the strategic triad in one system.

From Phantom to Pershing

The United States has always maintained a comprehensive range of tactical nuclear weapons for use against concentrations of troops and vital points along supply lines in Eastern Europe. During the early 1980s, this was provided by F-111 bombers, attack aircraft such as the F-4 Phantom and A-6 Intruder or surface-to-surface missiles (SSMs), the Lance and Pershing. The F-111 was the primary intermediate-range nuclear delivery system in Europe until the arrival of cruise missiles and the Pershing II in 1983-84, and still remains an important part of Nato's nuclear forces. The Pershing IA force is to be replaced during the decade by the Pershing II which is 10 times as accurate and possesses twice the range; this increased range brings the western Soviet Union as far as a line drawn from Leningrad to Sevastapol within the targeting area. The United States also deploys a comprehensive range of battlefield nuclear weapons, such as nuclear mines and artillery shells. Nuclear shells available in the 1980s included the enhanced radiation weapon, popularly known as the neutron bomb.

Where the United States' nuclear forces are influenced by their experience with strategic bombing concepts during World War II, the Soviet nuclear force (known as the Strategic Rocket Forces) was dominated at first by artillery thinking, with nuclear

Left: A group of Mirage F1 fighters of the French Air Defence Command being refuelled from a KC-135F tanker. Although a member of Nato, France retains an independent military policy, especially in the field of nuclear weapons.

Below: A Pluton S-3 intermediate-range nuclear missile mounted on its tracked mobile launcher. The Pluton constitutes the second element of a French nuclear triad which is completed by a fleet of five nuclear-missile armed submarines.

missiles seen as extremely destructive, long-range artillery. This has been reflected by the interest in reloading the missile silos after launching.

The Soviet strategic nuclear armoury is dependent on land-based ICBMs to a far greater extent than the US equivalent. In the 1980s, three missiles dominate the Soviet arsenal: the SS-17, the SS-18 and the SS-19. The SS-17 was initially deployed in 1977 and was the first Soviet missile to use the cold-launch technique (which uses compressed gas to force the missile out of the silo); it comes in two versions, a single six megaton warhead or four 750-kiloton MIRVs. The SS-19 is a similar missile but does not use the cold-launch technique; it carries either six 550-kiloton MIRVs or a single five-megaton warhead. The SS-18 is an enormous missile, over 30·5m (100 feet) high, carrying up to 10 MIRVs or a single warhead of 50 megatons; it also uses the cold-launch technique and is considered by US defence analysts to be intended to attack the Minuteman silos. The United States has expressed great concern over these missiles in arms-control negotiations, but the SS-18's earliest MIRV version had a very poor design for the vehicle carrying the warheads, casting doubt on its actual effectiveness.

The 60 SS-13s are the only solid-fuelled strategic missiles in service with the Soviet Strategic Rocket Forces. The Soviet weapons-makers seem to have had difficulties with the manufacturing technology involved in solid fuel and continue to use liquid fuel even though it is prone to leaks and spontaneous explosion. This preference extends even to the SLBM force, a dangerous situation for the sailors serving aboard the submarines. Experiments have been made with solid-fuelled ICBMs and SLBMs, but only the SS-13 has ever been put into production.

Compared to the United States' manned bombers and SLBMs, their Soviet equivalents play a less important role in the Soviet nuclear arsenal. The Soviets have a wide range of bombers but none are comparable in range to the B-52s or future B-1s of the US Air Force and, apart from the Tu-95 Bear, more properly belong in the intermediate weapons'

category. Apart from the problems with fuelling an SLBM, the Soviet submarine-based missile force is hindered by their difficulties in remaining at sea for any length of time because of engineering problems.

The Soviet Union does possess an excellent combination of intermediate-range nuclear delivery systems, based on the Tu-22M Backfire bomber and the SS-20 intermediate range ballistic missile (IRBM). The Tu-22M is a variable-geometry bomber with a range of 5500km (3420 miles), capable of carrying up to 12,000kg (26,455lb) of bombs. Many other Soviet aircraft have a nuclear capacity. The SS-20 is a solid-fuelled IRBM carrying three 150-kiloton MIRVs or a single 1·5 megaton warhead; its range is about 7500km (4600 miles). Soviet battlefield nuclear forces include a significant number of short-range SSMs.

France has a much smaller-scale arsenal than the two superpowers, but the ground, sea and air elements are all present. The latest French ground-based missile, the S-3, entered service at the beginning of the 1980s and incorporates some of the latest nuclear technology manufactured under licence from the United States. France is working on a new SLBM, the M-4, to enter service with a new class of submarines at the end of the decade, replacing the present fleet equipped with M-20 SLBMs. The French are also renewing their Mirage IV bomber force, some of which are to be converted to carry a short-range cruise missile of French design.

The other two major nuclear powers, the United Kingdom and China, do not presently attempt to maintain comprehensive nuclear forces. The United Kingdom has abandoned all nuclear weapons except for the SLBMs of the Polaris force. These have been improved by the Chevaline programme which gave the warheads manoeuvrable post-boost vehicles. Deployment of the first true Chinese ICBM began in the early 1980s with the CSS-X-4, a liquid-fuelled missile with a single warhead of possibly five megatons. The Chinese also successfully tested their first SLBM in 1982.

In addition to these dedicated nuclear warfare weapons systems described above, there are many additional systems which can be used to deliver a nuclear device, notably aircraft such as the Jaguar or the Tornado: these can be armed with nuclear bombs or air-to-surface missiles. If one has nuclear devices, there is no shortage of ways to deliver them.

Paul Szuscikiewicz

Below: US Army M110A2 8in self-propelled howitzers, capable of firing M753 rocket-assisted tactical nuclear rounds. Of questionable military value, tactical nuclear weapons are still important to the official Nato strategy of flexible response. Botom: A US cruise missile, mounted under the wing of a B-52G bomber.

World nuclear forces, 1983
Strategic, intermediate and medium-range systems

	Delivery systems	Number of warheads	Total mega-tonnage
United States			
ICBMs	1045	2145	1375
SLBMs	568	5152	333
Strategic bombers	328	c.2900	c.2000
IRBMs/MRBMs	16	16	0.6
	(108 by 1985)		
GLCMs	16	16	3.2
	(464 by 1988)		
SLCMs	44	44	8.8
	(900 by 1987)		
Intermediate bombers	156	936	c.900
Soviet Union			
ICBMs	1398	5678	5481
SLBMs	977	2857	914
Strategic bombers	145	290	290
IRBMs/MRBMs	600	1320	400
Intermediate bombers	815	n.a.	c.2000
China			
ICBMs/IRBMs	114	114	55
SLBMs	12	12	24
Strategic bombers	90	90	90
United Kingdom			
SLBMs	64	192	38
France			
IRBMs	18	18	18
SLBMs	80	80	80
Intermediate bombers	33	33	2

Key: ICBM – intercontinental ballistic missile; SLBM – submarine-launched ballistic missile; IRBM – intermediate-range ballistic missile; MRBM – medium-range ballistic missile; GLCM – ground-launched cruise missile; SLCM – sea-launched cruise missile

Left: Warsaw Pact military heads meet in Prague in 1983. Outwardly united, the Warsaw Pact faced a serious crisis over the events in Poland, and Romania contined to play its maverick role. Above: Soviet Minister of Defence Dimitri Ustinov.

Problems of the Pact

Moscow faces difficulties in Eastern Europe

As has often been pointed out by Western commentators, the Warsaw Pact is not a mirror-image of Nato on the opposite side of the Iron Curtain. The relationship between the Soviet Union and its Warsaw Pact allies is very different from that between the Western superpower and its partners. The Soviet Union dominates Eastern Europe both militarily and politically to a degree the United States could not achieve in the West, even if it wanted to. The Pact was designed as much to guarantee the maintenance of Soviet-style communist government in the member states as to augment the military power of the Soviet Union in its confrontation with Nato.

At the same time, the Pact is not the monolithic bloc that Moscow would perhaps ideally wish it to be. To maintain internal stability and at least a measure of popular support, each of the East European governments must be allowed to pursue its own initiatives, as long as these represent no fundamental threat to Soviet security. Thus, for example, Bulgaria has had a very different relationship with the

Soviet Union from neighbouring Romania, and East Germany has different priorities in its relations with West Germany than other Warsaw Pact states.

The Pact survived the 1970s without encountering any major crises, although Romania's President Ceaucescu continued to play the role of *enfant terrible* in the Eastern bloc. While maintaining a very hard-line regime at home, Ceaucescu's foreign policy expressed a fierce nationalism and a mistrust of Moscow common among Romanians. Romania was the only Pact country which had no Soviet troops or advisers on its soil. True to form, in 1979 Ceaucescu refused to agree to a Soviet proposal for all the Pact members to increase their defence budgets. Instead he actually cut Romania's defence spending in 1980 and 1981, and froze it at the reduced level for a further three years. This was not only a response to Romania's sorry economic plight, but also the expression of a policy which saw national advantage in an independent role within the alliance system.

The ability of Romania to get away with this

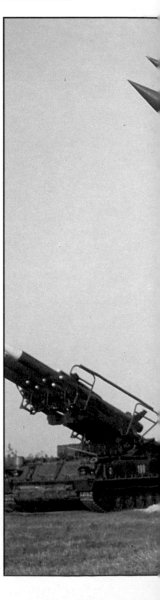

Right: A Polish Air Force Mi-24 Hind-E helicopter and its three-man crew. The formidable Hind gave the Warsaw Pact forces a powerful ground-support and anti-tank capability. Below: Two Polish SAM-6 missile launchers during Warsaw Pact exercises.

independent behaviour was perhaps a result of its strict adherence to Soviet ideology in domestic affairs and its relatively insignificant strategic position in Europe. The rise of the Solidarity movement in Poland in 1980 presented the opposite characteristics – it challenged Soviet political orthodoxy in a country of vital importance to Soviet military planning. With a population of 35 million, Poland was the largest country in the Warsaw Pact after the Soviet Union itself. Moreover, it lay across Soviet lines of communication with East Germany, thus threatening the Soviet Union's entire military position in Europe. With armed forces numbering some 340,000, Poland was also a substantial contributor to the Warsaw Pact's military power.

An unreliable ally

It was obvious that the Soviet Union would not allow Poland to become an 'unreliable' ally, but the Soviets were reluctant to intervene with direct military force. Instead, the Polish leadership was left to handle the crisis under a severely watchful eye and mounting pressure. The Warsaw Pact countries did not react in a uniform manner to the Polish situation. It was the East German leader, Erich Honecker, who was the most outspoken critic of developments in Poland. In October 1980, Honecker declared: 'Poland is and remains a socialist country…We, together with our friends, will make sure of that'. This was a barely-disguised threat of Warsaw Pact intervention to enforce the 'Brezhnev doctrine' – that no state in Eastern Europe could be allowed to reverse its commitment to Soviet-style socialism. Czechoslovakia was the other Warsaw Pact country in the forefront of the war of nerves over Poland, constantly broadcasting reminders of the events of 1968 in Prague as an example of what could happen.

In March and April 1981 Warsaw Pact forces held large joint manoeuvres in Poland, Czechoslovakia and East Germany. Code-named Soyuz 81, the manoeuvres lasted a record 22 days and had been timed to coincide with a predictably acute period of the Polish crisis. In August, during another climax of the crisis, a Soviet task force of 90 ships started exercises off the Polish Baltic coast, while the commander-in-chief of the Warsaw Pact, Marshal Viktor Kulikov, arrived in Warsaw for talks with Poland's commander-in-chief, General Jaruzelski. In September, as Solidarity was holding its first national congress, further Warsaw Pact manoeuvres were taking place, this time in Byelorussia, east of the Polish border.

Yet no invasion of Poland ever took place. At the cost of installing what was effectively a military dictatorship in Warsaw for a period, the crisis was controlled to the satisfaction of the Soviet leadership. This has to be counted as a success for the Pact, since the consequences of an invasion would almost certainly have been serious, both in terms of East-West relations and of the military cohesion of the Pact – the reaction of the Polish armed forces would have been unpredictable. Yet it was hardly encouraging for the Soviets to have the bankruptcy of a communist regime so publicly exposed.

Nato's nuclear deployment

The other major crisis confronted by the Pact in the 1980s was external – the Nato decision to deploy cruise and Pershing II missiles in Western Europe as a response to the Soviet Union's introduction of the SS-20 intermediate range ballistic missile. Recognising that deployment of the Nato missiles would threaten the clear superiority in nuclear forces in the European theatre which the USSR had established, the Warsaw Pact countries responded in 1980 with a call for a freeze of forces in Europe at their existing levels and a ban on the introduction of new weapons systems. The propaganda resources of the Pact were concentrated on encouraging opposition to the new missile deployment in the West. In an attempt to reinforce that opposition, a Pact summit meeting in Prague in January 1983 proposed the conclusion of a non-aggression treaty with Nato – a proposal rejected by Nato as meaningless. After the Nato missile deployment went ahead at the end of 1983,

the Soviet Union announced that in retaliation it was deploying 'operational-tactical' nuclear weapons – SS-21 and SS-22 missiles – at three sites in Czechoslovakia and East Germany.

On this question of East/West nuclear confrontation, Romania once more played a maverick role within the Pact, voicing outspoken criticisms of the Soviet Union's failure to pursue nuclear disarmament. Internal opposition to the perceived increase in the threat of nuclear war in Europe was generally restricted to officially-sponsored movements, which limited their criticisms to attacks on Nato policies, but in East Germany an important peace movement developed, centred on the Evangelical Church, which the government was not able to ignore.

The breakdown of detente between the two superpowers generated an interesting example of the continuing differences of interest between Warsaw Pact countries. Like its Western counterpart, East Germany appeared to view the deteriorating international situation as contrary to its interests. In the summer of 1984 the East German government concluded with the Federal Republic an agreement highly advantageous to itself, by which in return for easing various cross-border travel restrictions, it obtained new credits from Bonn. A visit by Honecker to West Germany was to follow. Neither the agreement nor the proposed visit should have come as a surprise to Moscow, yet they were both greeted with open disapproval. It took some weeks of sustained and barely disguised Soviet pressure to make Honecker abandon his planned visit to Bonn.

Despite such evidence of disagreements, the Warsaw Pact approached its 30th anniversary in 1985 still intact. If the fundamental political problem posed by the continuing failure of communist governments in much of Eastern Europe to establish genuine popular support for their rule remained unsolved, the military power of the alliance had grown with the years, as the level of equipment and training was steadily raised. Doubts expressed in the West as to the reliability of the Soviet Union's allies in a military crisis had still not been confirmed by any example of indiscipline or resistance to the chain of command in Eastern Europe. **Konrad Syrop**

Below: A huge Soviet Aist-class hovercraft disgorges a Naval Infantry tank during amphibious assault exercises on the Baltic coast. Similar exercises at the height of the Solidarity crisis in Poland were used to exert pressure on the Polish government to crack down on the free trade-union opposition.

Key Weapons

GRUMMAN A-6 INTRUDER

Grumman's ungainly-looking Intruder had its origins in a 1956 US Navy request for contractors' proposals for a carrier-borne all-weather attack aeroplane. The new aircraft's size was to be between the diminutive Douglas A-4 Skyhawk and the much larger Douglas A-3 Skywarrior. A prime requirement was long range at low altitude, as was the ability to engage targets at night and in bad weather. This all-weather capability was further stressed in a requirement for the type to be able to navigate in all conditions without reference to any external aids such as beacons; the specification was rounded out by an insistence on a nuclear capability.

Seven US manufacturers responded to the request and on 31 December 1957, Grumman's model 128 was chosen for development. To meet the specification, the company proposed a relatively small airframe housing a crew of two and a very extensive avionics suite known as the DIANE (digital integrated attack navigation equipment) system. Power was provided by a pair of Pratt & Whitney J52 turbojets and, to meet the range requirements, a total internal fuel capacity of 7230kg (15,939lb) was incorporated into the design. Five external stores stations were provided, one on the fuselage centre line and four beneath the moderately swept wings.

The DIANE avionics suite is at the heart of the Intruder's capabilities and allows the aircraft to engage targets situated in the widest variety of terrains in all-weather conditions without the crew needing to look outside the cockpit from launch to recovery. In practice, DIANE provided a fully automatic navigation facility which only required to be programmed with the relevant information to enable the aircraft to be flown 'hands off' if desired. In the attack mode, the system locates the target automatically, computes the launch parameters and generates stores release commands.

The A2F-1, as the A-6A Intruder was designated prior to 1962, made its maiden flight on 19 April 1960 and the type entered service with the US Navy's Attack Squadron 42 (VA-42, known as the 'Green Prawns') on 7 February 1963. A total of 488 A-6A aircraft (including prototypes) were built before production switched to the next major model, the A-6E, in the early 1970s. Between these two variants, a number of A-6A airframes were converted into a range of specialist variants which comprised the A-6B, the A-6C, the EA-6A and the KA-6D.

Both the A-6B and the A-6C were developed to meet specific requirements generated by the Vietnam War. The A-6B appeared during 1968 and was designed to improve the US Navy's surface-to-air missile suppression capability. Nineteen A-6B conversions were completed, with the aircraft falling into three distinct sub-variants, the Mod O of 1968 (10 aeroplanes), the PAT/ARM (passive angle tracking/anti-radiation missile) modification of 1969 (three aeroplanes), and the Mod 1 of 1970 (six aeroplanes). The Mod O had some of the DIANE electronics removed as the aircraft was adapted for the AGM-78 Standard ARM. The PAT system widened the AGM-78's search arc, and its performance was further enhanced in the Mod 1 by the introduction of the AN/APS-118 target acquisition and identification equipment. All 19 aircraft served throughout the remainder of the war and the survivors were reconverted to A-6A standard after the

Above: An A-6E from USS *Dwight D Eisenhower*; the TRAM (target recognition and attack multisensor) turret for laser-guided munitions is visible under the nose. Right: An Intruder is launched from the waist catapult of the USS *Constellation* during an exercise in the Indian Ocean in late 1974. The long projection from the nose is the in-flight refuelling probe.

United States withdrew its forces from Southeast Asia.

The A-6C was an attempt to improve the basic aircraft's ability to operate in poor visibility against Viet Cong supply routes in South Vietnam. Twelve A-6A aircraft were converted to this standard and featured the so-called TRIM (trails, roads, interdiction, multisensor) equipment alongside the standard DIANE suite. TRIM comprised a FLIR (forward looking infra-red) detector and an LLL-TV (low light level television) system mounted in an under-fuselage turret to detect movement in the light conditions experienced at dawn and dusk. The A-6C was the US Navy's equivalent of the US Air Force's B-57G aircraft and all the surviving TRIM aircraft were reconverted after the American withdrawal.

The EA-6A made its first flight on 26 April 1963 and was produced in response to a US Marine Corps requirement for a replacement for its ageing EF-10B ELINT/ECM (electronic intelligence/electronic counter-measures) aircraft. Entering service during 1965, the EA-6A is readily distinguishable from the standard A-6A by its fin-top pod housing the receiving antenna for the AN/ALQ-53 or ALQ-86 signals surveillance equipment. Other ELINT/ECM equipment carried by the type during its service life included signals recording systems, jamming pods, communications jammers, internal chaff dispensers and chaff dispensing pods. EA-6A conversions totalled 27 and they were operated by several US Marine Corps squadrons until their replacement by the EA-6B Prowler during the 1970s; the EA-6A saw service during the Vietnam War, as Marine aircraft were based at Da Nang from 1965 onwards.

The last of the A-6A derivatives, the KA-6D, is an in-flight refuelling tanker. The KA-6D retains a daylight attack/rescue control capability and features a hose-and-reel assembly in the rear fuselage, capable of delivering 1327 litres (350 gallons) of fuel per minute; to increase the aircraft's overall fuel capacity, the KA-6D can carry up to five 1136 litre (300 gallon) drop tanks, giving it a total tankage of

14,551 litres (3844 gallons), just over 11,356 litres (3000 gallons) of which is transferable. Additionally, the centre line drop tank can be replaced by the McDonnell Douglas D-704 'buddy pack' as a back-up to the main refuelling capability. The KA-6D entered service in 1970 and over 60 A-6A airframes have been converted to this version. A further six A-6A aircraft may be converted to KA-6Ds by 1986.

The current production strike model, the A-6E, appeared during 1970. Essentially an up-dated A-6A, the A-6E is powered by J52-P-8B turbojets in place of the earlier aircraft's P-6A or P-8A units and features an extensively revised navigation/attack suite using solid-state electronics to reduce maintenance. The two radars, the APQ-92 and -112, have been replaced by a single unit, the AN/APQ-148 multi-mode, track-while-scan set, as has the ASQ-61 computer by the AN/APS-133 navigation/attack system. To further improve the A-6E's capabilities, an AMTI (airborne moving-target indicator) was added to the radar equipment in the early 1980s and late production aircraft are fitted with a TRAM (target recognition and attack multisensor) turret under the nose. This installation provides an infra-red sensor for target identification, a laser ranger/designator and a laser-marked target detection system. As well as these refinements to the aircraft's attack systems, the A-6E carries up-dated communications, Tacan and IFF (identification friend or foe) gear, together with an improved ECM fit including the AN/ALE-39 chaff dispenser, the AN/ALR-50 radar warning receiver, the AN/ALQ-126 deception jammer and the AN/ALQ-130 communications jammer. By mid-1984, some 172 A-6E aircraft had been delivered or were on order and the US Navy had up-dated 240 A-6A aircraft to the new standard.

In mid-1984, an A-6E improvement programme was initiated which will radically alter the aircraft. Working from nose to tail, the upgraded Intruder will feature a new radar with twice the range of the present equipment and an air-to-air mode, a new nose radome shape, an offset refuelling probe to make

Page 2143: An A-6 aboard the USS *Enterprise* prepares to be catapulted into the air. Above: Over Vietnam, two Intruders from attack squadron VA-196 drop their bombs.

Below right: An A-6 Intruder from VA-65, based at Naval Air Station Oceana in Virginia. Apart from its carrier-based air wings, the US Navy also has a substantial number of shore-based squadrons.

contact with tanker aircraft easier, a completely revised cockpit layout, a revised wing format incorporating additional slats, two additional wing pylons to carry AIM-9 or AIM-120 air-to-air missiles and the deletion of the fuselage Doppler radar. New search/attack radar sets under consideration for the aircraft are the Hughes AN/APG-63 and APG-65, the Westinghouse APQ-68 and the Norden APQ-156 and APQ-164. In addition to these changes, the upgraded aircraft's engine is under review with General Electric proposing an F404 variant to replace the existing J52s. In 1984, the US Navy had not yet established exactly how many of the new model (possibly to be known as the A-6F) it required or determined which engine type would be used, decisions on both matters being expected early in 1985.

Completing the Intruder family is the EA-6B Prowler ELINT/ECM aircraft. First flown on 25 May 1968, the Prowler is based on the standard A-6 airframe but incorporates a 1·55m (4ft 6in) fuselage extension to make room for two additional crew members. Other changes include the deletion of the fuselage air brakes, the restressing of the wing structure to accept 5·5g manoeuvres and the use of the uprated J52-P-408 engines from the 31st airframe onwards. To suit it for the ECM role, the EA-6B carries an extensive electronics suite, the major element of which is the AN/ALQ-99 TJS (tactical jamming system).

Left: The large array of weapons that the Intruder can carry is shown here. Up to 30 Mk82 227kg (500lb) bombs, or 13 Mk 83 454kg (1000lb) bombs, or five Mk84 908kg (2000lb) bombs can be mounted on the weapons' stations.

Below: An EA-6A about to be launched by steam catapult. This was a conversion of the A-6 for the US Marine Corps which required an electronic warfare aeroplane and can be identified by the large housing on the top of the fin for the signals surveillance equipment.

The extremely powerful AN/ALQ-99 generates jamming signals against a wide range of emitters using a maximum of five external transmitter pods. The system as a whole is computerised and offers three operational modes; automatic, semi-automatic and manual. In addition to the TJS, the Prowler carries a range of sub-systems and the operational workload generated by all of this equipment demands the full attention of three of the aeroplane's four-man crew.

The EA-6B entered service with the US Navy's electronic warfare squadron, VAQ-132, in July 1971 and this unit made the first operational use of the type in Southeast Asia between June 1972 and February 1973. By the end of the Vietnam War, the Prowler had flown some 720 sorties, many of which were in connection with the Linebacker II raids of December 1972. The aircraft used in Southeast Asia were designated as Basic standard aircraft with a capability against three specific frequency bands. The 31st aircraft introduced the Excap (expanded capability) standard which broadened the TJS's cover to six bands. The first Excap Prowler was delivered in 1973 and total production of the model amounted to 25 aircraft.

The Excap aircraft were superseded by the Icap (improved capability) model in July 1976. Icap Prowlers have the same frequency coverage as the preceding model combined with a reduced response time to threats, new cockpit displays, an automatic carrier recovery system, improved communications and IFF systems and the A-6E's search radar. Icap production totalled more than 49 aircraft together with 21 Basic EA-6Bs brought up to the new standard between 1976 and 1979. A further Icap model, the Icap-2, appeared in 1980 and featured further improvements to the TJS. Icap-2 is the current standard for Prowlers under construction. For the future, work is in progress on an Advcap (advanced capability) configuration. Six prototype systems are expected to be available during 1986 with production Advcap aircraft being delivered from 1989.

In the attack role, the A-6 Intruder entered combat in June 1965 when the USS *Independence* steamed into the Gulf of Tonkin with the aircraft of VA-75 aboard. The 'Sunday Punchers' flew their first operational A-6 sortie early in the following month with a strike on targets south of Hanoi. Prior to the arrival of the Intruder, the US Navy had been hampered in its strikes against the North by the bad weather experienced over the area during a large part of the year. The A-6's DIANE equipment proved invaluable in overcoming this problem and gave the service an all-weather strike capability only really matched by the small number of F-111A aircraft deployed to the theatre. In November 1966, VA-75 was replaced by VA-85 aboard the USS *Kitty Hawk* and from then on Intruder strength in Southeast Asia built up and the type became the mainstay of the navy's strategic air campaign against the North for the remainder of the war.

This is not to say that all aspects of the A-6 were perfect; indeed, the DIANE suite caused considerable problems to begin with, especially in the radar sub-systems. The APQ-112 unit proved to be unreliable and many crews have preferred to rely on the APQ-92 alone. Equally, the EA-6B has proved to be a difficult aircraft to fly. Between November 1979 and February 1980, no fewer than 10 Prowlers were lost, resulting in the entire Intruder/Prowler fleet being grounded for a period early in 1980. After an extensive review of operational procedures, training methods and aircraft maintenance, the ban was lifted, but at least four more Prowlers have been lost in the ensuing years.

The Intruder went into combat again during the American attempts at peacekeeping in the Lebanon in 1983-84 – operations which resulted in the loss of a single aircraft to ground fire. At its height, the A-6 has seen service with 14 US Navy attack squadrons together with a further five US Marine Corps units, and the Prowler family looks set to provide a major component of the US Navy's air capability for many years to come.

Left: EA-6B Prowlers take off in the early morning. Below: A KA-6D fuel-tanker Intruder prior to launch from the USS *Coral Sea*. The KA-6D has most of the standard radars removed and carries up to 14,551 litres (3844 gallons) of fuel in five drop tanks under wings and fuselage.

DIANE (digital integrated attack navigation equipment)

At the heart of the Grumman A-6 Intruder's combat capabilities is DIANE, an extremely complicated electronic system. DIANE comprises a vast range of sub-systems, including the following items:

AN/APQ-92 Main search radar; provides both a navigation and an attack facility

AN/APQ-122 Tracking radar for terrain-mapping and target location

AN/APN-141 Low altitude (up to 1524m – 5000ft) radar altimeter

AN/APN-153 Doppler radar for navigation and to provide ground speed and drift angles for ballistic computer

AN/ASN-31 Inertial navigation system; provides data on heading, altitude and horizontal and vertical velocities

AN/ASQ-57 Integrated electronic control system

AN/ASQ-61 Ballistic computer; provides flight pattern data, cruise control and data for weapons selection, fuzing and delivery

AN/ASW-16 Three-axis autopilot

AN/AVA-1 Pilot's display unit; provides data on flight parameters, such as terrain clearance

CP-729A Air data computer which provides altitude, static pressure, Mach number and airspeed information for the ASW-16, the AVA-1 and the conventional flight instruments

Grumman A-6E Intruder

Type Two-seat carrier-borne all-weather attack aeroplane

Dimensions Span 16·15m (53ft); length 16·69m (54ft 9in); height 4·93m (16ft 2in)

Weight Empty 12,132kg (26,747lb); maximum take-off (catapult) 26,580kg (58,600lb)

Powerplant Two 4128kg (9300lb) Pratt & Whitney J52-P-8B twin-shaft turbojets

Performance Maximum level speed at sea level 1037km/h (644mph); cruising speed at optimum altitude 763km/h (474mph)

Range Combat range with maximum external fuel 5222km (3245 miles)

Ceiling 12,925m (42,400ft)

Armament Five external stores racks, each capable of carrying 1633kg (3600lb). Maximum external load 8165kg (18,000lb). Typical weapons loads are 30 227kg (500lb) bombs in five clusters of six or three 907kg (2000lb) bombs and two 1136 litre (300 gallon) drop tanks

Grumman EA-6B Prowler

Type Four-seat carrier-borne electronic warfare aeroplane

Dimensions Span 16·15m (53ft); length 18·24m (59ft 10in); height 4·95m (16ft 3in)

Weight Empty 14,588kg (32,162lb); take-off in stand-off jamming configuration 24,703kg (54,461lb)

Powerplant Two 5080kg (11,200lb) Pratt & Whitney J52-P-408 twin-shaft turbojets

Performance Maximum level speed at sea level with five external jamming pods 1002km/h (623mph); cruising speed at optimum altitude with five pods 774km/h (481mph)

Range Combat radius with maximum external fuel 3861km (2399 miles)

Ceiling 11,580m (38,000ft)

Armament None. Five external stores stations taken up with either jamming pods or drop tanks. Normal configuration is usually two or three pods and two or three drop tanks

Top left: The cockpit of the Intruder; the pilot sits on the left and the bombardier-navigator on the right. The operating complexity of the A-6 is shown by this array of instrumentation which has to be controlled by the crew. Above left: Intruders aboard the USS *Coral Sea* are washed down. Above: An A-6 about to be towed across the flight deck of the USS *Forrestal*. The folding wings of carrier-borne aeroplanes are necessary so that the maximum number can be provided in the confined space of the ship.

Between two wars

From civil strife to Israeli invasion in Lebanon

Even though the Israeli invasion of Lebanon in March 1978, Operation Litani, failed to achieve its prime objective of destroying the Palestinian military forces stationed across Israel's northern border, when the Israeli Defence Forces (IDF) withdrew in April 1978, Israel had won an effective buffer zone and sphere of influence in southern Lebanon. A 6000-strong United Nations peacekeeping force, known as the United Nations Interim Force in the Lebanon (UNIFIL), was soon stationed south of the Litani River, and between UNIFIL and the Israeli border a 310 sq km (120 sq mile) strip of territory was controlled by the men of Major Saad Haddad's pro-Israeli militia. Although the Palestinians rapidly infiltrated back into the area occupied by UNIFIL, it was now virtually impossible for them to mount commando raids over the border into northern Israel. The Israelis, on the other hand, continued to launch ground and air strikes against suspected Palestinian positions in southern Lebanon in an attempt both to hit at the Palestine Liberation Organisation (PLO) and to turn local opinion against the Palestinians by indiscriminate destruction.

In the rest of Lebanon, the confused situation left by the events of the 1975-76 civil war continued to simmer with hostility and occasionally break into open conflict. The government of President Elias Sarkis was quite incapable of establishing control over the country's warring groups. The partial defeat suffered by the Druze and Muslim leftists at the end of the civil war kept them relatively subdued, with the main focus of the complex confrontations shifting to the Christian Maronites and the Syrian forces in Lebanon.

During the Lebanese civil war, Israel had accepted intervention in Lebanon by its bitter enemy, Syria, because both countries had a mutual interest in preventing an outright military defeat of the Lebanese Christians by their Lebanese Muslim and Palestinian opponents, and because Syria unofficially agreed to recognise the existence of vital Israeli strategic interests in southern Lebanon. In what became known as the Red Line agreements, sponsored by the United States in 1976, Israel had accepted that Syria would be allowed to station a peacekeeping force in Lebanon, but no nearer than 24km (15 miles) to the northernmost point of the Israeli border and without air support or air-defence missiles. In effect, Israel was to guarantee its interests by retaining control of Lebanese airspace.

The Israelis also kept up their strong links with the Lebanese Maronite Christians, whom they had trained and armed during the civil war. Mossad, the Israeli secret service, had particularly close relations with the rising strong-man of the Maronite community, Bashir Gemayel. Bashir was the younger son of the Phalangist leader Pierre Gemayel, but though he owed much of his original influence to his father, he had exploited his opportunity as commander of the Phalangist militia to create his own power-base, largely independent of the Phalangist establishment. The Lebanese Forces, as Bashir's militia was known, were recruited mainly from among young working-class Maronites from East Beirut and from the ranks of Christian refugees who had fled their homes during the civil war. Uprooted and freed from their otherwise unquestioning loyalty to the traditional Maronite chieftains, including Pierre Gemayel, they provided Bashir with the military muscle to carry out his plans for undisputed lead-

Top: A pall of thick smoke rises above the bombed ruins of the Lebanese capital, Beirut, during the Israeli invasion of June 1982. This climax to decades of Israeli-Palestinian confrontation followed the partial Israeli invasion of Lebanon, Operation Litani, in March 1978. Between the two Israeli invasions, internal Lebanese politics were dominated by the efforts of Phalangist militia leader Bashir Gemayel (above) to achieve dominance not only over the Lebanese Christians, but over the whole country.

ership of the divided Lebanese Christian forces.

The rival Zghorta Liberation Army, led by former President Sulieman Frangieh's son Tony, was a major obstacle to this ambition. Based in the north Lebanese town of Zghorta, the Frangiehs were jealous of their local power and blocked attempts at infiltration by Bashir's supporters. The Frangiehs were also critical of the Gemayels' reliance upon Western and Israeli support, and favoured a rapprochement with Syria and reconciliation with the Lebanese Muslims. If Bashir was to impose his control over the whole Christian community, and then to impose Christian control over the whole of Lebanon, the Frangiehs had to be eliminated.

On 13 June 1978, Bashir's men mounted a raid upon the Frangieh summer palace in Ehden, in the heart of their northern stronghold. Tony Frangieh, his wife and baby daughter were all killed in the fighting, which effectively removed the threat of a Frangieh challenge to Bashir's claims to leadership. Maronite opinion was outraged, however, and Sulieman Frangieh swore vengeance, but Bashir was saved from complete isolation by the clumsiness of the Syrian reaction to the Ehden killings. Realising that the murder of Tony Frangieh was a challenge to its own policy in Lebanon, Syria attempted to administer a warning to the Maronites by shelling the Christian areas of East Beirut. But the bombardment merely re-united the Maronites and power continued to slip into the hands of Bashir. The Lebanese Christians had by now turned completely against the Syrians, who in 1976 had saved them from disaster. Convinced of the backing of both Israel and the United States, the Christians failed to realise the relatively minor role they played in the regional policy of both countries.

In the autumn of 1978, the United States and Israel were preoccupied with an Israeli-Egyptian disengagement in the Sinai, which was ratified by the Camp David agreement of September 1978. After Camp David, both powers turned their attention northwards, with contradictory results. Israel began to pursue a more aggressive policy on its northern border, but the United States sought to restore its influence with Syria, which meant that President Jimmy Carter was extremely hostile to further direct Israeli intervention in Lebanon. As a result, when fighting broke out between the Syrians and Phalangists in October 1978, Israeli support, on which the latter had counted, was totally absent, and the Christians were forced to accept a ceasefire.

In 1979, however, Israel's attitude to the Lebanon situation hardened. In January, Minister of Defence Ezer Weizman announced that Israel would henceforth not merely react to Palestinian attacks with retaliatory raids on PLO positions in Lebanon, but would also carry out pre-emptive strikes whenever and wherever necessary. Then, in March, Prime Minister Menachem Begin took over as his own minister of defence. Begin was a firm believer in the use of military power to achieve political solutions and saw the defeat of the Palestinians in Lebanon as a necessary prelude to the eventual absorption of the West Bank of the Jordan into Israel. His belief in military solutions was in the end to give such 'hawks' as Israeli Chief of Staff Lieutenant-General Rafael Eitan effective control of policy, but between August 1979 and April 1980 US pressure on the Israeli government was still sufficient to prevent any pre-

emptive strike into Lebanon.

Direct intervention was not the only option available to Israel, however, and support for Haddad in southern Lebanon and Bashir Gemayel in the north became increasingly important. When Haddad's Israeli-supplied artillery shelled UNIFIL positions in April 1979 in order to prevent the Lebanese Army from reasserting central government authority along the border, it was clear that he had acted with Israeli approval. Haddad then proceeded to declare his area the 'Republic of Free Lebanon'.

Bashir Gemayel, meanwhile, continued to extend his control over his Maronite rivals, though not without opposition. On 23 February 1980, for example, a car-bomb meant for him killed his daughter. But the only major independent Christian military force remaining was the Tiger militia of Camille Chamoun's National Liberal Party (NLP), led by Chamoun's son Danny. Bashir's Lebanese Forces totally crushed this last obstacle to undisputed military leadership of the Lebanese Maronites in an assault upon Tiger militia positions and NLP offices which began on 7 July 1980 and cost over 500 lives.

Conflict with the Syrians

Bashir Gemayel now turned his attention to the non-Maronite Christian communities, but his next move brought him into direct and fateful conflict with the Syrians. In the spring of 1981, the Phalangists, allegedly transported in Israeli helicopters, took up positions in and around the largely Greek-Catholic town of Zahle in the Beqaa Valley, and attempted to construct a road through the mountains to connect it with the Maronite heartland north of Beirut. The Syrians, realising that a Phalangist-controlled Zahle would threaten the vital Beirut-Damascus road, opened an assault upon Zahle on 1 April. On 25 April, a helicopter-borne Syrian unit captured the key ridge which overlooked the town, but three days later, Israeli jets shot down two Syrian helicopters over the Beqaa Valley in apparent reprisal for the defeat of their Phalangist allies.

Though the Red Line agreements were never made public, it was widely believed that they had not prohibited the Syrian use of helicopters in Lebanon, and that the Israeli action was simply a punishment for the Syrian frustration of the Phalangist expansion into Zahle. Syria was not intimidated, however, and

Above: Palestinian fighters carefully maintain a Soviet-built 73mm RPG-9 recoilless rifle at a PLO base in southern Lebanon. The 1978 Operation Litani had been unsuccessful in destroying the PLO in the south of the Lebanon, and in the next four years the Palestinians reorganised, with heavy weapons supplied by the Russians.

Above: Israeli ambassador to London, Shlomo Argov, whose attempted assassination by hitmen of the breakaway Palestinian group of Abu Nidal on 3 June 1982 provided the pretext for the Israeli invasion of Lebanon. The Israeli General Staff had been planning such an operation for over a year, and rumours of an impending Israeli assault had been rife in Beirut for months.

Above: US special envoy to the Middle East Philip Habib, who sought to reach a compromise settlement to the conflict over Lebanon between Israel and Syria. American pressure on the Begin government to prevent a further invasion of Lebanon was significantly weaker under President Reagan than his predecessor Jimmy Carter, and ultimately proved incapable of averting a new Middle East war.

on 29 April moved three batteries of SAM-6 anti-aircraft missiles over the border into the Beqaa Valley. The protection which these missiles provided the Syrian forces in Lebanon against Israeli air attack was more symbolic than real, but they represented a clear Syrian abrogation of the Red Line agreements, to which the Begin government replied with dire warnings and demands for their immediate removal.

In the run-up to the June 1981 Israeli general elections, the confrontation with Syria came as a god-send to the Begin government, which was trailing far behind the opposition Labour Party in the opinion polls. The danger of a diplomatic crisis escalating into a full-scale war between Syria and Israel brought US special envoy Philip Habib flying in from Washington on the first of his several missions to the Middle East. His task was to avert war and restore US links with the Syrian regime of President Hafez Assad. But Syria too had gained advantage from the confrontation with Israel which had helped rally support from other Arab states and allowed Assad to assume the mantle of the main Arab opponent to Israel, abandoned by Egypt after the Camp David compromise.

Habib therefore faced a difficult task, and the impotence of his efforts was emphasised within 24 hours of his return to Washington towards the end of May 1981, when Begin ordered new airstrikes against Palestinian targets south of Beirut. The immediate crisis was defused, however, and the popularity of the Begin government was restored

anyway by the Israeli destruction of the Iraqi nuclear reactor outside Baghdad on 7 June. On 30 June, the Begin-led Likud coalition was re-elected.

The Israeli government seems to have considered the possibility of a full-scale invasion of Lebanon soon after the June election, and this would certainly explain the heavy Israeli air attacks on southern Lebanon which took place on 10 July, during which eight of the nine bridges across the Litani were destroyed. The failure to destroy the Litani bridges had been a much-criticised weakness of the 1978 invasion which had allowed the PLO forces to withdraw across the river intact. The Palestinians, for their part, used 130mm artillery and Katyusha multiple rocket-launchers to bombard Israeli settlements in northern Galilee. Yet no Israeli invasion occurred. On 24 July the Israeli government agreed to what was in effect a ceasefire with the PLO, negotiated through Philip Habib. Israel denied that the agreement represented formal contact with or recognition of the PLO, but the ceasefire nevertheless represented an unusual departure in Israeli policy.

Thoughts of invasion

An invasion had not been mounted in July 1981, perhaps because of US pressure, but from August 1981, with the appointment of Ariel Sharon as Israeli minister of defence, planning began in earnest for the invasion of Lebanon. During the winter of 1981-82, rumours abounded in Beirut of the probability of such an Israeli invasion, and in January 1982 Sharon himself visited Beirut in secret to inform Bashir Gemayel of his plans and to carry out a personal on-the-spot reconnaissance.

In February 1982, Israel recommenced its arms supplies to the Lebanese Phalangists, and early in April US reconnaissance satellites detected suspicious Israeli troop concentrations along the Lebanese border. Israel continually alleged Palestinian breaches of the ceasefire, but it seems to have been carefully observed by the PLO, who were doubtless able to read the regular newspaper forecasts of an imminent Israeli invasion. On 21 April 1982, the Israeli Air Force struck targets in Lebanon in retaliation for the death of an Israeli officer killed by a landmine while on patrol in southern Lebanon (where, of course, he had no right to be) but there was no PLO response to the raids. Heavy Israeli raids on Damour and Zahrzani on 9 May did provoke a Palestinian reply, however, and the PLO heavy artillery around Tyre loosed off some 30 rounds towards Israel. On 20 May 1982, Sharon visited Washington for talks with US Secretary of State Alexander Haig, during which he later alleged he informed Haig of the Israeli intention to invade Lebanon in order to remove the PLO threat to northern Israel.

It was in this atmosphere of tension, rumour and threats that the Israeli ambassador in London, Shlomo Argov, was the victim of an unsuccessful assassination attempt by agents of renegade Palestinian terrorist leader Abu Nidal on 3 June 1982. At last the Israeli government had a public justification for its long-planned invasion of Lebanese territory, and within 48 hours Israeli tanks were rolling northwards across the border into Lebanon on the first day of what Israel called Operation Peace for Galilee.

Robin Corbett

The Palestinians in Lebanon

The Palestinian refugee camps in Lebanon dated back to the earliest exodus from Israel in 1948, but it was only after the Palestine Liberation Organisation (PLO) shifted its centre of activities there in 1971 that it became a focus of political attention. From that time, Lebanon offered the PLO the only remaining possible base for unfettered activity.

The Palestinians' involvement in the Lebanese civil war (1975-76) resulted in heavy casualties, direct conflict with one of their main Arab backers, Syria, and in the aftermath a distinct worsening of their relations with the host population. On the credit side, they gained fighting experience and some reinforcement to their armed strength – from the Palestine Liberation Army (PLA), a conventional military force which had previously operated as part of the Syrian Army but came under PLO influence after deployment in Lebanon, and from Saiqa, the Syrian controlled Palestinian guerrilla group, many of whose members defected to the PLO forces.

The Palestinians' relations with Syria were soon to be repaired. In November 1977 the Egyptian President, Anwar Sadat, began his unilateral peace initiative that excluded the Palestinians; the PLO was united with Syria and other radical Arab states in its rejection of Sadat's policies. After the Camp David accords there was even wider agreement in the Arab world, in which the PLO joined. Within the PLO, the dissident movements normally opposed to Arafat's Fatah leadership were generally reconciled to the movement's policies.

By 1982 the Palestinians in Lebanon numbered some 400,000 people, with schools and hospitals as well as armed camps and training sites. Such heavy weapons as Soviet T55 tanks and 130mm artillery had been added to their armoury, although these were far from the latest models and any idea of a Palestinian invasion of Israel was pure fantasy. In fact, Arafat was still playing for time, hoping that an Arab or US peace initiative would hand the Palestinians a homeland by diplomacy. The more militant groups, such as Ahmed Jibril's Popular Front for the Liberation of Palestine – General Command (PFLP-GC), occasionally rebelled against Arafat's moderation, but were brought back into line. By its own standards, the PLO was exceptionally united in 1982, although this unity would not survive the pressures of defeat in Lebanon.

'Peace for Galilee'

The Israelis invade Lebanon

The attempted assassination of Shlomo Argov, the Israeli ambassador to London, late on the evening of 3 June 1982, set into motion the preparations for the invasion of Lebanon which the Israeli Defence Forces (IDF) had been planning for at least a year under the code-name Pine Tree. This plan contained a number of options, including a limited operation in which the IDF would advance only as far north as the Awali River in order to destroy the Palestine Liberation Organisation's (PLO) military strength in southern Lebanon which the 1978 Operation Litani had left largely intact. A second option was an advance as far north as Beirut, but without the IDF entering the city. The mopping up of PLO forces within Beirut was to be left to the Israelis' Phalangist militia allies. Neither of these first two options involved armed conflict with the Syrian Army forces which were present inside Lebanon – confrontation with Damascus was to be strictly avoided.

A third option, however, favoured by Israeli Minister of Defence Ariel Sharon and Chief of Staff Rafael Eitan and known as the 'Big Plan', rejected the constraints of limited war and set the aim of defeating both the Palestinians and the Syrians. The IDF was to enter Beirut where it would cooperate with the Christian Phalangists in the final destruction of PLO power in Lebanon.

Despite his hardline attitude, Israeli Prime Minister Menachem Begin, whose main aim was to inflict a defeat on the PLO which would undermine its influence over the Arab population of the occupied West Bank of the Jordan, initially favoured a limited operation, and it was essentially a variant of the first option of Pine Tree which the Israeli cabinet sanctioned when it met to discuss the Argov shooting. But the ability of Sharon to influence events by his direction of operations on the ground was gradually to draw Israel into a situation where the temptations of implementing the Big Plan proved irresistible.

On Friday 4 June, Israeli aircraft carried out heavy raids upon suspected PLO targets in Lebanon, but there was still no final decision to invade. On Saturday 5 June, the PLO replied to the Israeli air attacks by bombarding 23 Israeli settlements in northern Galilee with heavy artillery, and the IDF continued to hit Palestinian targets in Lebanon with air and artillery counter-strikes. That evening, the Israeli cabinet met and gave the final go-ahead for the invasion to proceed. The aim was a swift limited war against the PLO without any confrontation with Syria, and no decision was taken to enter Beirut.

Eitan was ordered to move quickly, without waiting the 24 hours necessary to mobilise the IDF to 60 per cent of its full strength, much less the 48 hours needed to reach full mobilisation. The reason for such haste was less the government's desire to achieve surprise over the Palestinians than its fear that any delay would increase the possibility of the

Left: An Israeli M60 tank roars past a checkpoint in southern Lebanon manned by French UNIFIL troops. The Israelis had absorbed the lessons of the 1973 Yom Kippur War by integrating mechanised infantry and self-propelled artillery into armoured units, and by developing the Merkava tank, which proved more than a match for the Syrian T72s during the battles of 11 June.
Inset: Israeli Chief of Staff Lieutenant-General Rafael Eitan, who masterminded the invasion.

Below: An enormous column of smoke and dust towers over the Lebanese port of Sidon during the bitter battle between its Palestinian defenders and the invading Israeli forces.

United States intervening to prevent an invasion.

At 1100 hours on Sunday 6 June, Israeli forces crossed the border into Lebanon in three assault groups, responsible respectively for the coastal, central and eastern sectors of the invasion. The task of advancing northwards up the narrow coast road was entrusted to General Yitzhak Mordechai, commanding three brigades totalling some 22,000 men and 220 tanks. Progress in this sector was slow, and the IDF armoured columns were vulnerable to Palestinian ambush from the olive groves which lined the landward side of the highway. An advance guard, sent forward to cut off the Palestinian forces on the Tyre peninsula, drove by accident into the town of Tyre itself and was only extricated from its mistake by the arrival of the bulk of the main force. Tyre was blockaded and Mordechai's group continued its advance, bridging the Litani at around 1600 hours at the site of the Qasmiye Bridge, which had been destroyed during the air raids of 5 June.

In the central zone, where approximately 18,000 Israeli troops and 220 tanks were committed, the 36th Division, commanded by General Avigdor Kahalani, entered Lebanese territory from Metalla in a two-pronged attack whose immediate objectives were the capture of the strategic crossroads at Nabitiya and the occupation of the Arnoun Heights, including the key Palestinian strongpoint at Beaufort

Castle, which dominated the whole Israeli border and access to the Beqaa Valley to the north. While one column of Kahalani's force crossed the Litani River at Khardali Bridge, south of Beaufort Castle, and advanced into the Arnoun Heights, a second crossed the river to the north of the castle at Kakalet Bridge and moved on Nabitiya under heavy fire from the castle's Palestinian garrison.

Bypassing Nabitiya, a battalion-sized force continued to advance towards Jezzine, and the PLO forces stationed in Nabitiya withdrew before them. On the evening of 6 June, Beaufort Castle was subjected to a heavy air and artillery bombardment, and the elite reconnaissance battalion of the IDF's Golani infantry brigade detached from the main force to assault the castle from the rear. A frontal attack, up the high cliffs upon which the castle was perched above the Litani River, had been ruled out as impracticable, so under cover of darkness, the Israelis moved forward from the west over gently sloping ground. The battle for Beaufort Castle lasted six hours, and the Palestinian garrison was only overwhelmed after the fiercest hand-to-hand fighting.

The largest Israeli force was concentrated in the eastern sector, where some 38,000 men and 800 tanks moved forward towards the positions occupied by the Syrian Army in the Beqaa Valley. The 252nd

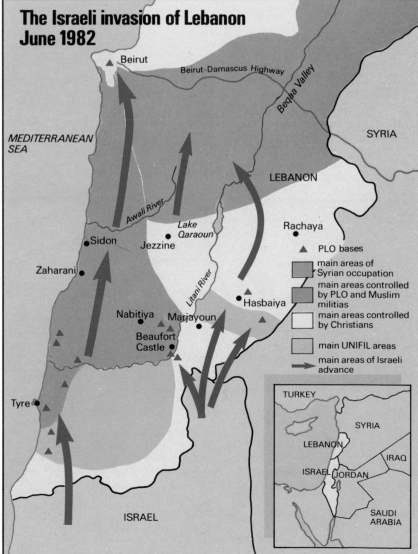

The Israeli invasion of Lebanon June 1982

MEDITERRANEAN SEA

Beirut
Beirut-Damascus Highway
Beqaa Valley
SYRIA
LEBANON
Awali River
Lake Qaraoun
Rachaya
Sidon
Jezzine
Zaharani
Litani River
Hasbaiya
Nabitiya
Marjayoun
Beaufort Castle
Tyre
ISRAEL

▲ PLO bases
main areas of Syrian occupation
main areas controlled by PLO and Muslim militias
main areas controlled by Christians
main UNIFIL areas
main areas of Israeli advance

TURKEY
SYRIA
CYPRUS
LEBANON
IRAQ
ISRAEL JORDAN
SAUDI ARABIA

Division, under General Immanuel Sakel, attacked through Wadi Cheba in the hills around Mount Hermon, carving out a 20km (12 mile) long passage through which its armour and artillery poured north. A second column advanced on Hasbiya and Kouka-ba. Meanwhile, IDF units also began to move towards the Lake Qaraoun area. The purpose of these operations was to outflank the Syrians, cutting them off from Damascus.

The invasion continued the following day, 7 June, with heavy Israeli bombing of PLO positions in Beirut and the coastal sector. While IDF units began to mop up Palestinian resistance bypassed in the initial advance, the junction of IDF forces from the central and coastal sectors at Zaharani took place in preparation for a combined assault on the PLO stronghold of Sidon. Around 2400 hours the previous night, the IDF had staged an amphibious landing north of Sidon in order to cut off its Palestinian defenders and link up with an armoured brigade advancing on Damour. With Sidon surrounded, the Israelis began to shell the town, fighting their way into the large Palestinian refugee camp at Ein Hilwe on its outskirts.

While the Israeli forces in the central zone continued their advance northwards on Beit ed Dein and Ajn Zhalta, with the ultimate objective of commanding the Beirut-Damascus highway, in the east the IDF flanking movements south of the Beqaa Valley further weakened the position of the Syrian units stationed there.

SAMs under attack

The most significant event of Monday 7 June, however, was the arrival of the Israelis' divisional artillery in the frontline area in the eastern sector, placing Syrian surface-to-air missile (SAM) batteries in the Beqaa Valley within range of IDF attack. Damascus responded by moving in more missiles. This was exactly the situation towards which Sharon had been manoeuvring. By massively threatening Syrian positions in eastern Lebanon, he had forced Damascus to make a move which he could now represent to Begin as a threat to the flank of the Israeli invasion. The Israeli cabinet, which until now had been insisting that the invasion was a limited operation, and that there would be no confrontation with Syria, gave the go-ahead to knock out the Syrian SAM batteries. Begin's government was now effectively committed to carry out its most ambitious plans in the Lebanon, including both war with Syria and the destruction of the PLO in Beirut.

This decision, taken on Wednesday 9 June, came after a day of relatively little action, during which the Syrians had refrained from using their SAMs against Israeli jets flying over eastern Lebanon. Israeli and Syrian fighters had engaged in dogfights over Beirut, however, and four Syrian aircraft had been shot down without any Israeli losses. On the afternoon of 9 June, Israeli aircraft attacked the SAM sites and took on the Syrian Air Force over the Beqaa Valley. Exploiting their superior technology and tactics, the Israelis scored a resounding success, knocking out 19 missile batteries and downing 22 Syrian MiGs without loss.

This was the decisive action of the 1982 Lebanese war, assuring Israel total air superiority over the Lebanon, depriving the Syrian and PLO ground forces of air support, and leaving them vulnerable to

the hammer blows of the IDF's continued advance. The Israeli air victory over the Beqaa Valley was swiftly followed by IDF ground forces advancing northwards around Lake Qaraoun and towards the Beqaa Valley itself.

The following day, while Israeli units began to mop-up Palestinian resistance in the south, bypassed by the rapid advance of the preceding week, the IDF advance guard continued its race towards the outskirts of Beirut, south of which the Syrian 85th and 62nd Brigades were now deploying. The Israeli advance was temporarily halted, however, by stiff Palestinian resistance around the Kafr Sill suburb of the Lebanese capital. In the central zone, the Israeli forces moved nearer to their target of the Beirut-Damascus road, although they began to encounter increasingly effective Syrian opposition, and in the east the Syrians were forced to retreat, even though they successfully destroyed a number of Israeli tanks using Gazelle anti-tank helicopters and special infantry teams armed with HOT anti-tank missiles. An Israeli tank battalion ambushed near Soultan Yaaquoub lost eight tanks and some 30 men in a fierce six-hour battle, but the Israelis continued to notch-up victories in the air, shooting down a further 26 MiGs and four helicopters.

Fire does not cease

On Friday 11 June, the Israeli government announced that it had agreed to a ceasefire with the Syrians, which did not, however, include the Palestinians, now trapped inside the Lebanese capital. Before the ceasefire came into operation, there were further clashes between the IDF and the Syrians, who attempted to move a column of T72 tanks into the Beqaa Valley to strengthen their forces there. Ambushed by the Israelis, nine of the Syrian T72s were destroyed, and the remainder forced to withdraw. The continued air battle cost the Syrians a further 18 aircraft, bringing their total losses to 70 since the beginning of the Israeli invasion.

The ceasefire, which had later been extended to include the PLO, broke down within hours, and by the afternoon of Sunday 12 June, the IDF was involved in a heavy battle with the Palestinians around Khalde, some 10km (6 miles) south of Beirut. Fighting between the Syrians and Israelis now developed in the area east of Beirut, as the siege of the capital was instituted, but there was no major battle until 22 June, when a bitter contest for the crucial Beirut-Damascus highway broke out. Until they seized control of this road, the Israelis would be unable to proceed with their aim of reducing the PLO inside Beirut without fear of a Syrian attack on their eastern flank.

Although the Syrians deployed large numbers of tanks and artillery, Israeli command of the air left them totally vulnerable to airstrikes. In one Israeli air attack alone, some 130 Syrian vehicles were reported to have been destroyed. By Friday 25 June, the Syrians were unable to sustain their positions along the road to Beirut, which was now largely dominated by the Israelis, and they began to withdraw eastwards towards the Beqaa Valley. With the announcement of a new ceasefire late on the 25th, the major operations of the Israeli-Syrian conflict in the Lebanon were over, and the IDF now turned its main attention to the battle against the Palestinians in the ruins of West Beirut. **Robin Corbett**

Above: Israeli APCs and tanks make an amphibious landing on the Lebanese coast during Operation Peace for Galilee. The Israelis were determined to prevent the PLO forces from withdrawing intact northwards as they had during the 1978 Operation Litani. The IDF made a number of landings (at Rachidya; north of Sidon; at Damour; and West of Beirut) in order to cut off the Palestinians' line of retreat. Left: PLO fighters advance during street-fighting in the Beirut suburb of Khalde.

Left: An observation post at Beaufort Castle, captured from the Palestinians during a night-time assault by the elite Israeli Golani infantry brigade, and subsequently handed over to the pro-Israeli militia of Major Saad Haddad. Right: Palestinian suspects being rounded-up in Sidon and transported to the large prison-camp at Al Ansar in southern Lebanon, where they were interned and interrogated by Shin Beth, the Israeli security service.

Battle over the Beqaa

Total victory for Israel in the air war

The air battles over the Beqaa Valley in 1982 between Israeli fighters and attack aircraft and Syrian air superiority fighters and surface-to-air missiles (SAMs) resulted in one of the most resounding victories in Israeli Air Force (IAF) history. In air combat the IAF claimed a total of 84 Syrian aircraft shot down, while on the ground more than a score of missile batteries were knocked out by air attack; Israeli losses were minimal.

These successes were achieved by a very different air force from that which had snatched victory from the jaws of defeat during the Yom Kippur War of 1973. The F-4 Phantoms and A-4 Skyhawks which had formed the backbone of the IAF of the mid-1970s, while remaining in service in appreciable numbers, had yielded pride of place to the new generation of American fighter aircraft – the F-16 Fighting Falcon and the F-15 Eagle. Furthermore, in response to the threat from Soviet-supplied SAMs and anti-aircraft artillery, which had proved such costly weapons to neutralise in 1973, the IAF had greatly expanded its electronic warfare capabilities. Command and control of the Israeli air forces was also vastly improved with the introduction of four E-2C Hawkeye airborne early-warning (AEW) aircraft into IAF service from mid-1978.

The F-15 Eagle air superiority fighter was the key weapon in maintaining Israel's qualitative edge over potentially hostile Arab air forces. A total of 40 was

supplied from the United States, with deliveries beginning in December 1976. In June 1979 the Eagles scored their first successes against Syrian Air Force MiG-21s, while escorting an IAF strike force operating against PLO bases in southern Lebanon, and over the next two years more than a dozen Syrian fighters were shot down in similar skirmishes. The victims included MiG-23 Floggers, as well as the older MiG-21s, but it was the MiG-25 Foxbat which presented the IAF with its most difficult problem of interception. Capable of flying at Mach 3 and operating at an altitude of more than 21,000m (70,000ft), Soviet Air Force MiG-25R reconnaissance aircraft had flown missions over Israeli-occupied Sinai with impunity in 1971-72. The interceptor and reconnaissance Foxbats operated by the Syrian Air Force a decade later were to enjoy no such immunity from interception and both the first and last IAF victories of the Lebanon campaign were MiG-25Rs brought down by the F-15's AIM-7 Sparrow missiles.

The F-16 Fighting Falcon lacks the Eagle's ability to engage targets at distances beyond visual range. However, it is a highly manoeuvrable dogfighting aircraft, with excellent ground-attack capabilities. As such it was well suited to the combat conditions of the Beqaa Valley fighting, where most air engagements were fought at close range. Israel's initial order for F-16s was for a total of 75 aircraft, sufficient

Below: A Syrian SA-6 launcher with missiles in the Beqaa Valley. The Israeli Air Force first encountered the SA-6 during the Yom Kippur War of 1973, when SA-6s destroyed considerable numbers of aeroplanes until tactics were devised to defeat them. The Israeli strike on the Syrian SA-6 batteries in June 1982 was a coordinated effort using electronic warfare, remotely-piloted vehicles, anti-radiation missiles and conventional bombs.

Left: During the strike on Syrian SA-6 batteries, US-supplied AGM-45 Shrike anti-radiation missiles like this were used by the Israelis to home in on the Syrian missile-control radars.

Below left: An Israeli Scout remotely-piloted vehicle (RPV) on its launcher. RPVs were used to trick the Syrians into revealing the positions of their tracking radars. Below: A Grumman E-2 Hawkeye of the Israeli Air Force. These airborne early warning aeroplanes controlled the operations of Israeli combat aeroplanes.

to equip three operational squadrons, and all of these had been delivered by the end of 1981. The Fighting Falcon's dramatic operational debut in Israeli service was the raid on Iraq's Osirak nuclear reactor in June 1981.

The four E-2C Hawkeye AEW aircraft delivered in 1977-78 played a crucial role in Israeli combat successes. When operating at an altitude of 9100m (30,000ft), the E-2C's radar can detect aircraft at distances of up to 320km (200 miles) and this target information can be rapidly relayed to ground control centres and fighter aircraft via a data link. Therefore the IAF enjoyed the considerable tactical advantage of being able to anticipate its opponent's moves well in advance.

Airborne self-sufficiency

Israel was very conscious that its command of the air during the early 1980s was largely dependent on American-supplied aircraft and weapons. Therefore there were strong pressures on the small indigenous defence industry to develop a degree of self-sufficiency in air armaments. Israel's ultimate objective was to design and build the Lavi dual-role, high-performance fighter for service in the mid-1990s. In the meantime, local industry had succeeded in producing the Kfir fighter, based on the Mirage III airframe mated to a General Electric J79 turbojet,

nearly 200 of which were in service by mid-1982. Israel also produced the Shafrir and Python air-to-air missiles and a range of avionic and electronic warfare equipment. Israel Aircraft Industries' Scout remotely-piloted vehicle (RPV) was to play an important part in anti-SAM operations in the Beqaa Valley, operating alongside the more advanced American Teledyne Ryan 147 RPV. The Israeli aircraft industry was also involved in modifying and upgrading the older aircraft in the IAF's inventory, which comprised some 140 F-4 Phantoms, 170 A-4 Skyhawks and 30 Mirage IIIs. One of the most important conversion programmes modified about a dozen Boeing 707 airliners for the electronic intelligence-gathering, airborne command post and in-flight refuelling tanker roles.

In theory the IAF's 600-plus combat aircraft were all capable of switching at will between air superiority, counter-air, or ground-attack missions. In practice the F-15s and F-16s tended to concentrate on the air-to-air missions, leaving ground-attack to the F-4s, Kfirs and A-4s. The latter were mainly operated by reserve pilots, in contrast to most IAF aircraft which were kept at a high state of readiness as the first line of defence against a surprise attack. The Syrian Air Force which confronted the IAF over Lebanon numbered some 680 combat aircraft.

The first aerial victory

The Israeli offensive in southern Lebanon opened on 4 June, but apart from ground-attack sorties in support of the army, the IAF saw little action for the first five days of the campaign. The first aerial victory against the Syrian Air Force, a MiG-25R shot down by an F-15 with an AIM-7 Sparrow missile, was scored on 7 June and the following day four Syrian MiG fighters were claimed as destroyed. Yet it was not until the IAF attacked Syrian SAM batteries in the Beqaa Valley that the Syrian Air Force was brought to battle in any appreciable strength. The heaviest air fighting took place between 9 and 11 June, with Syrian MiG-21s and MiG-23s vainly trying to penetrate the IAF's fighter umbrella of F-15s and F-16s to engage the ground-attack fighters which were systematically destroying the SAM batteries.

Syria had first deployed her mobile SAM systems in the Beqaa Valley in April 1981 and thereafter they constituted an ever-present threat to the IAF's freedom of action over the Lebanon. The majority of these missiles were Soviet SA-6 Gainfuls, supplemented by a number of older SA-2 Guidelines and SA-3 Goas. The SA-6 was a 37km (23-mile) range low-to-medium altitude missile, which had proved particularly effective against the IAF during the early stages of the Yom Kippur War. The missiles were mounted in threes on a tracked transporter and launch vehicle and so, unlike the SA-2 and SA-3, did not have to be transferred from transporter vehicles to launchers before they were ready for firing. The SA-6 operated in conjunction with the Straight Flush missile-control radar and was guided by a radio-command link, with semi-active radar terminal homing.

In 1973 the IAF had initially been unprepared to deal with the SA-6 and had suffered heavy losses in consequence, but by the later stages of the war they had already learnt how to cope with the missiles, which were by then recording very few kills. By

1982, improved Israeli electronic warfare capabilities, linked to careful planning and rehearsal of tactics, made the Syrian SAMs relatively easy to defeat. More striking was the ease with which Syria's aircraft were destroyed.

The basis of the Israeli success was their total victory in the electronic war. The IAF operated at all times with a precise knowledge of the location of their enemy and under coherent centralised direction; the Syrians, by contrast, were denied almost all the facilities of modern electronic air war, their command links jammed and their radar rendered ineffectual by Israeli counter-measures. Effectively, the Syrians fought blindfold against an enemy with his eyes wide open.

The destruction of the Syrian SAMs, begun on the afternoon of 9 June and completed the following day, was achieved by a coordination of the most up-to-date techniques. Modified Boeing-707s and the IAF's other electronic intelligence aircraft, Beechcraft RU-21s and Grumman OV-1 Mohawks, were used to identify missile-site radars. Scout and Teledyne Ryan 124 RPVs were sent in to locate the positions of the mobile SAM batteries and to act as decoys. As the RPVs approached the batteries, the Syrians tracked them with their radars and engaged them with their missiles. This gave the Israeli strike aircraft their opportunity. Guided towards their target by the E-2C Hawkeyes, and also protected from the SAMs by their own radar-warning receivers and jamming transmitters, they were extraordinarily effective. AGM-45 Shrike anti-radiation missiles were fired to home-in on the SAM radars, mostly still tracking the drones. The SAMs themselves were hit with free-fall bombs rather than stand-off weapons. The IAF attack pilots were amazed to find that the Syrians had made no attempt to protect their missile batteries by constructing field fortifications around

them. Instead the launch vehicles were parked in the open and Syrian attempts to mask them using smoke screens proved to be counter-productive by drawing attention to their positions. On 9 June the IAF claimed the destruction of 19 missile batteries and a further 11 missile sites were successfully attacked the following day.

Air combat in the valley

The IAF attacks on the Beqaa Valley SAMs provoked a strong reaction from the Syrian Air Force, operating from airbases out of bounds to Israeli attack. Waves of MiG-23 and MiG-21 fighters swept into the valley intent on intercepting the IAF's F-4, Kfir and A-4 attack aircraft. They were met by F-15s and F-16s operating under the control of E-2 Hawkeyes. The ensuing air combats were a resounding victory for the Israelis, with 22 Syrian fighters shot down on 9 June and another 26 on the following day. Further air battles took place on 11 June, in which 18 Syrian aircraft were claimed by the Israelis. In shooting down over 60 Syrian aircraft, the Israelis had not lost a single plane. Yet the MiG-23 in particular was an aircraft of very respectable capabilities. The Israeli pilots were inclined to attribute the failure of the Syrian fighters to tactical ineptitude, but it should be noted that the fact that Syrian communications with their ground controllers were almost entirely jammed by Israeli ECM

inevitably gave the IAF total tactical superiority.

After 11 June there was a lull in air-to-air combat until 24 June, when fighting briefly flared up again, with the IAF knocking out a new SA-6 battery in the Beqaa Valley, and also claiming two MiG-23s shot down during the course of the operation. Further SA-6 launchers were attacked two days later, but it was clear that the Syrians would be unable to re-establish an air defence system for their forces in Lebanon with this missile. Accordingly, the more advanced SA-8 Gecko low-altitude SAM, only recently received from the Soviet Union, was deployed in the Beqaa Valley late in July. The IAF were quick to respond to this challenge and on 24 July three SA-8 batteries were knocked out, at a cost of two Israeli drones and an RF-4C reconnaissance aircraft shot down. This combat marked the end of Syrian attempts to rebuild an area air defence system in Lebanon and thereafter the only tactical SAMs encountered by the IAF were SA-9 Gaskin point-defence missiles.

When the last of the 84 Syrian fighters to be shot down by the Israelis crashed near Beirut on 31 August, it was apparent that the air battles over Lebanon had fully vindicated the IAF's reputation as a formidable fighting force. Total air superiority throughout the fighting in the Lebanon made a vital contribution to Israel's overall military effort in 1982.

Anthony Robinson

Above: Beirut under bombardment: as a result of the aerial campaign over the Beqaa Valley the Israelis were able to achieve total air superiority over Lebanon; this enabled them to bomb Beirut without hindrance. The Israeli aerial operations during the 1982 invasion were another example of their air force's formidable fighting prowess.

Left: Casualties from Israeli bombing raids during Operation Peace for Galilee were heavy. The Syrian Air Force at first attempted to intercept Israeli aeroplanes attacking Beirut during the campaign, but were outfought by the Israeli pilots.

Below left: An Israeli Phantom is chased by a missile. Below: A Phantom flies unchallenged over Beirut.

Left: Palestinian air-defence artillery fires at Israeli aeroplanes bombing their positions. Syrian and Palestinian air defences were not notably successful in shooting down Israeli warplanes.

Beirut under siege

Israeli forces bombard the Lebanese capital

On 11 June 1982, five days after the Israeli Defence Forces' (IDF) invasion of Lebanon, Defence Minister General Ariel Sharon felt confident enough to announce the completion of Operation Peace for Galilee. His statement, however, did not indicate a timetable for the withdrawal of Israeli forces. Although the IDF had dealt its opponents a major blow by establishing a cordon sanitaire in southern Lebanon, it had been unable totally to remove the threat of Palestinian attacks on settlements in northern Israel. The Palestine Liberation Organisation (PLO) headquarters in Beirut remained intact, many frontline units remained beyond the limits of the Israeli advance and it seemed likely that a premature withdrawal would precipitate their reoccupation of the south. The hardliners of the Israeli government, led by Prime Minister Menachem Begin, continued to seek a military solution to the Palestinian threat regardless of the domestic and international repercussions. Their objectives were to remove the Syrian presence from Lebanon and install a pro-Israeli regime based on the Maronite Christian Phalangist Party. There could be no question of allowing the PLO to remain; it was to be expelled and, if possible, destroyed altogether. As a powerful lever in securing this objective, Beirut was placed under siege.

On 13 June, in contravention of a ceasefire agreed with the PLO on the previous day, Israel's armed forces systematically isolated Beirut from the outside world. As Israeli gunboats and aircraft resumed their bombardment of the capital, armoured units pushed up the coast road to reach the strategic road junction at Khalde, 10km (6 miles) south of the international airport. Opposition from local PLO units and Muslim militiamen was quickly subdued and elements of the column were sent northeastwards to the site of the presidential palace at Baabda. From Baabda, units moved eastwards through Kabr

Chamoun to cut the Beirut-Damascus highway near Aley. By 14 June, with Israeli troops to the south and in the mountains to the east, supported by Christian militiamen in the north and along the Green Line separating the Muslim and Christian halves of the capital, West Beirut was completely surrounded.

The speed of the Israeli advance trapped an estimated 13,000 troops and 250,000 civilians in West Beirut. Alongside 9000 PLO fighters commanded by Yassir Arafat – equipped with a handful of T34 tanks, 130mm cannon, 160mm mortars, SAM-7 missiles and rocket launchers – 1500 men of the Syrian 85th Brigade and 2000-3000 Muslim militiamen held a front line of sandbagged shelters, earth barricades and fortified buildings. The Israelis, however, had rejected the option of storming the capital. Experience in southern Lebanon had highlighted the difficulties of fighting in built-up areas and it appeared likely that any ground operations might result in the IDF suffering a politically unacceptable level of casualties. Consequently the PLO were to be ejected by the use of 'static fire' (the destruction of resistance by bombardment alone) and blockade.

The Israeli bombardment of West Beirut began on 13 June and, with the exception of two short intervals of about a week each at the end of June and in the middle of July, continued until 12 August. For the whole of the period the capital was subjected to air raids from Israeli F-15s and F-16s, naval bombardment, heavy artillery barrages from 155mm and 120mm howitzers, as well as fire from tanks, mortars and rocket launchers deployed in the Chouf mountains. The severity of the attacks was compounded by the use of the most up-to-date military hardware: phosphorus shells; Mk 20 Rockeye cluster bombs which scatter steel darts from 650 bomblets over 4200 sq metres (5000 sq yards); and suction bombs that implode rather than explode, causing buildings to collapse on themselves. Although the Israelis claimed that their attacks were carried out with pinpoint accuracy against military targets in open spaces, civilians accounted for an estimated 90 per cent of all casualties.

Indiscriminate bombardment

The attacks on the capital fell into four distinct phases during which the bombardment became heavier, more widespread and less discriminate. The first phase, from 4 June to 26 June, concentrating on targets in the southern suburbs of Khalde and Hay Saloum, was followed by the bombardment of the city's airport and the refugee camps at Ouzai and Borj al-Barajneh. This phase reached its peak on 11 July when Syrian forces in the capital began to hit back. Equipped with 40 large-calibre field guns and Katyusha rocket launchers, the Syrians hit targets in East Beirut and Baabda. In the 16 hours of almost continuous artillery exchanges before a ceasefire was agreed, 10,000 rounds were fired, leaving 200 dead in West Beirut. In the third phase, from 22 July until the beginning of August, the Israelis hit targets further north around the Corniche Mazraa. A 13-hour bombardment on 27 July caused 300 casualties before the first series of truces called a temporary halt to the fighting. Finally, the first two weeks of August saw the Israelis switch their attention to targets in the city's commercial centre and residential areas. On 1 August a 15-hour bombardment by the air force caused over 500 casualties.

This final phase of the bombardment heralded an Israeli attempt to push a little further into West Beirut. On 4 August, units of the IDF backed by tanks captured Museum Hill in the northeast corner of West Beirut, advanced into the Ouzai area 5km (3 miles) south of the city and attempted to occupy Ras Beirut at the northern end of the Green Line. Although the attacks were preceded by a six-hour rolling barrage that hit targets between the Green Line and Hamra, fighting was heavy. Over 1000 casualties were reported, including Israeli figures of 19 killed and 91 wounded which were the highest

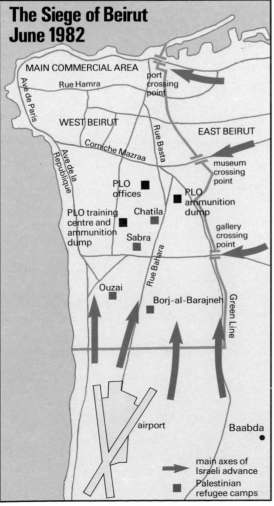

The Siege of Beirut June 1982

MAIN COMMERCIAL AREA
Rue Hamra
Ave de Paris
WEST BEIRUT
Corniche Mazraa
Ave de la Republique
Rue Basta
EAST BEIRUT
port crossing point
museum crossing point
PLO offices
PLO ammunition dump
PLO training centre and ammunition dump
Chatila
Sabra
Rue Bahara
gallery crossing point
Ouzai
Borj-al-Barajneh
Green Line
airport
Baabda

→ main axes of Israeli advance
■ Palestinian refugee camps

Below left: Israeli M107 175mm self-propelled guns and M110 self-propelled howitzers bombard Palestinian positions during the siege of Beirut. Above left: PLO Chairman Yassir Arafat studies the military situation at a frontline command post in beleaguered West Beirut. Below: A modern block almost destroyed in the course of the siege. The Israeli bombardment took its toll of the city's inhabitants, overburdening the limited medical facilities.

since the invasion began. On the following day IDF units around the Museum crossing and along the western edge of the port withdrew from over-exposed positions. The failure of the advance precipitated a renewal of the bombardment. On 6 August, the PLO offices at Sanajeh were hit by a laser-guided bomb which caused over 100 casualties, although the main target of the attack, Yassir Arafat, had left the building 15 minutes before it was hit. Six days later Beirut came under fire for the final time. Syrian troops were singled out as Israel was, by this stage, pressing for their withdrawal, but all areas of the city were hit during the 11-hour attack. Over 200 deaths were reported and 800 homes in Borj al-Barajneh and Sabra refugee camps were destroyed before a ceasefire was arranged. From the first air raid on 4 June to the final hours of bombing on 12 August, an estimated 15,000 people were killed in the attacks.

Total blockade

It soon became apparent that the bombardment itself would prove insufficient to break the PLO's will to resist. It was the imposition of a formal blockade in early July, after a month of intermittent power-cuts and water shortages, that contributed most to their eventual withdrawal. On 3 July Phalangist militiamen backed by Israeli troops had acted to prevent the supply of food and fuel to West Beirut by sealing off the two main crossing points with the East. Simultaneously aircraft had dropped leaflets urging civilians to leave the capital or suffer the consequences. An estimated 50,000 did go, but the majority, unwilling to leave either their homes or belongings, stayed behind. The following day IDF engineers cut off electricity supplies from the Karantina generating station and water from Achrafinyah.

Over the next few weeks shortages of food and, above all, fuel had made conditions intolerable. Unicef had set up five distribution centres for bottled water, but the majority of civilians made do with less hygienic supplies. Cholera and typhoid broke out in the city's poorer quarters, while the ending of refuse collections on 16 July because of fuel scarcity increased the likelihood of plague. West Beirut's 25 hospitals, manned by the Red Crescent, ran dangerously short of basic medicines with which to treat the 200 casualties a day they were receiving. The capital had been brought to the point of collapse by the beginning of August. However, on 8 August the Israelis partially lifted the blockade by reconnecting the water supply and easing the ban on the flow of foodstuffs. The International Red Cross was also allowed to bring in a lorry-load of supplies that included emergency rations and a mobile field hospital. By this stage it was clear that the blockade and bombardment had succeeded in forcing the PLO to agree to withdraw from Lebanon.

Negotiations relating to the PLO's departure began in the early stages of the siege, when President Reagan's special envoy Philip Habib paid a series of visits to several Middle East capitals to seek a solution that would find acceptance with all concerned parties. As early as 3 July Yassir Arafat had agreed to leave Lebanon on certain conditions, but further progress was delayed by Israel's insistence on the closure of PLO offices in Beirut and refusal to allow the absorption of 2000 Palestinians into the Lebanese Army. However, definite progress towards a settlement by the end of the month allowed Habib to put forward a plan in which the Palestinian fighters would leave over a period of two weeks. Their departure was to be supervised by a multinational peacekeeping force drawn from the United States, France and Italy.

In the early hours of 21 August, two days after the Lebanese government formally issued a request for the force's deployment and the Israelis had agreed to the withdrawal timetable, 350 men of France's 2nd Foreign Legion Parachute Regiment occupied the inner part of Beirut harbour. As US Marines landed by the airport and Italian units were deployed, the first Palestinians, 265 men from Arafat's Fatah, gathered in a stadium near the Arab University before embarking on a ship for Cyprus. Over the following days 9000 PLO members left West Beirut to settle in eight Arab countries as far apart as Iraq, South Yemen and Algeria. Arafat stayed in the city for a further two weeks before sailing to Greece on 10 September en route for Tunisia.

The same day that Arafat left Beirut, the multinational peacekeeping force was withdrawn. Yet the impression that an end had been reached to the turmoil in Beirut was a total illusion. Within a week the assassination of Lebanese President Bashir Gemayel would precipitate events that would shock the world and throw Israel into political and moral crisis. **Ian Westwell**

Below: Palestinian fighters drive through the rubble of West Beirut to the ships that will carry them into a new exile, scattered across the Arab world. Despite their high morale and jubilation at having resisted the might of the Israeli armed forces, their withdrawal from Beirut marked the virtual end of an independent Palestinian military organisation.

Key Weapons

AMPHIBIOUS VEHICLES

The world's first amphibious AFV (armoured fighting vehicle) was an experimental version of the British Tank Mk IX armoured supply and personnel carrier; it relied on cylindrical pontoons for flotation and was propelled when afloat by hinged paddles attached to its tracks. The vehicle was undergoing trials on the day World War I ended and did not see active service.

No further serious consideration was given to the ability of armoured vehicles to cross water obstacles until shortly before the beginning of World War II, when the Royal Armoured Corps carried out deep wading experiments with a sealed A9 cruiser tank. Deep wading involved the attachment of a snorkel to the tank, to supply air to the engine and the crew, and driving it across the bed of the river. The project was abandoned at the outbreak of the war, but a variant appeared during German preparations for Operation Sealion, their never-attempted invasion of Britain. The plan was to drive sealed PzKw IIIs and IVs, dropped into the water by light transports, along the sea-bed to the shoreline; air would be supplied by a flexible hose held on the surface by a buoy. The tanks were used during the 1941 German invasion of the Soviet Union and a snorkelling method was adopted by the Soviet Army for its postwar tanks' amphibious capability.

An alternative method to snorkelling tanks was developed by Nicholas Straussler in 1941; it consisted of a collapsible canvas screen that formed part of the vehicle. The screen would keep the AFV afloat when erected and a propeller would provide propulsion through the water. The idea was applied to M4 Sherman tanks used during the D-day landings; the arrival of supporting armour with the infantry assault wave proved invaluable. Since World War II a flotation screen has been incorporated into numerous AFV designs, including the British Ferret armoured car, the British FV432 APC (armoured personnel carrier), and the US M551 Sheridan light tank, but propulsion now is generally by means of the vehicle's tracks, which produce an approximate speed of four knots.

Since the war, the Soviet Army has been attentive to the provision of an amphibious capability for its vehicles and, building on its considerable experience of river-crossing operations during World War II, now possesses the world's largest fleet of vehicles of this type. The Soviet Army's first postwar amphibious vehicle was the PT76 tank, and its chassis

Previous page: An M113 of the 4th Armoured Cavalry Squadron of the Army of the Republic of Vietnam demonstrates its amphibious capability. Below left: This British Land Rover is fitted with a flotation kit that comprises four rubberised fabric airbags, inflated by the vehicle's exhaust system. Bottom left: An FV432 of the British Army with the flotation screen raised crosses a river in West Germany. Below: A French AMX30 in full snorkelling rig during an exercise: the gun-barrel is sealed and the air-intake is on the turret. When equipped with this type of gear, a tank can ford a stream to a depth of 4.5m (15 feet).

served as the basis for the first amphibious APC in Soviet service, the BTR-50. This vehicle, like most Soviet amphibious APCs and tanks, is hampered by a low freeboard which prevents it from swimming in anything but calm water; there is a trim-vane at the front that is raised when the vehicle is in the water to provide greater stability. The BTR-50, like the PT76, is propelled through the water by a system of hydrojets – two intakes in the hull have water pumped through them and the water is expelled out of exit ports at the rear. To steer, the driver partially closes one of the ports' covers by the required amount; however, this system is prone to failure if weeds get into the intakes. Other Soviet combat vehicles using hydrojet propulsion are the BTR-60 and the BRDM scout cars.

Another system of propulsion used by Soviet AFVs and those of other nations is that found on the BMP series of APCs and the MT-L family of vehicles. Unlike the BTR-50, when entering the water the tracks are not disengaged but continue to operate, thereby propelling the AFV. The BMP suffers from a low freeboard, and is easily swamped by the most moderate swell. These problems have not been rectified in the MT-LB which has a height of

Above: Cuban troops in Luanda wait for orders beside their K-61 tracked amphibious transporters. These vehicles are driven through the water at a speed of 10km/h (6mph) by two propellers. They can carry up to 50 passengers or a payload of 5000kg (11,000lb).

Right: BTR-60Ps of the Soviet Naval Infantry swim in a calm sea, heading for the coast. The trim vanes are extended and are marked with the flag of the Soviet Navy; trim vanes are used to give stability to the vehicle while afloat. Below: BMP-1s of the Soviet Naval Infantry ashore in wintry conditions.

1·8m (6ft) compared to the 1·9m (6ft 3in) height of the BMP. The MT-LB's chassis is used in the SAU-122 SPG (self-propelled gun), which is also amphibious.

Soviet engineering units have a variety of amphibious vehicles at their disposal, including the PTS/PTS-M amphibious transporter, the K-61 tracked amphibious transporter and the ZIL-485 BAV amphibious truck. Other nations of the Warsaw Pact have produced their own amphibious designs, such as the Polish MAV light truck and the Czech OT series of APCs.

Diverse and impressive as the Soviet amphibious fleet might be, few would dispute that the most versatile and successful design in this field is the US M113 tracked APC, of which more than 60,000 have been built in various forms by the Food Machinery Corporation (FMC) of San Jose, California; it serves in the majority of the armies of non-communist nations. The M113 is constructed from aluminium armour and can swim without preparation, propelled by its tracks at a speed of three knots. The vehicle gave fine service in Vietnam; whether acting as an APC or in another of the numerous roles it can perform, the M113 coped impressively with every kind of terrain, including the flooded paddy. The M113 is presently being replaced in the US Army by the Bradley series of MICVs (mechanised infantry combat vehicles) which are also amphibious. The MCV-80, now entering service with the British

Army, follows a very similar design concept. In fact, the majority of manufacturers in the highly competitive world arms market now recognise that a built-in amphibious capability is essential for all but the heaviest vehicles.

During the French campaign in Indochina from 1946-54 and during the Korean War of 1950-53, the DUKW-353 (also known as the Duck), which had served in World War II, returned to action. This vehicle had been designed in 1942; it consisted of a watertight hull built onto the mechanical chassis and engine of a 2·5 tonne GMC truck. Once in the water, a screw propeller drove the DUKW and the vehicle was steered by the combined action of turning both the front wheels and a rudder at the stern linked to the steering column. Some vehicles had a 0.5in Browning heavy machine gun on a ring-mount next to the driver.

Of somewhat different ancestry to the vehicles already described is the LVT (landing vehicle tracked) family. During World War II the Japanese garrisons of coral islands in the Pacific relied heavily on the surrounding girdle of coral reefs to keep the American landing craft from the shoreline, thus ensuring that those attempting to wade across the intervening lagoon would do so under fire all the way. To solve the problem the US Marine Corps turned to a vehicle known as the Alligator, which had been designed by a Florida engineer named Donald Roebling as an amphibious swampland rescue craft.

Below left: An M113A1 charges into a rice paddy in pursuit of Viet Cong, throwing up a large bow wave. The M113 performed well when called upon to use its amphibious capabilities in the rivers and rice paddies of Vietnam. Below: LVTH-6s of the US Marine Corps during Operation Deckhouse V in January 1967, part of a series of amphibious actions that were coordinated with ground offensives, in this case in Vietnam's Mekong Delta. The LVTH-6 is armed with a turret-mounted 105mm howitzer on the chassis of an LVTP-5, to provide mobile fire-support.

Top left: Troops debark from their French LVT during operations near Nam Dinh in Vietnam in 1954. Top right: A DUKW of the French Army in Vietnam. Above left: The LVTP-7 entered service with the US Marine Corps in the early 1970s. Above right: US LVTP-5s in Vietnam in 1965.

It did not take long to discover that the vehicle could also cope with reefs and lagoons and the military version of the design was built by FMC with the designation LVT or Amtrac (amphibious tractor). It was also soon apparent that until tanks could be landed, LVTs would provide a very adequate substitute, and a howitzer-armed close-support version was quickly introduced. Several versions were produced during the war, and many of these served in Korea with the US Marines and with British troops at Suez. The French employed the original Alligator series in Indochina, together with the M29 Weasel cargo-carrier, which they renamed Crabe

Since World War II the US Marine Corps' concept of the LVT has been extended to include command, weapon carrier, recovery and assault engineer versions. The Corps' Armored Amphibious Tractor Battalions saw action in Vietnam with the box-like LVTP-5A1. They are now equipped with the more streamlined but still bulky LVTP-7, manned by a crew of three and carrying up to 25 fully-equipped Marines. The vehicle has 30mm frontal armour and is armed with a 0·5in heavy machine gun. It has a road-speed of 63·4km/h (39·5 mph) and when afloat can achieve 7 knots, being propelled by hydrojets. Nonetheless, weapon systems such as this are appropriate only to superpowers with global responsibilities, and for other nations they represent something of an expensive luxury. Consequently, the LVTP-7 is little used outside the US Marine Corps. One exception is Argentina's Naval Infantry Corps, which deployed a squadron of them during the invasion of the Falkland Islands, one being knocked out by a Royal Marine anti-tank team as it entered Port Stanley. The remainder were withdrawn to the mainland on completion of the occupation. The LVTP-7 has also seen action with US forces in Beirut in 1982-84 and in Grenada in 1983.

Below left: An FV620 Stalwart shows its amphibious capabilities; a splash board has been erected at the front of the vehicle. Below: An M29 Weasel negotiates heavy mud while moving ammunition and supplies for the US 1st Marine Division in Korea in 1952. Bottom: A Transportpanzer Fuchs of the West German Army during Nato manoeuvres in September 1984.

The disputed islands

The background to the Falklands conflict

The Falkland Islands, which dominate the passage around Cape Horn, became a target for the ambitions of France and Britain during the 18th century. In spite of their recognition of Spanish sovereignty over the islands in the Treaty of Utrecht in 1713, France established a colony on East Falkland in 1764, and the British flag was planted on West Falkland in the following year. In 1766, a British contingent landed to establish a fort on West Falkland, and a dispute developed with the French.

France subsequently sold its colony to Spain, however, which re-asserted its claim to the whole of the Falklands in 1769, expelling the small British garrison. The resulting diplomatic crisis was resolved by Spain allowing the temporary return of a British force to West Falkland between 1771 and 1774, although Britain effectively recognised the Spanish claim to sovereignty. Spanish control of the Falklands, known in Spanish as Islas Malvinas, was interrupted by the Napoleonic Wars, and totally broke down with the 1816 declaration of independence by the Latin American colony which was the forerunner of the modern Argentina. The nationalist government which took over from Spain in Buenos Aires insisted that it had inherited Spain's rights to the islands and established a garrison there in 1820.

The British government never relinquished its claim to the sovereignty of the islands and in 1833 a British force landed on the Falklands and expelled the Argentinian garrison. The British government thereafter exercised continuous control of the islands until April 1982. While Argentina insisted that the British occupation of the islands was illegal, the

British settlement was no more than a minor irritant to Anglo-Argentinian relations until the nationalist government of President Juan Perón revived Argentina's claims in the 1940s. The ensuing anti-British propaganda campaign excited Argentinian feelings so much that the slogan 'The Malvinas are Argentinian' became a matter of national honour. The claim to the Falklands was a useful tool in the hands of the succession of military governments which followed Perón, allowing them to divert the attention of the Argentinian masses away from their internal grievances.

Argentina's campaign for the 'return' of the islands to its sovereignty registered a significant

Above: The three-man Argentinian military junta (from left to right: General Leopoldo Galtieri, Brigadier Basilio Lami Dozo and Admiral Jorge Anaya). Argentina's economic and political crisis had undermined the country's military rulers, who sought to strengthen their position by launching an invasion of the Falklands. Below: Port Stanley, capital of the Falkland Islands.

success when, in September 1964, the United Nations Committee on Decolonisation recommended negotiations between Argentina and Britain over the future of the islands. In December 1965 the General Assembly followed this up by calling on both parties 'to proceed without delay with the negotiations recommended'. Preoccupied with her difficulties with the UN over Rhodesia, Britain agreed to the opening of negotiations with Buenos Aires, thereby tacitly giving some credence to Argentina's claims.

The talks did not begin in earnest until July 1966 when there were several meetings between British and Argentinian diplomats. The secrecy in which these discussions were conducted aroused fears among the islanders that British sovereignty was to be sacrificed on the altar of improved trade between Britain and Argentina, and these fears were conveyed to the influential Falklands lobby in London which consisted of members of parliament and businessmen with interests in the islands. The en-

Above: British governor of the Falkland Islands, Rex Hunt, wearing full official uniform as he leaves the islands after his surrender to the invading Argentinians.

suing fuss in the Falklands and in parliament led Prime Minister Harold Wilson's government to decide that the issue of sovereignty was not negotiable, a decision confirmed by Michael Stewart, the British foreign secretary, in parliament on 11 December 1968. Any transfer of sovereignty would require the prior approval of the islanders.

However, the Foreign Office minister dealing with South American affairs, Lord Chalfont, decided on a different approach to the issue – one which sought to strengthen economic, social and cultural ties between the islands and the Argentinian mainland, in the hope that the islanders would gradually become reconciled to Argentinian citizenship under conditions that would allow them to keep their British identity. Argentina proved willing to try this gradualist approach in the belief that this would lead ultimately to it securing sovereignty over the islands, and during the early 1970s the two countries hammered out a set of principles which were intended to govern future relations between the islands and the mainland. These included the lifting of travel restrictions for islanders visiting Argentina, their exemption from Argentinian income tax and military service obligations, the improvement of telephone and postal links between the islands and the mainland and Argentinian assistance to improve health, agricultural and educational facilities on the islands. Finally, Argentina was to provide a regular air service between Buenos Aires and Port Stanley (where Britain was to construct an airfield), while Britain was to finance a regular shipping service between the islands and Argentina.

During the early 1970s, the two sides attempted to translate these principles into more concrete form. Prospects for success were not improved by the British Treasury's refusal to pay for the airstrip at Port Stanley (a short temporary airstrip was eventually constructed by Argentina), or for the promised shipping service. Argentina's growing doubts about

The islanders

Above: Proudly patriotic Falklanders.

The most important factor in the British government's resistance to Argentinian claims to the Falkland Islands was the stubborn insistence of the islanders themselves upon remaining under British sovereignty and administration. Without this Britain might well have come to a compromise agreement with Buenos Aires in the interests of improved diplomatic and economic relations both with Argentina and the rest of Latin America.

Most of the 1800 islanders were descendants of British settlers who had established themselves on the Falklands in the 19th century. Over 1000 of them lived in the islands' only town, Port Stanley. The main economic activity was sheep-farming, carried out on large estates controlled by absentee landlords, the largest of whom was the Falkland Islands Company, based in Britain.

In the Camp (from the Spanish *campo*, meaning countryside), as the area outside Stanley was known, sheep-

farmers lived isolated lives on small scattered farmsteads. The islanders faced a serious emigration problem – the population had declined continuously since 1931. Young women were particularly loath to stay, and there were twice as many men as women on the islands.

A report drawn up by Lord Shackleton in 1976 was extremely critical of the lack of investment in the Falklands, and suggested a number of measures to revitalise the islands' economy, including the development of a fishing industry, oil exploration and the construction of an airfield capable of taking medium-range aircraft. The latter proposal also had military implications, as it would have been hoped that it would allow the rapid reinforcement of the Falklands' otherwise tiny garrison in the case of a threatened Argentinian invasion. The local population could muster a territorial defence force which numbered some 120 men, although only 23 of them presented themselves for action in April 1982.

British commitment to the Communications Agreement were fuelled by Lord Shackleton's report on the future of the islands in 1976. This talked about the need for long-term British investment if the islands were to become economically viable and further aroused Argentina's suspicions by mentioning as a distant possibility the prospect of oil exploration in Falklands waters. The British Foreign Office persevered with discussions with Argentina in the late 1970s, but by this time Argentina's impatience over the failure of British diplomacy to make any concession on the crucial sovereignty issue was causing a rapid deterioration in relations between the two countries. There were rumours of an impending Argentinian coup against the islands and a growing anger in the Falklands and its lobby in London over the British government's willingness to continue the negotiations with Buenos Aires.

Focus on the Falklands

Argentina's deteriorating economic situation during the 1970s and bitter internal divisions encouraged Argentina's military rulers to focus publicly on the Falklands issue as a means of drumming up some semblance of popular support for their regime. In December 1981 a new military junta took power in Buenos Aires, led by army strong-man General Leopoldo Galtieri, who was determined to settle the Falklands issue once and for all by force. Galtieri became convinced that the US administration of President Ronald Reagan, which was eager to enlist Argentinian support for its anti-communist policies in Latin and Central America, would not oppose an Argentinian seizure of the islands.

Meanwhile the new Thatcher government elected in Britain in 1979 continued the efforts of its predecessor to find a solution to the seemingly intractable problem of the Falklands. Foreign Office minister Nicholas Ridley became the most recent convert to the view that Britain could not be expected to guarantee the defence of the islands in the long term and could not afford to provide the enormous investment that Shackleton had deemed to be essential if the future of the islands was to be secured. Ridley revived a compromise plan that had already been mooted by the Foreign Office during the 1970s – the transfer of sovereignty of the islands to Argentina but with Argentina agreeing in return to lease them to Britain for 99 years. This proposal was bitterly attacked by both the islanders and members of parliament during a House of Commons debate on 2 December 1980.

It seemed clear to Buenos Aires that the British would concede nothing in the Falklands, although Anglo-Argentinian talks on the subject continued in 1981. At the same time, Britain's decision in that year to withdraw the ice-patrol vessel HMS *Endurance* from Falklands waters as an economy measure, and the reduction of its surface fleet, which would deprive Britain of an out-of-Nato area naval capability, suggested to Argentina that Britain had lost both the will and the means to defend its colony.

Britain nursed similar illusions about Argentina – despite bitter Argentinian press attacks on British policy in early 1982 and threats to invade the islands, British intelligence considered that Argentina was too preoccupied with its internal problems to contemplate an attack. Argentina's willingness to continue negotiations also suggested to London that there was no imminent danger. Warning signs, such as the activities of an Argentinian scrap-metal dealer on South Georgia in February and March 1982, were either ignored or treated with some levity by sections of the British press. Towards the end of March the British government at last began to wake up to the seriousness of the threat to the islands and started to prepare contingency measures, but these were a little too late. On 2 April 1982 Argentinian seaborne forces began to land on the Falklands.

Michael Dockrill

Below: Men of the Royal Marine detachment stationed on the Falklands train with a GPMG prior to the Argentinian invasion. By chance, at the time of the invasion there were two Marine detachments on the islands, the resident garrison and its relief.

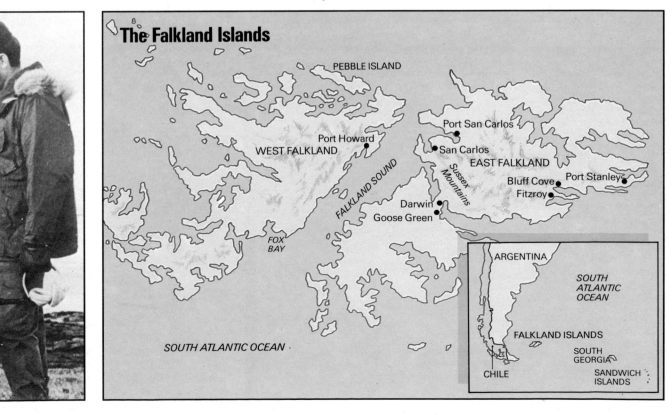

The Falkland Islands

PEBBLE ISLAND

Port San Carlos

Port Howard
WEST FALKLAND

San Carlos

EAST FALKLAND

Bluff Cove
Port Stanley
Fitzroy

FALKLAND SOUND

Sussex Mountains

Darwin
Goose Green

FOX BAY

SOUTH ATLANTIC OCEAN

ARGENTINA

SOUTH ATLANTIC OCEAN

FALKLAND ISLANDS

SOUTH GEORGIA

CHILE

SANDWICH ISLANDS

Britain unprepared?

British defence policy, 1979-82

Above: Defence Secretary John Nott at a press conference in London during the Falklands War. His decision to concentrate British military resources on its Nato commitments and reduce its 'out-of-area' capability had provoked widespread controversy. The decision to drastically reduce the Royal Navy was particularly criticised, and may have helped persuade the Argentinian junta that Britain was no longer prepared to fight for the Falklands.

When Margaret Thatcher's Conservative government entered office in May 1979, Britain's defence policy seemed to have settled down into a stable pattern, reflecting the priorities established by Labour's defence minister Roy Mason four years earlier. His 1975 review had laid down that Britain's defence effort was to be geared firmly towards Europe and that this was to be achieved by a steady withdrawal of forces from remaining overseas bases. By 1979 this appeared to have been carried out – in that year, for example, Britain withdrew from Malta and ceased to maintain naval forces east of Gibraltar on a permanent basis – and defence spending, as a result, had declined to a more manageable 4·75 per cent of the country's annual gross national product (GNP), in line with Mason's projection.

But this was something of a facade. With British forces still deployed as far afield as Hong Kong, Belize, Cyprus and the Falkland Islands, the full-scale withdrawal to Europe implied in the Mason review had not been achieved, necessitating a 'mix' of global and regional defence capability which the country could not afford. Moreover, it soon became obvious that the reduced defence budget had only been maintained because the outgoing Labour government had either deferred or ignored the need for

decisions in two key areas of defence costing. The most pressing of these concerned the pay of servicemen, for the effects of continued inflation and government restraint had produced a discernible reduction in recruitment figures. The Conservatives immediately introduced improvements and awarded phased rises of some 30 per cent over the next two years, a move that added nearly £1000 million to the annual defence bill for little tangible gain.

Much more important in the long term, however, was the need to plan for a replacement to Polaris as Britain's strategic nuclear deterrent. The missiles themselves, with their recently-developed and very expensive Chevaline warheads, could probably last into the 21st century, but the submarines that carried them would have to be replaced by the early-to-mid 1990s, when their hull-life would expire. A lengthy process of research and development necessitated an early decision about replacement and, whatever the final choice, the cost was likely to be high. Mrs Thatcher announced her decision in March 1981, opting for the US-made Trident missile, to be carried aboard four new submarines. This, it was estimated, would add £5000-6000 million to the defence budget, spread over the next 10-15 years. In itself, Trident was not outrageously expensive – at the height of its cost, it was unlikely to absorb more than five per cent of the annual defence budget – but when it was taken in conjunction with the pay rises, to say nothing of the spiralling expense of just maintaining existing force levels, the need for firm financial control was apparent. A new secretary of state for defence, John Nott, was appointed to cast a merchant banker's eye over the defence establishment.

The new minister approached his task of projecting Britain's defence policy into the late 1980s with a certain ruthless rationality. Despite widely-voiced fears, he was not a 'hatchet man', determined to save money by a simple process of cutting the size of the armed forces; rather he was intent upon laying down precise role-allocations which could be used as a more accurate basis for long-term financial calculations. In the process, he was forced to make some 'hard decisions', but the result was a clear definition of Britain's security role, reiterating Mason's priority towards Europe and taking the process one stage further to cope with the new realities of financial strain. For there can be no doubt that the driving force behind the subsequent review, presented to parliament on 25 June 1981 and entitled *The United Kingdom Defence Programme: The Way Forward*, was financial, as Nott was the first to admit. He pointed out that defence spending was currently running at approximately 5·2 per cent of the annual GNP – 'one of the highest figures anywhere in the (Nato) Alliance' and one that would translate into about £14,500 million in actual cash for the financial year 1982-83. Moreover, the government was committed to an annual spending increase of three per cent in real terms, in line with a Nato agreement to help offset the ravages of inflation, and when this was added to the myriad of other pressures, it was apparent that something quite drastic was required to avert a financial crisis over defence.

Nott's solution was based on two interconnected beliefs. On the one hand, it was clear that Britain had neither the resources nor the need to deploy large forces outside the Nato geographical area; on the other, it naturally followed that any remaining global

Below: A British Aerospace Nimrod Mk 2 long-range maritime patrol aircraft. Despite the defence cuts, the Mk 2 Nimrod was to be introduced in order to enhance Britain's maritime strike and reconnaissance capability. The inability to operate such aircraft along with the Falklands Task Force was a weakness which left the British naval force vulnerable to surprise air attack, and made it difficult to monitor the movements of Argentinian vessels. Bottom: The Antarctic survey vessel *Endurance* in Leith harbour, South Georgia. *Endurance* was a symbol of the British commitment to the defence of its remote colony. Its proposed withdrawal as part of the Nott defence cuts was seen by Buenos Aires as a sign that that commitment had been weakened.

capability could be reduced to save money. Thus it was stressed from the beginning that the Nato alliance was 'at the top of the government's priorities' and this was reflected in the list of defence roles which formed the structure of the review: 'an independent element of strategic and theatre nuclear forces committed to the Alliance; the direct defence of the United Kingdom homeland; a major land and air contribution to the European mainland; and a major maritime effort in the eastern Atlantic and Channel.' Mention was made of commitments 'beyond the Nato area', but these were clearly of secondary importance and, whenever possible, were to be carried out in conjunction with Nato allies. The key to British policy was collective defence against the Soviet threat.

As far as both the British Army and the RAF were concerned, this represented little change to the prevailing situation. Both services had already redeployed to a largely European commitment in the late 1970s and Nott could find few ways to cut their costs. I (Br) Corps in West Germany was directed to be reorganised yet again, this time from four back into three armoured divisions, with some savings resulting from a decision to relocate one armoured brigade and the fourth divisional headquarters in the UK, but

no regiments were disbanded and the size of Britain's commitment to mainland Europe – set at 55,000 men as long ago as 1954 – was unchanged. Even so, the army was to lose about 7000 men overall by 1986 and, with an increase to the strength of the Territorials, more of its wartime tasks were to be carried out by volunteer reservists who cost less to maintain during peace. The RAF fared no worse, for although a projected replacement for the Jaguar strike aircraft was cancelled, air potential remained, with an increase in orders for the new Tornado and a promise of 60 American-designed AV-8B variants of the V/STOL Harrier. Indeed, it could be argued that Britain's air strength was improved, with a new emphasis upon fighter protection of the UK, enhanced maritime strike and reconnaissance through the projected deployment of the Nimrod Mark II, and a host of new or improved air-to-air and air-to-surface missiles. As a result, the RAF was to lose 2500 men only over the next five years.

Naval cuts

The main weight of Nott's revision therefore fell squarely on the navy and although he did not, as some critics made out, sound the death-knell of the Senior Service, he did re-assess its role in the light of European priority. If non-European commitments were to be reduced, there was clearly no need to maintain a large global navy, and Nott used this argument to justify his announcement that in future Britain would deploy only two instead of the projected three aircraft carriers and would cut her destroyer/frigate fleet from 59 to 'about 50' vessels, dedicated principally to the Nato role. This, in turn, would have a number of unavoidable 'knock-on' effects. With fewer ships in commission, the size of the Royal Fleet Auxiliary could be cut, dockyards could be run down or closed and up to 10,000 sailors made redundant.

The full impact of these changes became apparent in the immediate aftermath of the review. The amphibious assault ships HMS *Fearless* and *Intrepid* – of little use in a purely regional role – were ordered to be mothballed with a view to eventual sale or scrap; the recently completed aircraft carrier HMS *Invincible* was offered to the Australians and the older commando carrier HMS *Hermes* was earmarked for reduction; the Royal Dock Yard at Chatham was ordered to close by 1984 and a whole range of support facilities were run down. Most important of all in the context of the future, the ice-patrol ship HMS *Endurance* – the only naval vessel on permanent duty in the South Atlantic – was directed to return home at the end of her current tour (March 1982) and was not to be replaced.

Although this was undoubtedly a bitter pill for the Royal Navy to swallow, it did represent a logical rebalancing of Britain's defence capabilities. With decolonisation virtually complete, the economic and political reality of Europe accepted and the need for financial savings unavoidable, it was inevitable that defence should suffer, and Nott's response, representing the 'continental' rather than the 'maritime' school of strategic thought, was the only sensible one to follow. Unfortunately it was slightly premature, put into effect at a time when Britain still retained overseas responsibilities that required protection. The Argentinian invasion of the Falkland Islands on 2 April 1982 had not been foreseen. **John Pimlott**

Galtieri's gamble

The Argentinians invade the Falklands

An Argentinian plan for the invasion of the Falklands had existed since the late 1960s. It was drawn up by a politically-minded naval officer, Captain Jorge Anaya, who had been greatly impressed by the speed with which India's occupation of the former Portuguese colony of Goa in 1961 had presented the world with a *fait accompli*. Anaya's plan, code-named Goa, was endorsed by a subsequent head of the Argentinian Navy, Admiral Emilio Massera, who also expanded his service and made its political influence equal to that of the army.

As Britain's influence in world affairs declined, so Argentina's attitude towards the Falklands hardened. A number of provocative incidents were staged to test British resolve, including the occupation of Southern Thule in the South Sandwich Islands in 1976. Further sabre-rattling the following year prompted British Prime Minister James Callaghan to despatch two frigates and a submarine to the Falklands and the Argentinians modified their attitude.

In March 1982 Jorge Anaya, now an admiral and head of the Argentinian Navy, was a member of the three-man junta which ruled Argentina, the other two being General Leopoldo Galtieri, commander of the army and president since December 1981, and Brigadier Basilio Lami Dozo of the air force. At this period, the junta was enjoying the favour of the United States, partly because it had displayed total ruthlessness in stamping out left-wing guerrilla activity within Argentina, and partly because of the backing it was giving Washington over Central America. The Americans viewed Galtieri as a strong leader who could help prevent the spread of communism in Latin America.

The citizens of Argentina saw their rulers differently. The campaign against the guerrillas, known as the Dirty War, had been waged with no regard whatever for human rights. Thousands had been murdered or tortured and the disappearance of thousands more was the subject of daily protests in Buenos Aires. In addition, the military had proved wildly inept at running the country, so that soaring unemployment was coupled with raging inflation and the whole economy was staggering towards total collapse. The ferocity of street riots was such that the junta's survival seemed increasingly unlikely.

At this point, Galtieri accepted Anaya's suggestion that Plan Goa should be implemented on the grounds that, while it would not solve the junta's long-term problems, it would certainly restore its popularity for some time to come. Foreign Minister Nicanor Costa Mendes believed Great Britain had finally lost interest in the South Atlantic, a fact apparently confirmed by the decision to withdraw the ice-patrol vessel HMS *Endurance*, and that a military response by the Thatcher government was extremely unlikely. In any event, he believed that the United States could be relied upon to exercise a restraining

Above: Royal Marines from the garrison at Port Stanley are marched off as prisoners, under the guard of a member of the elite Argentinian Buzo Tactico unit. The 68 Marines, under the command of Major Mike Norman, put up a fierce fight against the invasion force, and a surrender was negotiated before they could be overwhelmed. Above right: Admiral Bussa, deputy commander of the Argentinian invasion force, who negotiated the surrender with Governor Rex Hunt at Government House. Right: Argentinian troops, supported by an LVTP-7 amphibious APC, advance down a street in Port Stanley shortly after the invasion.

influence on the British. Anaya himself would certainly have preferred to wait until later in the year, when the navy would have received its full quota of Exocet-armed Super Etendard aircraft, as well as the modern submarines and frigates being built in foreign yards. However, with the deteriorating political situation within Argentina, the sooner the invasion took place the better.

The junta was keen to test the likely British reaction to such a venture, and found an opportunity in the unlikely form of a contract negotiated between the Argentinian scrap-metal merchant Constantino Davidoff and the Scottish-based Christian Salvesan company to dismantle the abandoned whaling station at Leith on the Falkland Islands' Dependency of South Georgia. Davidoff's men landed from the naval transport *Bahía Buen Suceso* on 19 March 1982, hoisted the Argentinian flag and steadfastly refused to apply for authorisation from the British Antarctic Survey base at Grytviken. London's reaction was surprisingly prompt. *Endurance* was despatched from Port Stanley and on 24 March a small Marine detachment under Lieutenant Keith Mills was put ashore at Grytviken. The previous day, the Argentinians had raised the stakes when the *Bahía Buen Suceso* was replaced by the armed survey vessel *Bahía Paraíso* off Leith and an Argentinian Marine unit under Captain Alfredo Astiz was landed to 'protect' Davidoff's workmen.

Plan Goa goes ahead

With the British government alerted by these events on South Georgia, the junta appreciated that if the crisis was prolonged the British garrison at Port Stanley would undoubtedly be reinforced, thus making the task of the invasion force that much more difficult. The decision to activate Plan Goa was taken on 26 March and during the next few days the Argentinian Navy put to sea, ostensibly for combined manoeuvres with the Uruguayan Navy, while troops embarked aboard transports. Two A69 corvettes were detached from the main body of the fleet and headed steadily southeastwards towards South Georgia.

The Argentinian armed services had not fought a foreign enemy for a century and displayed an unbelievable amateurism in some of their operational procedures. For example, despite Anaya's fear that a British hunter-killer submarine might be lurking in the vicinity, ready to put an end to his ancient but prized aircraft carrier the *Veinticinco de Mayo*, the voyage to the Falklands was accompanied by continuous radio chatter between ships in clear. By 31 March signals intelligence, diplomatic sources and information provided by *Endurance* had made Argentina's intentions as clear as crystal to the British government. In Buenos Aires, a jubilant junta abandoned all pretence of secrecy and instructed the press to prepare victory editions before the landings had even taken place.

The Argentinian plan for the seizure of the islands was based on the elimination of the token Royal Marine garrison at Moody Brook barracks, just outside Port Stanley, following which the governor, Rex Hunt, would be arrested and the invasion fleet would sail into the harbour. However, once the inevitability of invasion became apparent, the garrison commander, Major Michael Norman, deployed his 68 Marines in small detachments around Port

The bitterness of surrender

Major Mike Norman, the Royal Marine commander on the Falklands at the time of the invasion, later described the meeting between Admiral Bussa, the deputy commander of the invasion force, and Governor Rex Hunt at which the decision to surrender was taken.

'Bussa came in and wanted to shake his hand, but the Governor pointedly refused. Before Bussa could say anything, this little dapper man pulled himself up to his full height and said "This is British property. You are not invited. We don't want you here. I want you to leave and to take all your men with you." And Bussa looked at him, smiled and said "I've got 800 men ashore at the moment. I've got another 2000 about to land. The only sensible thing that you can do is tell these brave men to stop fighting…" Bussa was a professional soldier, he wasn't a politician. And after we'd surrendered, he couldn't have been nicer.

'The Governor didn't confer with me at this point, nor should he have done. I'd given him my military advice, and he decided to go for the option of a truce. But the Argentinians weren't interested… Their reaction was, if you don't want to stop fighting, carry on fighting and it's entirely up to you. But Bussa pleaded with the Governor to stop, because he said "I don't want to damage civilians and I don't want to kill these men, and if we continue that's what you're asking me to do because we're not going to stop. They're not going to win either." And as I'd already told the Governor that, he thought about it for a while and then said "You've given me no option. I will order my men to lay down their arms."

'As a professional I didn't like it. When I went round telling my Marines to lay down their arms, they were very angry and some of them said afterwards that we should have continued. But if you talk to those lads now, they will tell you they were very relieved. I was very relieved, as a commander, that it wasn't my decision, because there is no way that, as a military man, I could have come to that decision. I'd have fought. That's what our job is. It's not our job to surrender.'

Major Norman and many of his men were soon to return to Port Stanley, where they would enjoy the pleasure of hoisting the Falklands flag once more over Government House.

Stanley, concentrating most of his resources for the defence of Government House. No one had any illusions as to how the battle would end; but nor was anyone prepared to make a present of the Falklands to Argentina.

The poor performance of the Argentinian forces during the execution of Plan Goa was later excused by the junta on the grounds that the invasion was made in overwhelming strength in the hope that this would induce prompt surrender, and that their men were equipped with blank ammunition. This was a complete fabrication, for although it is true that stern punishments were threatened if any islander was killed or injured during the fighting, the enemy's intentions towards the Royal Marines were less pacific. At 0430 hours on 2 April, 150 men of the Buzo Tactico, an elite Marine unit, were lifted by helicopter to Mullett Creek and from there marched across country to Moody Brook. At 0600 hours, they hurled phosphorus grenades into the barrack rooms, which were then raked with automatic weapon fire. To their chagrin, the Argentinians discovered that they had in fact been attacking buildings that were completely empty.

At Government House, however, the Buzo Tactico met fierce resistance and a two-hour gun-battle ensued in which at least two Argentinians were killed and several more wounded. A three-man squad, sent in to capture the governor, was itself made prisoner. As the light became stronger, LVTP-7 armoured amphibious assault vehicles, each mounting a 12·7mm heavy machine gun and capable

of carrying 25 fully-equipped infantrymen, drove up the beach at York Bay and into Port Stanley. The leading vehicle was knocked out by a Marine section with 66mm LAW and 84mm MAW anti-tank rockets; these are blast-effect weapons and, since no one emerged, the British estimate of Argentinian casualties at Port Stanley as being five killed and 17 wounded is very probably conservative. Inside Government House, Major Norman told the governor that he and his men were prepared to break out and continue fighting in the interior of the island. By now, however, the LVTPs had reached positions from which a decisive attack on the building could be launched. Hunt, feeling that the British had made their point and not wishing to cause the Marines unnecessary casualties, negotiated a surrender through the agency of an Argentinian airline official resident in Port Stanley, and at 0925 hours Major Norman's detachment was ordered to lay down its arms. There were now 2800 Argentinian troops ashore and more were arriving. The governor, wearing his ceremonial uniform, was driven to the airport, from which he and the Marines were flown to Montevideo on the first leg of their journey back to the United Kingdom.

The British garrison at Grytviken should also have been attacked on 2 April but bad weather conditions forced Captain Astiz to postpone this operation for 24 hours. At 1030 hours on 3 April the *Bahía Paraíso* arrived off Grytviken and the corvette *Guerrico* sailed into the harbour to provide direct gunfire support for the Argentinian Marines landing by helicopter. Lieutenant Mills and his 22 Royal Marines had been told to force the enemy to fight for the island and, if possible, to hold out for half an hour.

Mills considered this to be too modest an objective and swore that he would 'make their eyes water'. For an hour he and his men fought a battle which was an epic even by the exacting standards of their corps, shooting down two helicopters, killing approximately 15 of the enemy and wounding an unknown number, and damaging the *Guerrico* so seriously that she would spend the remainder of the war in the dockyard – one 84mm MAW round had blown a hole in the corvette's side, while another had hit an Exocet launcher but failed to explode; two 66mm LAW rounds had jammed the 3·9in gun in elevation and there were 1275 strikes with smallarms ammunition on the superstructure. When Mills eventually surrendered only one of his men had been wounded. Lieutenant Mills was awarded the Distinguished Service Cross shortly after the detachment was repatriated via Uruguay.

In Buenos Aires, the news that the Malvinas had been recovered and South Georgia captured was greeted with an immense outburst of unfettered joy. The popularity of the junta soared as crowds danced in the streets until dawn. Yet many of the dancers were to view the next few days with an uneasy disbelief, for the British were not reacting as the Portuguese had when Goa was seized, and all the signs were that Argentina had unwittingly been pitched into a full-scale war with one of the world's major powers.

Bryan Perrett

Far left: Major Mike Norman, commander of the Royal Marine garrison at Port Stanley, looking understandably dejected after the surrender.

Below: General Galtieri acknowledges the enthusiastic applause of a crowd in Buenos Aires as the successful outcome of the invasion is announced. Bottom: The Falklanders were left with little to smile about as the Argentinian forces made themselves at home, and Argentinian armoured vehicles lined the streets of Port Stanley.

Left: There was a carnival atmosphere in the streets of Buenos Aires as Argentinian civilians and military celebrated the repossession of the 'Islas Malvinas'. But jubilation was to be shortlived.

Britain strikes back

The Task Force and the retaking of South Georgia

The news of the Argentinian invasion of the Falklands on 2 April caused a furore in Britain. During a special session of the House of Commons the following day, the government of Prime Minister Margaret Thatcher was the object of attacks from all sides for having allowed the seizure of the islands to take place, and there were demands for immediate action to restore British control. In the wake of this outcry, Foreign Secretary Lord Carrington and Defence Secretary John Nott both offered their resignation, along with two less senior colleagues. The prime minister persuaded Nott to continue in his post, but Carrington was replaced by Francis Pym.

In fact, by the time these demands for military action were voiced, and satisfaction promised by the prime minister, an armed response was already under way. Signals intelligence and satellite reconnaissance pictures routinely passed to Britain by the Americans had given a clear indication of Argentinian military preparations in the last week of March. In an effort to deter the Argentinians, a hunter-killer submarine was ordered to the South Atlantic on 29 March. Within 48 hours HMS *Spartan* had been equipped with live torpedoes and had set off from Gibraltar. HMS *Splendid* followed on 1 April and HMS *Conqueror* sailed on the 4th. However, travelling at an average speed of 23 knots, HMS *Spartan* did not reach Port Stanley until 12 April – too late to deter invasion.

On the same day that the submarines were ordered

southwards, 29 March, the First Sea Lord, Admiral Sir Henry Leach, looked into the option of providing a Task Force for the South Atlantic. His operations staff agreed that a Falklands undertaking was not to be considered without using every resource including aircraft carriers and amphibious assault elements. They also noted that the largest concentration of warships conveniently placed for a venture in the South Atlantic was the First Flotilla of some 20 ships which was exercising off Gibraltar; this would be a useful start to putting together a more balanced fleet. At a meeting of senior government ministers on 31 March, Leach was able to assure the politicians that by 5 April the ageing aircraft carrier HMS *Hermes*, which was in Portsmouth for a refit, and the newer HMS *Invincible*, just returned to Britain from exercises, could be ready to set off for the Falklands. It was the beginning of a frantic period of preparations involving improvisation at all levels.

As planned, the *Hermes* and *Invincible* were made ready in record time and despatched from Portsmouth on 5 April to follow the First Flotilla ships southwards. The principal vessels of the First Flotilla were three Type 42 destroyers – *Coventry*, *Sheffield* and *Glasgow* – and two Type 22 frigates – *Brilliant* and *Broadsword*.

At this stage there were no fixed plans for the procedure of the Task Force or any conviction that it would eventually be necessary to employ force. Certainly it was not envisaged that British infantry

Above left: 2 Para leaves Aldershot for the Falklands. Both 2 and 3 Para were attached to 3 Commando Brigade, which sailed from Portsmouth on *Canberra* and *Norland*. Above: Stores being loaded onto the assault ship *Fearless* in preparation for the voyage to the South Atlantic.

would need to be disembarked in the Falklands in sufficient force to defeat an Argentinian garrison of 12,000. On the other hand, the Admiralty realised that a contingent of infantry might well be useful: if necessary an under-garrisoned area of East Falkland could be seized and turned into a temporary airstrip for Phantom aircraft which would ensure total air superiority. Because the Royal Navy had been the first service to understand the implications of the Falklands crisis, the entire venture was organised and conducted under naval command. Naturally enough the Admiralty turned to their own soldiers first and the Royal Marines' 3 Commando Brigade was alerted for embarkation to the South Atlantic on 2 April. The brigade was quickly beefed up with the addition of the 2nd and 3rd Battalions of the Parachute Regiment and two troops of the Blues and Royals with light tanks, together with additional gun batteries, special forces and logistics units.

For these soldiers to get ashore in the face of enemy resistance the amphibious assault ships *Fearless* and *Intrepid* with their complement of landing craft were also necessary to the Task Force. With them sailed the navy's six logistic landing ships: *Sir Bedivere*, *Sir Galahad*, *Sir Tristram*, *Sir Geraint*, *Sir Percivale* and *Sir Lancelot*. In an imaginative stroke, the troops themselves were embarked in a requisitioned cruise liner, the *Canberra*, and a North Sea ferry, the *Norland*. There is no doubt that the facilities of these civilian ships ensured that the infantry were in better fighting shape after a long sea voyage than they would have been if smaller vessels had been used. One of the most impressive features of the gathering of the Task Force was the speed with which these civilian ships were requisitioned and refitted with everything up to and including helicopter landing-pads before joining the growing armada.

From the beginning of the venture Admiral Leach and his staff had been clear that a very large fleet would be required. Ever since 1944 movements of the Royal Navy have been accompanied by the supply vessels of the Fleet Train to make them independent of land bases. By 1982 the numbers of tankers and support vessels deployed by the Royal Fleet Auxiliary (RFA) were not great enough to supply dozens of warships and troop carriers at the other end of the globe. However, contingency plans had been laid to cope with a national emergency and the Admiralty had powers to requisition or charter ships from the British merchant fleet which were designated Ships Taken Up From Trade (STUFT). As Leach's concept became reality – a fleet commanded at sea by Rear-Admiral John 'Sandy' Woodward and controlled from Fleet Headquarters at Northwood by Admiral Sir John Fieldhouse – the Northwood STUFT cell was increased in size to deal with a massive workload.

An extraordinary feat

Besides the 14 RFA tankers, replenishment ships, stores ships and casualty ferries, the Task Force would need no less that 54 civilian ships in its support – an enormous fleet. The impression of a single-minded purpose, of speed and efficiency was indelible as the STUFT were fitted with helicopter pads or with facilities for replenishment-at-sea (RAS). It was an extraordinary feat of logistics to select the ships, acquire the stores and provide naval specialist personnel to assist the civilian crews to RAS or to deal with ciphering.

The certainty with which plans to raise the Task Force were carried out contrasted with the uncertainty of plans for its use. On 7 April the British government had declared that a 200-mile (320km) Maritime Exclusion Zone (MEZ) would be enforced around the Falklands from 12 April, when the first of the submarines would be on the spot, but Chief of the Defence Staff, Admiral of the Fleet Sir Terence Lewin later admitted that, even after the Task Force was in being, 'We had no plan . . . for the reoccupation of the Falkland Islands'. This ambivalence was reflected throughout the senior command. Even in Thatcher's War Cabinet there were some who believed it might not come to a real fight. The Cabinet's

Below: County-class destroyer HMS *Antrim*, which led the group of vessels assigned to the recapture of South Georgia. Right: Grytviken, which was garrisoned by Argentinian Marines who also held the settlement at Leith, such terrain made operations perilous.

chief military adviser was Admiral Lewin and beneath him were the chiefs of the three services – responsible for assembling and supplying their relevant sections of the Task Force but not with the detailed planning of violently expelling the Argentinians from the Falklands. Beneath the defence staff came Fieldhouse at Northwood and then, crucially, the sea and land commanders on the spot – Admiral Woodward and Brigadier Julian Thompson, who was later superseded by Major-General Jeremy Moore. It was these operational commanders who had the duty of planning the conduct of the war and this was done during the 12,870km (8000-mile) journey south, which included a substantial pause at Ascension Island.

Demands for action

Whatever approach was adopted, it was clear that no early victory could be expected in the Falklands, but the British government was in need of some striking military success, both to satisfy the popular demand for action and to reinforce diplomatic pressure on Argentina. South Georgia offered an obvious target, since it was outside the range of Argentinian air cover and its garrison was not substantial. It could also provide shelter from South Atlantic storms for the repair of damaged ships or to concentrate troop-carrying vessels.

As early as 6 April work began on organising a combined force at Ascension Island to retake South Georgia, consisting of the destroyer *Antrim*, the frigate *Plymouth* and the tanker *Tidespring*. Troops for the South Georgia operation – which was code-named Paraquat after the potent and dangerous weedkiller – were flown direct to Ascension Island from Britain; they comprised M Company, 42 Commando under Major Guy Sheridan, the Mountain and Boat Troops of D Squadron, the 22nd Special Air Service Regiment (22 SAS) under Major Delves, and 2 Section, Special Boat Squadron (SBS).

The Argentinian garrison on South Georgia consisted of two Marine detachments based at Grytviken and Leith, beyond which the harsh terrain and

harsher weather offered scant inducement to stray. Consequently, several members of the British Antarctic Survey (BAS) Team remained at liberty, as did two television journalists, Cindy Buxton and Annie Price. Nor was a British military presence entirely absent, for HMS *Endurance* remained in the offing ready to rendezvous with Task Force units when they reached the South Atlantic.

The assault group sailed from Ascension Island on 10 April and met up with *Endurance* 1600km (1000 miles) north of South Georgia on the 12th. The sea approaches to South Georgia were scouted and declared clear first by the submarine *Conqueror* and then by an RAF Victor. By 21 April the ships were within easy helicopter range of the island and *Antrim* took on board one of the British Antarctic Survey scientists, who provided information on Argentinian positions.

The opening stages of the operation in fact came within a hair's breadth of catastrophe. The first phase

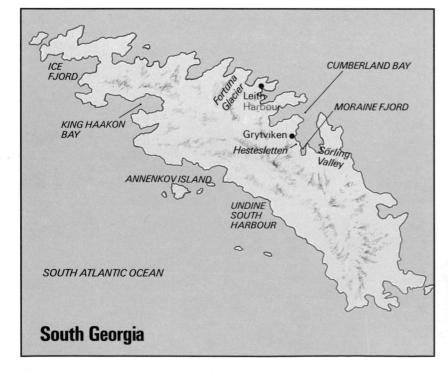

South Georgia

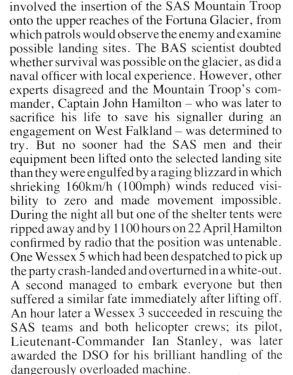

Above: Wasp and Lynx helicopters operating from *Antrim* and *Plymouth* during the assault on South Georgia. Left: The Argentinian submarine *Santa Fe* lies in Grytviken harbour after being severely damaged in an attack by British helicopters. Hit by missiles, depth-charges and machine-gun fire, the *Santa Fe* limped into the harbour where it was beached by its crew. Below: The crew of a Wessex helicopter examine the wreckage of another Wessex which crashed on South Georgia while transporting an SAS team. Right: Men of 42 Commando who took part in the recapture of Grytviken.

involved the insertion of the SAS Mountain Troop onto the upper reaches of the Fortuna Glacier, from which patrols would observe the enemy and examine possible landing sites. The BAS scientist doubted whether survival was possible on the glacier, as did a naval officer with local experience. However, other experts disagreed and the Mountain Troop's commander, Captain John Hamilton – who was later to sacrifice his life to save his signaller during an engagement on West Falkland – was determined to try. But no sooner had the SAS men and their equipment been lifted onto the selected landing site than they were engulfed by a raging blizzard in which shrieking 160km/h (100mph) winds reduced visibility to zero and made movement impossible. During the night all but one of the shelter tents were ripped away and by 1100 hours on 22 April Hamilton confirmed by radio that the position was untenable. One Wessex 5 which had been despatched to pick up the party crash-landed and overturned in a white-out. A second managed to embark everyone but then suffered a similar fate immediately after lifting off. An hour later a Wessex 3 succeeded in rescuing the SAS teams and both helicopter crews; its pilot, Lieutenant-Commander Ian Stanley, was later awarded the DSO for his brilliant handling of the dangerously overloaded machine.

That night the Boat Troop also narrowly avoided disaster. The outboard motors on two of its five Gemini inflatable assault boats failed and the craft vanished into the storm. One crew was picked up next morning, the other three days later, after switching on their emergency radio beacons. The remaining three craft reached their objectives on Grass Island, from which they were soon withdrawn when ice began tearing the rubber hulls. The news, however, was not all bad, for an SBS patrol was successfully inserted by helicopter into the Sorling Valley and moved the next day to Moraine Fjord.

On 24 April the group's commander, Captain Brian Young of the *Antrim*, was advised by satellite link that an Argentinian submarine was now known to be in the vicinity and that enemy C-130 Hercules were patrolling the area. It therefore seemed safe to assume that the Argentinians were aware of the British group's presence, and since he could achieve little until his helicopter losses had been made good, Young decided to withdraw temporarily to a point north of the island, where he was joined that night by the frigate HMS *Brilliant* and her two Lynx helicopters. Then, leaving *Tidespring* with most of M Company aboard, he turned south again and instituted an anti-submarine search.

At 0630 hours on 25 April, Lieutenant-Commander Stanley's Wessex picked up a radar contact 8km (5 miles) from the coast. It was the Argentinian submarine *Santa Fe* leaving Cumberland Bay, having reinforced the Grytviken garrison with a further 40 Marines. Stanley attacked at once, dropping two 112kg (250lb) depth-charges which exploded close to the submarine's port casing, evidently causing such internal damage that the *Santa Fe* immediately reversed course and headed back towards Grytviken, trailing smoke and a lengthening oil slick. Summoned by Stanley's contact report, a Lynx from *Brilliant* and the Wasps from *Plymouth* and *Endurance* all continued to strafe the stricken vessel with machine-gun and missile fire; an AS 12 missile fired by *Endurance*'s Wasp penetrated the conning tower, crossed the interior and emerged the other side before detonating. Inside the harbour, the submarine was run ashore near the jetty and hastily abandoned.

The time for painstaking reconnaissance and carefully planned attacks was clearly long past and the moment had come to exploit the shock, confusion and dismay which the incident had caused within the

enemy's ranks. Although the major part of M Company was still absent aboard *Tidespring*, Major Sheridan formed an *ad hoc* 75-strong company with every soldier he could lay his hands on, including his commandos, members of the ships' own Royal Marine detachments, SBS and SAS personnel. The Wessex and Lynx helicopters began lifting them ashore to Hestesletten, where a tactical headquarters and a mortar position was set up. Then Sheridan led an advance around the shoulder of Brown Mountain, which separated Hestesletten from Grytviken, while a Wasp lifted Captain C. Brown of 29 Commando Regiment Royal Artillery, the Naval Gunfire Support Officer (NGSO), to a point from which he could direct the fire of the warships against the enemy's positions. Altogether, *Antrim* and *Plymouth* fired a total of 235 rounds, expertly controlled by Brown so that they fell in an obvious pattern around the target area in an impressive display of the technique of minimum force. It was quite clear to the Argentinians that the Royal Navy could place its shells exactly where it wanted and this, together with their previous experiences, knocked all the fight out of them. When Sheridan and his men came within sight of the settlement white flags were already flying; the first troops to arrive were regarded with some awe since they had apparently just walked through a minefield.

The *Santa Fe*'s captain and the Marine company commander were entertained to dinner aboard *Antrim* and the following day the enemy detachment at Leith, which had broadcast its defiance overnight, surrendered promptly when the SAS arrived, supported offshore by *Plymouth* and *Endurance*. The surrender formalities were concluded in *Plymouth*'s wardroom in the presence of both British captains.

The Argentinian signatory was Captain Alfredo Astiz, whose troops had been so badly mauled by Lieutenant Mills' little command only three weeks previously; he qualified the document by inserting that he had submitted to 'overwhelming' force. As group commander, Captain Young despatched the following signal to the Ministry of Defence: 'Be pleased to inform Her Majesty that the White Ensign flies alongside the Union Jack on South Georgia. God save the Queen!'

The recapture of South Georgia had cost the British some equipment but, miraculously, no casualties. One enemy crewman was wounded during the attack on the *Santa Fe*, and one was shot dead in error when the submarine was being moved, his guard being under the impression that he was about to scuttle the boat. The remaining 156 Argentinian service personnel and the 38 scrap-metal merchants were repatriated via Uruguay, leaving the island aboard the *Tidespring* on 30 April. The one exception was Astiz, who had acquired a sinister reputation and the nickname of Captain Death as a result of his activities as an interrogator at the Buenos Aires Escuela Mecanica Naval (Naval Engineering Institute), which was used as a political detention centre during Argentina's 'Dirty War'. The French and Swedish governments wished to interview him regarding the disappearance of some of their nationals in Argentina and he was flown to England. However, there was no legal basis upon which he could be held and he was repatriated. He has since been brought to trial in Argentina.

The loss of South Georgia took the Argentinian junta by complete surprise and for a while they refused to acknowledge the event. For British Prime Minister Margaret Thatcher the success of Operation Paraquat was the first vindication of her South Atlantic policy, and her relief at the outcome was obvious. On board HMS *Hermes* Admiral Woodward looked confidently to the future: 'South Georgia was the appetiser . . . . This is the run up to the big match which, in my view, should be a walkover.' The admiral himself was shortly to admit that these words, spoken in the euphoria of the moment, were not entirely appropriate.

P. J. Banyard and Bryan Perrett

Below left: British troops raise the Union Jack and White Ensign after the surrender of the Argentinian garrison on South Georgia. Below: Argentinian commander on South Georgia, Captain Alfredo Astiz, signs the surrender document in the presence of Captain Barker of the *Endurance* and Captain Penreath of the *Plymouth*.

Key Weapons

BOLT-ACTION RIFLES

When World War II ended in 1945 the majority of military rifles in use were bolt-action magazine weapons. Only the US Army had a semi-automatic rifle, the Garand M1, as standard issue; the German and Soviet armies had small numbers of semi-automatic and selective fire (fully-automatic and single shot) rifles issued to particular units, largely on an extended trial basis, since not all the designs were as good as had been hoped. For the remainder, bolt-action rifles were standard issue: the British and Commonwealth troops used the Lee Enfield in ·303in calibre, Germany had the Mauser Model 98 in 7·92mm calibre, the Soviet Army had the Mosin Nagant M1891/30 in 7·62mm calibre, and the French had the MAS 36 in 7·5mm. Other involved countries used various Mauser or Mannlicher designs.

The bolt action in all these rifles was similar. The bolt assembly would be pulled back by means of a handle. This opened the chamber to the magazine, which fed in a round pushed up by a spring at the base of the magazine. The bolt was then pushed back and the rifle was ready for firing. A bolt-action rifle such as the Lee Enfield could be fired by a trained soldier at a rate of 15 rounds per minute, but the poorly-trained conscripts and volunteers that made up the majority of the armies of World War II could only be mediocre shots with the bolt-action rifle.

The experience of the US Army in the war had proved that a semi-automatic rifle was a practical weapon in the field. Soldiers did not empty their magazines as soon as they saw some movement, as had been feared, and the robust mechanism of the Garand showed itself capable of withstanding all the various rigours of active service. Moreover, some of the designs which appeared in Germany – the parachutists' FG42 and the MP43/44 Sturmgewehr, for example – indicated that it was not necessary to mill expensive pieces of steel into shape to make a semi-automatic rifle. As a result every army began studying semi-automatic rifles and by the mid-1950s the bolt-action rifle was no longer a first-line weapon in the armies of the major powers. By 1960 it had also vanished from second-line and support units; the semi-automatic rifle had taken over from the bolt-action in the most advanced nations' armies.

In the early postwar years, the bolt-action rifle still saw service with, for example, the French during their 1946-54 campaign in Indochina. However, it was a weapon progressively confined to the armies of developing nations. The Viet Minh and Viet Cong used them throughout the French and US interventions in Vietnam, both Arabs and Israelis used them in their 1948 and 1956 wars, and Indian and Pakistani forces were armed with them during their 1947, 1965 and 1971 wars. The increasing spread of semi-automatic rifles such as the Belgian FN FAL, the US M16 and the Soviet AK-47 has steadily reduced even those Third World armies using bolt-action rifles until by 1983 none were in use as the first-line standard weapon in any of the world's armies. Poorly-equipped guerrilla forces were its main users. The bolt-action rifle had had its day.

For a weapon classified as obsolete there are still many survivors in the world's arsenals, and on examination this is found to be for two reasons: they make useful training weapons and many armies are reluctant to believe that the semi-automatic weapon is capable of fulfilling sniping duties.

The training aspect of the bolt-action rifle is partly an economic matter and partly technical. Economically it makes sense to use up older rifles for as long as they remain serviceable and ammunition stocks exist. Technically, the recruit can learn elementary safety and marksmanship on a simple weapon, he can become used to the recoil of a service cartridge, and he can learn the basics of fire discipline which will be reinforced by the need consciously to load each round.

It is, however, the sniping role which has led to

Page 2183: These Afghan rebels have an unusual collection of weapons, including a Lee Enfield Pattern 14 rifle in the foreground and a Russian Mosin Nagant on the left. Left: Indian soldiers advancing on Dacca, in Bangladesh, during the 1971 Indo-Pakistan War; they are armed with Lee Enfields. Below far left: Bolt-action rifles such as this Lee Enfield Rifle No 1, Mark VI, are now confined to irregular fighting groups, such as guerrillas. Below left: Lee Enfield rifles were still used in Chad in 1978 alongside AKs. Below centre: Arab Legionnaires with Lee Enfield rifles take up positions in Jerusalem in 1948. Below right: The armed forces of modern nations still make use of the bolt-action rifle for drill, as demonstrated by these West German sailors.

the 7·62mm rifles came into service the existing ·303in Lee Enfield sniping rifles were retained until such time as a new 7·62mm sniper could be produced, the change in ammunition being required because of the advantages of standardisation. The eventual issue was the L42A1 rifle, which is simply the old Lee Enfield Rifle No 4 converted to 7·62mm Nato calibre. There is a new cold-forged heavy barrel, and the wooden fore-end and handguard are reduced in length, leaving the forward half of the barrel exposed. A telescope sight mount is fitted on the left side of the receiver to take the standard sighting telescope; it will also accept any night-vision sight with the standard Nato dimensions. There is a 10-round magazine, and the shoulder-stock has a wooden cheek-piece fitted. The normal 'iron' sights are retained and can be used in an emergency.

The Royal Small Arms Factory also manufacture the Enfield Enforcer, a police version of the L42A1. The difference lies in the stock, which is of a more sporting appearance, and in the iron sights which use a tunnel foresight and a target-type aperture rear sight.

The Parker-Hale Company of Birmingham produce their Model 82 bolt-action rifle for sniping, which has been adopted by the Australian, Canadian and New Zealand Armies. This uses a Mauser bolt action and a heavy barrel, has a butt with an adjustable cheek-piece, and can be fitted with whatever iron sights or telescope mounts the purchasers demand.

Fabrique National of Herstal in Belgium were originally set up in the 1890s to manufacture Mauser rifles for the Belgian Army, and their expertise has never been allowed to fade. As a result they offer a Mauser bolt action in their Model 30-11 sniper rifle. This also has a sports-gun appearance, in that the barrel is largely exposed and there is merely a half-length fore-end underneath it. The barrel is very heavy, for stiffness and accuracy, and carries a flash eliminator. The butt is adjustable, by means of spacers, for length and for height of cheek-piece so

manufacturers producing new designs of bolt-action rifles for military and police use. The modern semi-automatic rifle is not expected to perform well at long range, and therefore is unlikely to meet the rigorous specification demanded by sniper rifles. Although there are plenty of experts who can produce impressive figures to prove otherwise, most soldiers instinctively feel that they can shoot more accurately with a bolt-action rifle than they can with a semi-automatic.

The British Army never attempted to use its FN FAL-derived SLR rifle as a sniping weapon; when

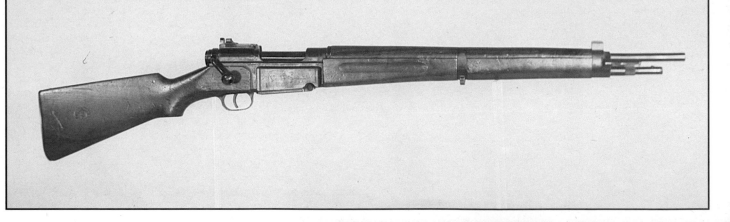

that it can be made to fit almost any stature. A telescope sight is fitted as standard and the normal iron sights are retained. There is also an optional light bipod which can be fitted under the fore-end, a useful accessory for those times when the sniper must remain at the ready for long periods.

The Mauser Waffenwerke also manufacture a sniper rifle, using their short-action bolt mechanism. This has the bolt handle fitted towards the front end of the bolt, which reduces the bolt movement by some 90mm (3·5in), giving less overhang behind the rifle and less need for the firer to move his head when operating the bolt to reload. The heavy barrel is fitted with a muzzle brake and compensator which resists the usual upward jump on firing, so allowing the sniper to re-aim very quickly. The wooden stock is very luxurious, having a well-shaped thumb-hole pistol grip; the butt is fully adjustable and every area likely to be gripped is roughened to a non-slip surface. The Mauser SP66 is in use by the West German Army and by at least 12 other armies throughout the world.

The last of the three major bolt actions is the Mannlicher, and this is preserved in the Steyr SSG-69 sniping rifle made in Austria by the company that made the original Mannlicher rifles in the 1890s. The SSG is unusual in using a plastic stock which is normally a drab green but which can be provided in other colours – such as sand or black – as required. The bolt is a turnbolt, and the magazine is normally a rotary spool holding five rounds, though a 10-round box can be provided for those who prefer it. The rotary magazine is another old Mannlicher design: it is fed from the top with single rounds which, as they go in, wind up a spiral spring. As the bolt is operated, so the spring turns the spool and feeds a new round; the whole magazine can be removed from beneath the rifle, and the rear face is of transparent plastic so that the firer can immediately see how many rounds remain inside it. There are iron sights for emergency use only; the normal sight, supplied with the rifle, is a 6-power telescope.

The French Army more or less followed the British example by taking their existing service bolt action, the MAS 36 rifle in 7·5mm calibre, and modifying it for sniping use, naming it the FR-FI. The 7·5mm calibre was retained in the first models, though later production has been in 7·62mm Nato calibre. As with the other sniping rifles, the stock has been shortened to leave the forward half of the heavy barrel exposed, and there is a muzzle brake and flash eliminator on the muzzle. A light bipod is per-

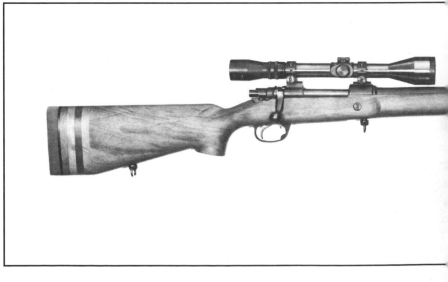

Left: The French MAS 36 was the last bolt-action rifle to be adopted as a standard service arm in the Western world, in 1936; it was still in use with the French troops in Indochina during 1946-54. Right: The British Army's sniper rifle, the L42A1, a modified Lee Enfield. Below right: The Belgian FN FAL Model 30-11 sniper rifle uses a Mauser bolt action and adjustable butt.

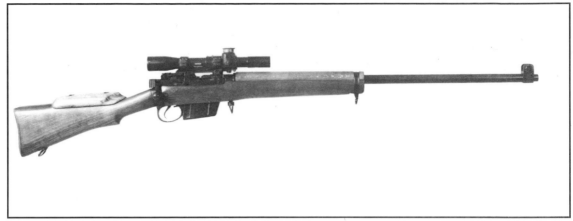

Left and right: The Austrian Steyr SSG-69 uses a Mannlicher bolt action and has an unusual plastic stock. The exploded view shows both the rotary spool magazine that carries five rounds and the 10-round box magazine. Below: The British Parker-Hale Model 82 has been successfully exported to Canada, New Zealand and Australia. Below right: The wooden stock of this Mauser SP66 has a thumbhole pistol grip for the shooter's comfort.

Left: Afghan insurgents show a determined face for the photographer as they advance, armed with AK-47s and short magazine Lee Enfields. The bayonet emphasises the antiquated character of some of the armaments used by guerrilla forces. Below: This Yugoslav sniper is aiming his Model 1948, a Yugoslav version of the Mauser Model 98. Below left: The Soviet Dragunov SVD is one of the few service sniper rifles in the world to use a semi-automatic action; the action is similar to that used in the AK-47 family of weapons. Bottom left and bottom: The French FR-F1 is a modification of the MAS 36; the stock is cut back and a flash eliminator added. It uses a 4-power telescope, and there is also a bipod.

manently fitted to the fore-end, there is a pistol-grip, and the butt has an adjustable cheek-piece and is adjustable for length. Iron sights are fitted but are normally folded down out of the way and a 4-power telescope is the normal method of sighting.

Since World War II new semi-automatic sniping rifles have become available, although only one has so far been adopted in any numbers (the Soviet-made Dragunov SVD sniper rifle, in service with the armies of most Warsaw Pact nations). These demonstrate the concern over accuracy of semi-automatic rifles versus bolt-action, since although two of them (the SVD and the Yugoslav M76 7·92mm rifle) use existing service-pattern semi-automatic mechanisms, the rifles are designed specifically for sniping and are not adapted standard-issue weapons. The third model, the Walther WA2000, uses a totally new system of construction, reinforcing the belief that an ordinary military semi-automatic rifle is not acceptable. However, these semi-automatic sniping rifles have one characteristic in common: they are expensive; and as long as they stay that way, the bolt-action rifle will have a home in the military armoury.

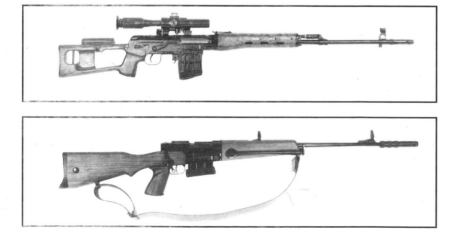

Race against time

Diplomatic efforts to stop the Falklands War

General Leopoldo Fortunato Galtieri, army chief of staff, president and head of the three-man military junta which ruled Argentina, decided to end the long-running and fruitless negotiations with Great Britain over Argentina's claim to the Falklands by invading the islands in 1982. He reasoned that economically enfeebled Britain, which was busily engaged in cutting its out-of-Nato-area naval capability, would do no more than protest at the *fait accompli*. British complacency about the possibility of such a coup, reinforced by the failures of her intelligence services, enabled Galtieri's invasion force to seize the islands virtually unopposed on Friday, 2 April 1982. Margaret Thatcher's Conservative administration, angry and humiliated, and faced with bitter recriminations from the House of Commons on 3 April, assembled and despatched a naval Task Force to the islands and at the same time froze Argentina's financial assets in London and cut off all trade with that country.

British politicians, haunted by the fate of many World War II amphibious operations, did not relish the prospect of a possibly disastrous outcome to the expedition in the bleak and inhospitable waters of the South Atlantic. Many government ministers hoped that during the time which the Task Force would take to sail to the islands, knowledge of its approach would persuade the Argentinians to withdraw their forces. Accordingly, the British Foreign Office mobilised its diplomatic armoury to increase the pressure on Argentina.

British ambassador to the United Nations Sir Anthony Parsons had already succeeded in diplomatically outflanking Argentina by persuading the Security Council to call on both sides to show restraint in their dispute over the Falkland Islands on 1 April, before the invasion had even taken place. The Argentinian seizure of the islands therefore placed Buenos Aires in open breach of UN policy, and Parsons hastily drummed up sufficient Security Council votes to secure the passage of Resolution 502 which called for the immediate cessation of hostilities, the withdrawal of Argentinian forces from the islands and for the two countries to resolve their differences peacefully under the terms of the UN Charter. It was this important resolution which enabled Britain to claim throughout the ensuing crisis that it had the support of the international community in its efforts to repel aggression in the event that the Argentinians did not withdraw.

Britain followed its United Nations victory by persuading the EEC to impose economic sanctions (including the banning of arms exports) on Argentina for 6 weeks. Britain's triumph was not complete, however, for the United States equivocated, torn between its desire to maintain its recently improved relations with Argentina and its loyalty to its British ally. With President Reagan's blessing, Secretary of State Alexander Haig embarked on a gruelling air shuttle between London and Buenos Aires in the period 8-19 April, during the course of which he put forward four sets of compromise proposals. These were all variants on the same theme – the withdrawal of the Argentinian military forces from the islands and the recall of the British Task Force, the setting up of some form of Anglo-Argentinian interim administration for the islands, while negotiations would take

Below: An Argentinian soldier on the Falklands keeps watch for the arrival of the British Task Force, which set sail for the South Atlantic within days of the Argentinian invasion of the islands in April 1982. As the diplomats searched for a peaceful solution to the crisis, Argentinian reinforcements were flown in from the mainland in preparation for the expected British counter-blow.

place between the two sides for a long-term settlement of the islands' future, which (on British insistence) would take into account the wishes of the islanders themselves.

Negotiations in London took place mostly between Haig and Francis Pym, foreign secretary after Lord Carrington's resignation on 5 April. Pym appeared to be more ready to consider a compromise settlement than Prime Minister Thatcher, but both were at one in insisting that Argentinian forces must be withdrawn from the islands before any negotiations could begin, and that Britain must not be tied down to a deadline on the issue of future Argentinian sovereignty over the islands (Haig had proposed six months) since this would provide Argentina with the opportunity to reoccupy the islands on the expiry of the deadline.

Stalemate over sovereignty

Even when Haig tried to still British fears by offering United States participation in the interim administration, London refused to budge on its opposition to conceding sovereignty to Argentina at the outset of the negotiations, a point on which Galtieri insisted. On 19 April, after intensive negotiations in Buenos Aires, Haig managed to secure an Argentinian concession of sorts when the latter finally agreed to the mutual withdrawal of both Argentinian land and British naval forces from the area, the setting up of an interim administration under United Nations supervision, consisting of an equal number of British and Argentinian citizens – there were about 20 of the latter on the islands before the invasion – and negotiations for the transfer of sovereignty, which were to be completed by the end of 1982. This latter demand, together with Argentina's insistence that its citizens should be permitted to purchase land and settle on the islands, was completely unacceptable to the British government, suggesting as it did the relatively speedy transfer of sovereignty to Argentina. Haig thereupon abandoned his shuttle diplomacy but not his peace efforts: on Thursday 22 April he put forward another proposal, worked out with Pym, who had flown to Washington for the purpose, which provided for a somewhat lengthier negotiation process over the sovereignty issue than had been suggested in any of his earlier plans. This in turn was rejected by Argentina, which continued to insist that sovereignty be conceded at the outset of the negotiations. On 30 April, the United States, blaming Argentina for the impasse, applied limited economic sanctions against Buenos Aires, and began to supply fuel and military equipment to the British Task Force.

The willingness of either party to make concessions – however limited – depended very much on the ebb and flow of military and naval events. At first, Argentina doubted British determination to reconquer the islands and believed that in any case, even if they tried, they could be easily repelled. With the arrival of the British Task Force in the South Atlantic in mid-April, the British announcement of a Total Exclusion Zone (TEZ) of 200-miles (320km) radius around the Falklands, and the British recapture of the island of South Georgia on 25 April, Galtieri became more willing to compromise, at least to the extent of agreeing to the withdrawal of Argentinian forces from the islands.

Britain's position weakened, paradoxically, when a British submarine sank the Argentinian cruiser *General Belgrano* on 2 May, with the loss of 368 Argentinian lives, even though the vessel was some 64km (40 miles) outside the TEZ. International opinion was horrified by this demonstration of British ruthlessness, and many echoed Argentina's accusations that the action breached the spirit of Resolution 502. Already on 26 April, the Organization of American States (OAS), meeting at Argentina's request, had passed a resolution which was critical of Britain's behaviour. Ireland, West Germany and other EEC countries, sensing that Britain's actions were not going to be confined to a peaceful blockade of the islands as they had anticipated, began to demand the lifting of EEC sanctions against

Top: US Secretary of State Alexander Haig (left) confers with Argentinian President Galtieri (centre) and his foreign minister, Nicanor Costa Mendes (right) during a visit to Buenos Aires in April 1982.

Above: Haig and British Foreign Secretary Francis Pym during a meeting in Washington on 22 April. Below: Vessels of the British naval Task Force steaming southwards towards the Falklands.

Argentina. These pressures, together with evidence of US disapproval of the escalation of the conflict, caused the British government momentarily to reconsider its attitude to a possible compromise and this feeling was reinforced when on 4 May an air-launched Argentinian Exocet missile sank the British destroyer HMS *Sheffield*, thus emphasising to British ministers, and to British public opinion, the hazardous nature of the enterprise.

The most serious diplomatic effect of the sinking of the *Belgrano*, however, was in ending the hopes for a negotiated settlement which had been raised temporarily by a set of proposals put forward by the president of Peru, Fernando Belaúnde Terry. The Peruvian president's plan was a variant of Haig's proposals – the withdrawal of both sides' military forces from the area, the setting up of an interim administration with Latin American participation, and subsequent negotiations under United Nations supervision to settle the long-term future of the islands – and like Haig's initiative, skirted round the delicate and crucial issue of sovereignty. Eventually, after the sinking of the *Belgrano* and the *Sheffield* had been followed by the withdrawal of the Peruvian initiative, attention focussed on a plan put forward by the UN secretary-general, which became the basis for the subsequent feverish negotiations in New York. Argentina's insistence on a time limit for the conclusion of the negotiations on sovereignty in order to prevent Britain from prolonging the discussions indefinitely was once again the chief stumbling-block.

By mid-May, it was evident that both sides were playing for time. Britain, despairing of any agreement with Argentina, continued to go through the motions of negotiation at New York in order not to arouse the suspicions of the EEC and the United Nations while she continued to prepare for the reoccupation of the islands. The Argentinians also calculated that prolonged discussions would sap the morale of the British Task Force and at the same time enable Argentina to replenish its depleted stocks of Exocet missiles. Fresh British proposals on 17 May, which included the acceptance of an interim United Nations administration for the islands, broke down over continued Argentinian insistence on the prior settlement of the sovereignty issue. On 20 May, Britain abandoned the negotiations on the secretary-general's proposal.

By this time, the British War Cabinet had approved the timetable for the landing of British forces at San Carlos on 21 May, and neither the increasing restiveness of the EEC, which only agreed to the renewal of sanctions on a voluntary basis for one week on 17 May, nor an OAS resolution condemning Britain, nor a spate of anti-British resolutions sponsored by Latin American countries at the United Nations altered British resolve. A joint Spanish-Panamanian resolution of 4 June calling for a ceasefire and the implementation of negotiations under Resolution 502 was vetoed by Britain, backed by the United States in the Security Council.

There were bitter divisions within the Reagan administration over its policy towards Argentina. As Argentina's defeat loomed closer, Reagan wanted to put forward a new face-saving peace formula at the Versailles economic summit which was to begin on 3 June. Faced with defeat in the Falklands, Argentina was now more than willing to climb down: the Reagan plan proposed the positioning of a joint United States-Latin American peacekeeping force in the Falklands after the withdrawal of both British and Argentinian troops, an interim United Nations administration and open-ended negotiations between the British and Argentinians for a long-term settlement. The Argentinians, on the brink of disaster, accepted this plan, despite the fact that it overturned all their previous preconditions on the sovereignty issue. But the logic of military developments and the determination of the British to liquidate the affair were against any diplomatic settlement. After all the diplomatic efforts, the Falklands conflict was to be ended only by a clear military victory.

Michael Dockrill

Defeat of the Armada

The naval war and the sinking of the *Belgrano*

Even discounting the Polaris submarines which provide the United Kingdom's independent nuclear deterrent, the Royal Navy and the Armada Argentina are fleets intended for totally different roles. On the eve of the Falklands War, the Royal Navy comprised two anti-submarine warfare (ASW) carriers, 16 destroyers, 44 frigates and 31 hunter-killer submarines – of which force a dozen frigates and the same number of submarines were either refitting or laid up in reserve – plus an amphibious warfare squadron consisting of two assault ships and six logistic landing ships. In support was the Royal Fleet Auxiliary, whose tankers, supply and ammunition ships enable warships to stay on station for long periods without the need to return to harbour. The principal task of the Royal Navy was (and remains) the security of the eastern Atlantic, a role executed jointly with the navies of its Nato allies, with a heavy emphasis on ASW.

Because of this assigned role, the Royal Navy was not ideally prepared for a conflict in which air attack was likely to be the major risk. The two British carriers in commission in April 1982 were the 24,000-ton *Hermes*, which was on the brink of retirement, and the 16,000-ton *Invincible*, which was due to be sold to Australia. Neither ship was a fleet carrier capable of flying all types of aircraft from its decks, but they could both manage a small complement of Sea Harriers. Normally, each ship would have carried five Sea Harriers and nine Sea King helicopters, but during the war the Sea Harrier complement was virtually doubled. The commanders of the Task Force were uncomfortably aware that they possessed no airborne warning and control system (AWACS) aircraft, and as a consequence frigates would have to be deployed well forward as radar-pickets, with disastrous results.

The fleet's frigates and destroyers were also, on the whole, better equipped for the ASW than the air-defence role. A modern vessel depends for its defence on its missile systems and its electronic counter-measures (ECM) but is unarmoured and has little capacity to absorb damage. Most of the British vessels were armed with the obsolete Sea Cat short-range surface-to-air missile (SAM) system or the equally obsolete Sea Slug long-range SAM. In these circumstances, the most important ships were considered to be the Type 42 destroyers – such as *Coventry* and *Sheffield* – which possessed the relatively modern Sea Dart long-range SAM and the two Type 22 frigates – *Brilliant* and *Broadsword* – which had the superb modern short-range Sea Wolf SAM system. Most of the escort vessels were also armed with one or two 4.5in guns, Exocet surface-to-surface missiles (SSMs) and 20mm or 40mm high-angle AA guns.

For offensive action the Royal Navy had available the Valiant and Swiftsure classes of nuclear-powered attack submarines, capable respectively of 28 and 30 knots submerged, and the Oberon and Porpoise diesel-electric boats, which were appreciably slower. All were armed with 21in torpedoes, and their presence was to have a decisive effect on the campaign.

Although the fleet had not been involved in a major action since the Suez operation of 1956 it was, like every British armed service, an all-volunteer force which maintained the highest professional standards. Even so, it faced an almost 13,000km (8000-mile) journey to the war zone, following which it had to wrest control of the sea from an enemy who himself possessed a considerable navy as well as apparently overwhelming air superiority, and then carry out a major amphibious landing and support the ground troops in every possible way until the Argentinians surrendered. Many would have regarded

Left: A Sea Harrier returns to HMS *Hermes* after a combat air patrol over the Falklands. The two aircraft carriers attached to the Task Force, *Invincible* (below) and *Hermes* (bottom), played a vital role in providing the air cover without which the operation to recover the Falklands could not have been mounted in the face of heavy opposition from shore-based Argentinian aircraft. Above: British Task Force commander, Rear-Admiral John 'Sandy' Woodward.

Royal Navy Task Force

Aircraft Carriers

Hermes

Invincible

County Class Destroyers

Antrim
Glamorgan

Type 42 Destroyers

Sheffield
Glasgow
Coventry
Exeter
Cardiff

Type 82 Destroyer

Bristol

Type 22 Frigates

Broadsword
Brilliant

Type 21 Frigates

Antelope
Ardent
Arrow
Alacrity
Ambuscade
Active
Avenger

Rothsay Class Frigates

Yarmouth
Plymouth

Leander Class Frigates

Minerva
Andromeda
Penelope
Argonaut

Submarines

Conqueror
Spartan
Splendid·
Onyx
Courageous
Valiant

Amphibious Assault Ships

Fearless
Intrepid

Ocean Survey Ships

Hydra
Hecla
Herald

Offshore Patrol Vessels

Dumbarton Castle
Leeds Castle

Ice Patrol Ship

Endurance

such demands as excessive, yet Rear-Admiral John Woodward, the Task Force commander, obviously felt that these aims could be achieved, although he predicted the loss of six ships, including at least one major unit. This proved to be an accurate forecast.

In contrast, the Argentinian Navy was essentially a coastal defence force with a small amphibious warfare capability which had been stretched to the limit by the occupation of the Falklands and South Georgia. It regarded itself as the rival of the other armed services in the internal struggle for political power, and could be counted upon to preserve itself to that end, regardless of the situation at sea. It was with this in mind that a contemporary American observer commented that the Armada Republica Argentina was 'a one-shot navy – sink one of their ships and you've sunk the lot'.

The largest unit of the fleet was the carrier *Veinticinco de Mayo*, which had been completed in 1945 as HMS *Venerable* and then sold to the Royal Dutch Navy, in which she served until 1968 as the *Karel Doorman*. The *Veinticinco de Mayo* carried a complement of 12 A-4Q Skyhawks as well as several ASW aircraft; as Argentina's sole carrier she contradicted the fundamental tenet of air-sea warfare that to be effective one carrier must have the support of another, but her principal role had always been to enhance the prestige of the navy. The second most important vessel in the fleet, the 13,645-ton cruiser *General Belgrano*, was even older – she had been launched in 1939 as the USS *Phoenix* and was the last survivor of Pearl Harbor. Her armament consisted of 15 6in guns, eight 5in, two 40mm and two quad Sea Cat SAM systems, and she was the only warship on either side which possessed an armoured belt. The Armada also owned some second-hand but modernised ex-American destroyers armed with 5in and 3in guns and Exocet SSMs, and its modern warships

included two Type 42 destroyers recently delivered from British yards and three French Type A69 corvettes. Of the four Argentinian submarines, one is reported to have been in the hands of the dockyard at the start of the war, but this has never been confirmed. Finally, the Argentinians could muster a flotilla of small attack craft, patrol vessels and minesweepers.

Following the occupation of South Georgia and

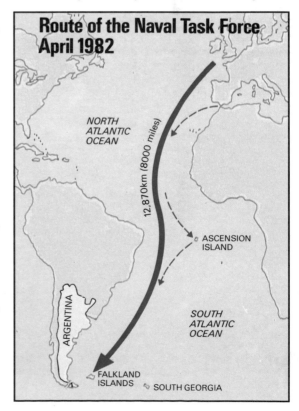

Route of the Naval Task Force April 1982

NORTH ATLANTIC OCEAN

ARGENTINA

12,870km (8000 miles)

ASCENSION ISLAND

SOUTH ATLANTIC OCEAN

FALKLAND ISLANDS   SOUTH GEORGIA

Left: The Argentinian cruiser *General Belgrano*, which was detected at sea by the British submarine *Conqueror* on 1 May. *Conqueror* continued to shadow the *Belgrano* until the following day, when she received an order from London to sink the Argentinian ship. Below left: The *Belgrano's* commander, Captain Hector Bonzo.

the Falklands, which cost the Argentinians the corvette *Guerrico*, the Argentinian Navy withdrew to its home bases, worried by the possibility that British submarines might be operating in the area. In fact, the first nuclear submarine, *Spartan*, did not arrive off the Falklands until 12 April, when Britain declared a Maritime Exclusion Zone (MEZ) around the islands. The submarines *Splendid* and *Conqueror* soon followed, and they were subsequently reinforced by *Valiant* and *Onyx*. Once the Exclusion Zone was declared, the flow of seaborne traffic between the mainland and Port Stanley was reduced to a trickle.

Meanwhile, the Task Force continued on its way south, pausing briefly to regroup at Ascension Island. Little of note occurred at sea until South Georgia was recovered on 25 April. During this operation the enemy submarine *Santa Fe* was caught on the surface near Grytviken, and was severely damaged and driven back into the harbour where she was abandoned by her crew. The following day the Task Force declared a Defence Zone around itself, and on 30 April the Maritime Exclusion Zone was declared a Total Exclusion Zone (TEZ). By 1 May the Task Force was able to begin hitting the Argentinian garrison on the Falklands, and Argentinian airstrikes against the British fleet began.

The progress southwards of the Task Force tempted the Argentinian Navy out to sea once more. Admiral Jorge Anaya deployed his ships in two groups to execute a pincer movement north and south of the Falklands. The northern group consisted of the *Veinticinco de Mayo* and five escorts including the two Type 42 destroyers, while to the south were the cruiser *Belgrano* and two escorts. Admiral Anaya's intentions are not fully known, but it seems that the plan was for the carrier group to launch an airstrike, receiving air cover from the mainland airbases while its aircraft were away; if the British withdrew to the south they would run into the *Belgrano* group, which would inflict further damage with gunfire and Exocet SSMs before disengaging.

It is clear that the British had at least general intelligence of the Argentinian movements. On 26 April the British submarines *Conqueror* and *Splendid* were patrolling to the west of the Falklands; on that day *Splendid* sighted several enemy destroyers off the mainland coast and began shadowing them but was instructed on the following day by Fleet Headquarters at Northwood, which retained immediate command of submarine operations, to break off and search for the *Veinticinco de Mayo* in an area still further north. Simultaneously *Conqueror* was ordered to search for the *General Belgrano* to the south.

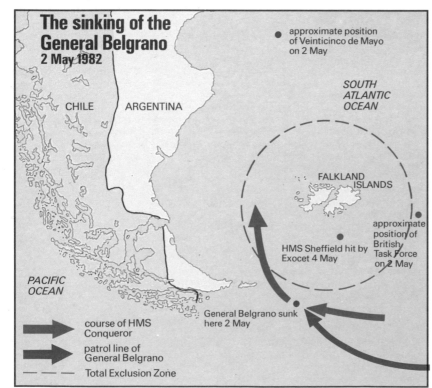

The sinking of the General Belgrano
2 May 1982

- approximate position of Veinticinco de Mayo on 2 May

CHILE ARGENTINA

SOUTH ATLANTIC OCEAN

FALKLAND ISLANDS

approximate position of British Task Force on 2 May

HMS Sheffield hit by Exocet 4 May

PACIFIC OCEAN

General Belgrano sunk here 2 May

→ course of HMS Conqueror
→ patrol line of General Belgrano
--- Total Exclusion Zone

Conqueror, captained by Commander Christopher Wreford-Brown, sighted the *Belgrano* and her escorts during the afternoon of 1 May and began shadowing them. This was the time when intense air and sea activity started around the Falklands and Anaya's pincers were beginning to close on the British ships, while a third group was thought to be in position west of the Falklands.

Searching in the dark

That night each of the opposing carrier groups flew off reconnaissance aircraft to search for the other. A Grumman S-2 Tracker located the Task Force on radar about midnight, and some time later one of *Invincible*'s Sea Harriers picked up the emissions of enemy missile-control radar and took evasive action, returning briefly to a point at which its own active scanner revealed the *Veinticinco de Mayo* and its five escorts. By dawn the Argentinian carrier was only 320km (200 miles) from the Task Force and in position to launch her airstrike. She was, however, almost as old as the *Belgrano* and equally unable to attain her theoretical maximum speed of 25 knots. This, coupled with the fact that the wind had fallen away to nothing, prevented her fully-laden Skyhawks from taking off. Rear-Admiral Juan Lombardo, controlling the operation, ordered the carrier group to retire towards the mainland and await better flying conditions. Far away to the south, the *Belgrano* group conformed. Both groups then established a holding pattern.

Meanwhile, *Conqueror* was still shadowing *Belgrano*. Discussion between Admiral Woodward and Admiral Sir John Fieldhouse, the C-in-C Fleet, resulted in the conclusion that the Argentinian Navy could be eliminated if the cruiser was sunk, although she was presently outside the TEZ. The British Cabinet approved the necessary change in the rules of engagement and their decision was communicated to Wreford-Brown. At 1600 hours on 2 May, *Conqueror* fired a pair of conventional Mark 8 torpedoes at a range of 2000 yards (1800m). Two exploded against the cruiser's port side, the first causing the bow to collapse almost as far back as A turret, the second in the after machinery spaces inflicting the warship's death blow. Within 20 minutes the *Belgrano* was listing so severely that Captain Hector Bonzo, her commander, ordered the ship to be

Top: Hit by two torpedoes fired by HMS *Conqueror*, the *General Belgrano* rapidly developed a heavy list and began to sink. Within an hour, she had rolled over and sunk. Above: Argentinian crewmen take to their liferafts. 368 lives were lost in the sinking of the Argentinian cruiser, which put an end to any naval threat to the British Task Force. Right: Survivors of the *Belgrano* arriving home in Argentina.

abandoned, and at 1700 hours she rolled over and sank. Poor damage-control probably contributed to the casualties; the highest estimate put the death toll at 368. The *Belgrano*'s two escorts launched an unsuccessful counter-attack and then wisely left the scene. The survivors were picked up 30 hours later.

In purely military terms, the sinking of the *Belgrano* achieved the desired result – the major surface units of the Argentinian Navy withdrew to their bases and remained there for the duration of the war. However, the heavy loss of life generated a wave of shock around the world which forfeited the United Kingdom a degree of international goodwill, until HMS *Sheffield* fell victim to an Exocet attack two days later. **Bryan Perrett**

Softening up the defences

Britain wears down the Argentinian forces

When Admiral Sandy Woodward's battle fleet arrived off the Falklands on the last day of April 1982, the British commanders were still not certain as to the type of campaign that lay before them. Besides this, they had no idea about the strength and dispositions of the Argentinian forces occupying the islands or the likely tactics of the Argentinian Air Force and Navy. It was obviously going to be a matter of feeling their way towards a military solution by gradually increasing pressure in every fashion possible. The only certainty was that the object against which they were to turn their strength was the Argentinian garrison on the islands – not Argentina itself. The surrender or expulsion of the garrison would accomplish everything required.

Admiral Woodward's first priority was to try to cut the garrison off from any attempt to resupply or reinforce it from the mainland. This in itself would have a disastrous effect upon Argentinian morale and, as supplies ran low, upon fighting effectiveness. The sea cordon around the islands was already effective but, with the forces at his disposal, Woodward was less able to interrupt the air link, maintained by the Argentinians' Hercules, Electra and Fokker Fellowship transports. For the blockade to become absolute, it would be necessary to knock out the runway at Port Stanley. The Task Force could attack the airfield with Harriers and 4·5in naval guns, but something heavier was needed to smash the concrete runway beyond easy repair.

It was decided to employ the RAF's ageing Vulcan bombers, each capable of delivering a load of 21 450kg (1000lb) bombs. The only problem was the immense distance from their nearest base at Ascension Island to the target. In an extremely complex operation the RAF managed to put up 17 refuelling tankers and a single Vulcan to reach the Falklands at dawn on 1 May. Immediately after the Vulcan's bomb run at 3000m (10,000 feet), Sea Harriers unleashed a series of raids against Stanley airfield and the grass airstrip at Goose Green, and HMS *Glamorgan*, *Arrow* and *Alacrity* carried out a daylight bombardment of Argentinian positions. The Argentinians countered with airstrikes against the British ships, and *Glamorgan*'s stern was lifted out of the water by two bombs which narrowly missed her. In the air battle which ensued, Harriers shot down a Dagger, a Mirage and a Canberra at no cost to themselves, while another Mirage was destroyed in error by Argentinian anti-aircraft gunners at Stanley airport. These successes did not obscure the fact of Argentinian airpower, however, and the British Navy never indulged in daylight shore bombardment again, although they made every night as uncomfortable as possible for the Argentinian garrison with randomly timed shelling.

The following day, 2 May, witnessed the loss of two Argentinian Z-28 patrol craft which had put out from Port Stanley to search for shot-down aircrew. They were engaged by Task Force helicopters and one, the *Rio Iguazu*, was sunk while the other, the *Islas Malvinas*, was damaged and run ashore. The next day two small gunboats, the *Comodoro Somellera* and the *Alferez Sobral*, emerged to look for survivors and unwisely initiated a further engagement with helicopters. Both were hit by AS 12 missiles; the *Comodoro Somellera* sank at once but the *Alferez Sobral* managed to struggle into Puerto Deseado on the mainland.

Along with the news of the sinking of the *Belgrano* that same day, it appeared as if the Task Force was taking control of the situation. But on 4 May the British Navy experienced its first loss of the campaign. Because there was no airfield on the Falklands from which Argentina's Mirage IIIs, Daggers and Skyhawks could operate, they were restricted to flying from the mainland airbases, virtually at the limit of their range; Woodward was therefore able to hold his carrier group in comparative safety some 95km (60 miles) east of Port Stanley, although the bombardment groups and radar-picket vessels remained exposed to danger. On 4 May the *Sheffield* was hit by an air-launched Exocet missile while on radar-picket duty south of the islands. The missile's warhead did not explode but the ignition of its residual propellant rapidly turned the interior of the vessel into an inferno which could not be brought under control and she was abandoned with the loss of 21 of her crew. During the rescue operation enemy torpedo tracks were sighted and anti-submarine measures were promptly put into effect, though with unknown results. The whereabouts of the surviving

Type 42s and Type 22s, but as the sinking of the *Sheffield* had shown, this was a dangerous game. On 12 May the Task Force suffered another serious setback when Argentinian Skyhawks launched an attack against HMS *Glasgow* which the destroyer was lucky to survive; a bomb passed clean through the ship without exploding. The *Glasgow* was still badly enough damaged to have to withdraw from the conflict. The attack on the *Glasgow* cost the Argentinians three Skyhawks, but on the whole they refused to be drawn by the British tactics. If they encountered a Harrier CAP, they withdrew without entering combat, and the lack of an airborne early warning system meant that the Harriers were lucky if they caught incoming aircraft. The worrying failure to establish air superiority was mitigated, however, by the success achieved by British special forces on the Falklands at Pebble Island, the islands' third airstrip.

From 1 May, teams from both the 22nd Special Air Service Regiment (SAS) and the Special Boat Squadron (SBS) had begun to land on the Falklands for the purpose of intelligence-gathering. At that time, the British military commanders had no idea about Argentinian strengths and dispositions. In the words of Brigadier Julian Thompson, commanding officer of 3 Commando Brigade, 'We started out with a blank map of the Falklands and fired special forces like a shotgun across the islands to see what they found'. This made the initial landings of the British teams hazardous, in that they never knew whether or not they might stumble into strongly-held Argentinian positions. However, six SBS teams and seven SAS patrols were deployed undetected. They were landed at night by fast inflatable boat or from helicopters whose pilots were equipped with the latest American Passive Night Goggles (PNG) which gave them an astonishingly clear view through the darkness. The SBS were chiefly engaged in reconnoitering possible landing sites on the coast, while the SAS trudged off into the hills to observe the dispositions of the garrison. Two SAS teams went to West Falkland, one to Darwin, one to Bluff Cove and three to the area around Stanley.

Apart from the intelligence they gathered the

Argentinian submarines was to provide Admiral Woodward with cause for concern for the rest of the war.

Another setback for the Task Force was the downgrading of the effort to soften-up the Falklands with aerial bombardment. A further Vulcan attack on 4 May failed to hit Stanley airfield, and the same day the first Sea Harrier was lost, shot down over Goose Green. Two more Harriers failed to return from a mission in bad weather conditions on 6 May. The Task Force was now reduced to only 17 aircraft and it was obviously far too hazardous to risk this residual strength on low-level bombing runs in the teeth of strong Argentinian air defences. Raids were limited and Harriers kept primarily for the duty of defending the Task Force against air attack. The Argentinian transport aircraft continued to fly into Stanley, at night and often under appalling weather conditions – it had not been possible to impose an aerial blockade.

Running the blockade

The naval blockade was very effectively maintained, however. On 7 May the Total Exclusion Zone was extended to within 20km (12 miles) of the Argentinian coast. Two days later, a Harrier intercepted and strafed the enemy's spyship *Narwal*, which surrendered but sank while under tow. During the night of 11 May HMS *Alacrity*, probing into Falkland Sound, caught the blockade runner *Islas de los Estados* and destroyed her with gunfire. Two more blockade runners, the *Rio Carcamia* and *Bahía Buen Suceso*, bombed and strafed by Harriers off Fox Bay on 16 May, were abandoned by their crews.

Meanwhile, the attainment of air superiority had become a prime objective for the Task Force. Land commanders were especially insistent that it should be achieved before a landing was attempted. Woodward planned to sap the strength of the Argentinian air forces by drawing them into encounters with Harrier Combat Air Patrols (CAPs). The Harriers were far superior in air combat, both because the Argentinian aircraft had fuel for a mere three minutes of dog-fighting over the Falklands and because the British aircraft were far more manoeuvrable.

The bait to tempt the Argentinian aircraft were the Task Force's best-equipped air defence ships, the

Left: An RAF Vulcan bomber in action. On 1 and 4 May, the Argentinian-held Stanley airfield was bombed by single Vulcans operating from Ascension Island, over 5500km (3400 miles) away. Above: Smoke rises above Stanley airfield after a British air-raid. Below: Argentinian prisoners of war at work repairing damage to Stanley airfield after the surrender of the islands' Argentinian garrison. Despite repeated bombing attacks by Vulcans and Harriers, the airfield remained operational throughout the war, and the Argentinians were able to use it to supply their troops on the islands.

special forces teams were enormously useful to British Psychological Operations (Psyops), who began to broadcast in Spanish to the Argentinian garrison during May. It is not easy to determine whether the broadcasts were widely listened to, but their message certainly seemed to be disseminated through the garrison fairly quickly. There is now evidence of a widespread neurosis among the Argentinian troops, some of whom suspected every stranger in Argentinian uniform of being a fifth columnist. The atmosphere of uncertainty was another crack in morale, which was to be shattered when the serious contest with British infantry began.

The resourcefulness of the special forces was so great and their training so thorough that it would have been foolish to restrict them to an intelligence-gathering role when there were still the three Falklands airfields that could operate Pucará aircraft. The Pucará was a light aircraft which had been designed for counter-insurgency operations and could carry a useful weapons payload of 1620kg (3520lb) – enough to give British troops serious problems if it could be used extensively in the ground-attack role. It was not known how many Pucarás the Argentinians had, but it was known that a substantial number were based at Pebble Island off the northwest coast of West Falkland. It was decided that the special forces would destroy these planes, both to whittle down the Argentinians' airpower and to undermine their confidence by demonstrating that the British could make damaging raids on their positions.

Special forces strike

On the night of 14 May 45 SAS men and a naval gunfire support team were landed by helicopter within striking distance of the airfield, where they joined an eight-man SAS team landed on the night of the 11th. They destroyed six Pucarás, four Turbo-Mentors and a Skyvan lined up beside the grass runway with explosive charges and drove off a counter-attack by the garrison in a brisk firefight. All the raiding party returned safely, although two were slightly wounded, and the raid was accounted an outstanding success.

It would appear that the activities of the special forces were not restricted to the Falklands but spread to the Argentinian mainland. On 16 May the discovery of a wrecked Sea King helicopter and the appearance of its crew in neutral Chile gave rise to

Below: Sea King helicopters and a Sea Harrier on the flight deck of HMS *Hermes.* Sea Harriers operating from the two British aircraft carriers flew missions against Argentinian targets on the Falkland Islands during the period of softening-up which preceded the landings at San Carlos.

Above: The destroyer HMS *Sheffield* after being hit by an Argentinian Exocet missile. Although its warhead failed to explode, the missile caused a fire which raged amidships, filling the vessel with thick fumes and smoke.

Left: An injured member of *Sheffield's* crew is helped to the sick-bay on board *Hermes*. Most of the casualties on *Sheffield* had suffered severe burns, and 21 crewmen were killed, with 40 injured.

In the course of its duties . . .

At 0945 hours on the morning of 4 May 1982, Lieutenant-Commander Augusto Bedacarratz and Lieutenant Armando Mayora were ordered to take off from the Argentinian Navy's air command base at Río Grande on the barren Tierra del Fuego. Each of the two French-supplied Super Etendard aeroplanes of the 2nd Naval Fighter and Attack Squadron carried a single Exocet missile under its starboard wing, balanced by a drop tank on the port wing. Their target was the British Task Force, whose position had been reported by a P-2 Neptune reconnaissance aircraft to be some 160km (100 miles) south of Port Stanley, about 560km (400 miles) away from the airbase.

At 1004 hours, the Super Etendards rendezvoused with a KC-130 Hercules tanker, about 400km (250 miles) from the British Task Force, to top up their fuel tanks; they then continued towards the British, directed by the Neptune which was still shadowing the Task Force. Flying at very low level – 15m (50 feet) – at 1030 hours they received a report of three targets: two medium-sized and one large vessel. At about 1100 hours the aeroplanes pulled up to a height of 35m (120 feet) to lock their radars onto their targets, dropped back down and launched their missiles before turning and flying back to base at top speed.

Just after 1100 hours, the officer of the watch aboard HMS *Sheffield*, Lieutenant Peter Walpole, saw smoke on the horizon, shortly after the *Sheffield's* operations room had informed him of a brief radar contact. He realised it was a missile but it was too late to do anything and five seconds later the Exocet hit the *Sheffield's* hull amidships, 2m (8 feet) above the waterline at an oblique angle. The missile smashed into the forward engine-room on Deck 2 without exploding, but the unused rocket-fuel began a hot fire that spread rapidly along the electrical cables as the PVC insulation ignited. The air below decks was filled with suffocating black smoke; it soon poured out of the drifting ship, to mark its position for those ships of the Task Force nearby.

HMS *Sheffield's* captain, Sam Salt, reached the bridge to find that the missile had knocked out the ship's communications system. Further reports indicated that the electrical power was out of action and the watermains fractured. There was little hope of saving the ship, but damage-control teams struggled on. A portable gas-turbine pump was brought out but the engine's start-chain broke, and water had to be supplied by submersible pumps lowered over the side to fill buckets with sea water. Some of the ship's surviving complement made their way to the upper deck, while those fighting the fire went below, breathing through respirators. The heat was so severe that the paint of the superstructure blistered and the decks were almost too hot to stand on.

Two frigates, HMS *Yarmouth* (thought to be the target of the second Exocet, whose fate is unknown) and HMS *Arrow*, came alongside. Captain Salt established communications with the *Arrow's* captain by walkie-talkies; 40 casualties, primarily suffering from smoke inhalation and burns, were evacuated. After four hours the fires neared *Sheffield's* magazines, so Captain Salt gave the order to abandon ship. Men began to jump onto the *Arrow* or were winched up into hovering Sea King helicopters. There were 21 dead. The *Sheffield* drifted for three days after the fires had burnt out; HMS *Yarmouth* took it in tow on 9 May and headed for South Georgia, but high seas early on 10 May caused *Sheffield* to sink.

speculation. The official line was that the helicopter had suffered damage to its navigation equipment during a storm and had force-landed on the mainland. Given the distance between the British fleet and the mainland this was inherently unlikely and, in any case, the crew appeared to contain members of the special forces. It was at least a possibility that the helicopter had been flown deliberately to a remote part of neutral Chile (which was conveniently near the vital Argentinian airbases) with an intelligence-gathering team. After the war the defence secretary denied that Britain had broken international law by using the territory of neutral Chile in such a fashion.

By 18 May, it was reckoned that all that was possible had been done to prepare for a landing on the Falklands. Argentinian airpower had not been neutralised, but the Argentinian Navy was effectively out of the conflict. Naval and aerial bombardment, along with the activities of the special forces, had lowered the morale of the Argentinian garrison. The flow of information from the SAS and SBS teams, along with electronic intelligence (ELINT) and signals intelligence (SIGINT) had allowed the British to build up a picture of the enemy's strengths and weaknesses, and in particular of the areas where a landing would produce the best results. During this period, the Task Force had perhaps not achieved as much as it had hoped to soften up Argentinian defences, but on 20 May the assault group detached itself from the main body of the Task Force and sailed for Falkland Sound.

P. J. Banyard and Bryan Perrett

Beachhead San Carlos

The landings on the Falklands begin

As British special forces built up an intelligence picture of the situation on the Falklands during May 1982, it soon became apparent that the Argentinians intended to conduct a concentric battle of defence in the hills around Port Stanley. Such a decision was almost inevitable, given that they could not be strong everywhere. It was estimated that Major-General Mario Menendez, the garrison commander and military governor of the Malvinas, could deploy approximately 10,000 men and their supporting arms. In and around Port Stanley were the 3rd, 4th, 6th, 7th and 25th Infantry Regiments, plus the 5th Battalion of the Naval Infantry Corps in general reserve; a field artillery regiment and a medium artillery troop; the major part of an anti-aircraft battalion, and an armoured car squadron. At Goose Green, there were elements of the 2nd and 12th Infantry Regiments, plus field artillery and anti-aircraft detachments. On West Falkland, the 5th Infantry Regiment and an engineer company was at Port Howard, the 8th Infantry Regiment and an engineer company was at Fox Bay, and the airstrip on Pebble Island was held by a 120-strong naval-air detachment. Menendez also possessed a respectable helicopter fleet consisting of two heavy-lift Chinooks, nine Hueys, three Agusta A109s and eight Pumas. This gave him the capacity to use his reserves in the strategic counter-attack role wherever the British landed.

The reports received by the Task Force from the SAS and SBS generally described an army which was well-enough equipped for its task, but which was suffering from steadily declining morale. Many of the 18-year-old conscripts who filled the ranks had received little training and seemed unable to look after themselves or their weapons in the field. They were perpetually hungry and carried out their garrison duties in a half-hearted manner; it was clear that the majority would be only too happy to leave the frozen, wind-blasted uplands of the Malvinas.

In addition to observing the state of the enemy, the SBS had the specialist task of assessing potential amphibious landing sites around the islands, including their defences. The actual landing itself, code-named Operation Sutton, was the subject of detailed planning by Brigadier Julian Thompson, commanding 3 Commando Brigade, and his staff, with expert advice on the SBS reports being provided by Major Ewen Southby-Tailyour, who had sailed extensively around the Falklands' coast when he commanded the Royal Marine garrison there four years previously.

Three possible landing sites received serious

consideration. The first was at Port North on West Falkland: while a landing here would undoubtedly have succeeded, however, it did not take into account the prime necessity of engaging and defeating the main mass of the enemy, which lay across Falkland Sound. With this is mind, the second alternative, that of a landing close to Port Stanley, received serious consideration. In this case it was felt that the Argentinians were present in such numbers that a reverse during an opposed landing was a distinct possibility which could not be contemplated. In fact, it was this alternative which Menendez believed the British would take, and he laid extensive minefields to cover the approaches. The third choice was San Carlos Water, a deep-water inlet off Falkland Sound which pushed twin arms inland to Port San Carlos in the north and San Carlos settlement in the south. San Carlos lay a difficult 105km (65 miles) from Port Stanley but was seldom visited by the Argentinians and offered several natural tactical advantages. These included adequate landing beaches and a sheltered anchorage ringed by hills which denied the use of air-launched Exocet missiles and severely curtailed the time that the Argentinians' mainland-based fighter-bombers could hold their targets in view. The choice of San Carlos was finally approved by the War Cabinet on 10 May, two days after the amphibious group had left Ascension Island for the final leg of the voyage south.

The soldiers had spent the period at Ascension Island in training, planning and reorganisation. While the troops maintained a high level of physical fitness by exercising on the decks of their transports, preparations for an amphibious assault on the Falklands were made by practising landing-craft drill and by live weapons-firing. The staff of the landing group worked around the clock to draw up plans for an eventual landing, but there was a certain amount

Above left: Royal Marines of 3 Commando Brigade race towards the shore at San Carlos from HMS *Fearless* in an LCU. The landing, code-named Operation Sutton, began on 21 May, and was carried out without opposition from the Argentinians on land, who had only a small patrol in the area. Above: A British paratrooper escorts an Argentinian prisoner of war, captured near San Carlos on 23 May. Left: Heavily laden Marines of 42 Commando at San Carlos.

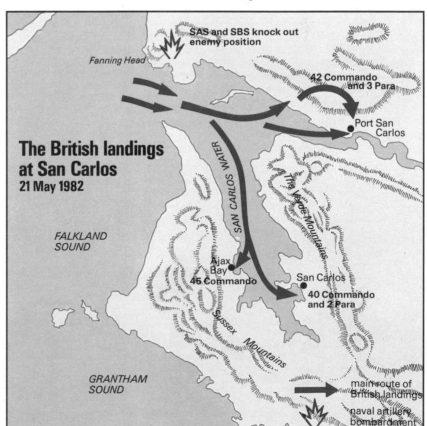

The British landings at San Carlos
21 May 1982

SAS and SBS knock out enemy position

Fanning Head

42 Commando and 3 Para

Port San Carlos

SAN CARLOS WATER

The Verde Mountains

FALKLAND SOUND

Ajax Bay
45 Commando

San Carlos

40 Commando and 2 Para

Sussex Mountains

GRANTHAM SOUND

main route of British landings

naval artillery bombardment

of friction with Admiral Woodward who, as commander of the naval battle group, seemed to the officers of 3 Commando Brigade to have little conception of the problems which they would face in retaking the islands. Equipment was meanwhile restowed in a massive cross-decking operation to ensure that the most vital items would be immediately available once the landings had taken place – in fact, many crucial pieces of equipment remained inaccessible and were returned to Britain unused.

On 18 May, the amphibious group joined Admiral Woodward's battle group in the vicinity of the Falklands and the final sorting-out process and cross-decking between ships fully occupied the next 24 hours. During this 22 men were drowned when a bird smashed into the engine of a Sea King helicopter, causing the machine to crash into the sea. Twenty of the dead belonged to the SAS and some had taken part in both the recapture of South Georgia and the recent raid on Pebble Island.

Operation Sutton goes ahead

Woodward had been given permission to initiate Operation Sutton at his own discretion. On 20 May there was poor visibility and therefore ideal conditions for the amphibious group's final approach, while clear weather had been predicted for the days which followed. The only possible decision, therefore, was to proceed immediately. The amphibious group entered the Sound during the night of 20 May, the enemy's attention being fully occupied by a series of special forces diversionary operations and naval bombardments elsewhere around the islands. At dawn on 21 May, covered by its escorts, 3 Commando Brigade went ashore in landing craft: 40 Commando, the Royal Marines, and the 2nd Battalion, the Parachute Regiment landing at San Carlos settlement, 45 Commando, the Royal Marines at Ajax Bay on the opposite shore, and the 3rd Battalion, the Parachute Regiment at Port San Carlos. The troops pushed quickly inland to secure the high ground and consolidate the beach-head perimeter. Soon, by landing craft and by helicopter, men, vehicles, guns and equipment of every description were streaming ashore, including the vital Rapier surface-to-air missile (SAM) systems, the position-

Above: Brigadier Julian Thompson, commanding officer of 3 Commando Brigade. Thompson's men were experts in winter warfare, and their high level of training and fitness made them ideal troops for the campaign in the Falklands, where conditions were harsh and the physical and mental demands made upon the ordinary soldier tested stamina to the limit. Below: Paras coming ashore at San Carlos under cover of a .50 calibre Browning heavy machine-gun. The beachhead at San Carlos was vulnerable to air attack by Argentinian aircraft, but the raids which began on the day of the landing were directed mainly at the Royal Navy combat vessels in San Carlos Water.

ing of which had been predetermined by computer some days previously.

The landing was not quite without incident, however. The night before, the thermal-imager aboard *Antrim*'s helicopter had revealed an Argentinian outpost on Fanning Head, dominating the entrance to San Carlos Water. Equipped with 106mm recoilless rifles and 81mm mortars, this post was capable of inflicting a great deal of damage. A heavily-armed attack force, consisting of 32 SBS men and an SAS team, was helicoptered onto the hillside above the outpost, which was then engaged with sustained machine-gun fire and naval gunfire support from *Antrim*. The Argentinians abandoned their weapons and at dawn nine men surrendered, three of whom were wounded; 12 more had been killed and the rest had fled.

The men probably belonged to a company based at Goose Green which was visiting Port San Carlos on a routine patrol. The remainder of the company, some 40 strong, was spotted and engaged at extreme range by 3 Para as they escaped eastwards from the hamlet. At this precise moment, two of the commandos' Gazelle helicopters were unwisely inserted into the area and brought down by the enemy's smallarms fire – three of the four crew were killed. At 0815 hours the British had their revenge when a Chinook and two Pumas were destroyed by cannon fire on the slopes of Mount Kent by a pair of RAF Harrier GR3s.

This was all the action on the ground that accompanied the landing, but the Argentinian response from the air was a different matter. The first air attacks came in at 1000 hours and soon some of the fiercest fighting of the campaign was under way. The air battle over San Carlos Water was to be perhaps the crucial encounter of the Falklands conflict.

Bryan Perrett

Key Weapons
AERIAL GUNS

At the end of World War II, the machine gun and more especially the cannon (any aerial gun with a calibre of 20mm or above) reigned supreme as the armament for interceptor aircraft. The conflict highlighted three basic requirements for the next generation of weapons and these have remained more or less constant to the present day.

The first consideration was calibre. Quite early on in the war it had become obvious that small-calibre machine guns had little value against targets with metal structures and equipped with armour. Thus by 1945, most of the combatants had settled on weapons with calibres between 13 and 30mm as being the most effective in air-to-air combat. Within this range, the most favoured figures were between 20 and 30mm, a standard still kept today.

After calibre, a weapon's muzzle velocity and rate of fire were considered crucial. The former is the measure of the speed at which the bullet or shell leaves the weapon's barrel and affects both the accuracy of the weapon and its ability to penetrate and destroy armoured targets over useful ranges. Rate of fire is the number of projectiles fired in a given period (usually expressed as 'rounds per minute' or rpm); it is equally important both as an aid to target destruction and as a means of maximising firepower since high-performance jet aeroplanes are too fast to remain targets for any length of time.

In the immediate postwar years, the gun designers of the victorious Allies embarked on the creation of new weapons fulfilling these criteria. In this they were helped by the existence of the German Mauser MG213 20mm cannon. This weapon began as a specification issued in 1942 which called for a gun

with a rate of fire of 1000rpm and muzzle velocity of at least 1000mps (3281fps). Some idea of the advanced nature of this requirement can be gauged when it is compared with the performance of the Luftwaffe's standard 20mm weapon at the time, the MG151/20, which had a theoretical maximum rate of fire of 780rpm and a muzzle velocity of 810mps (2656fps).

To meet this exacting requirement, Mauser fitted the MG213 with a five-round revolving chamber. Previously, most guns used belted ammunition with each round being individually fed into the breech. In the MG213, the ammunition belt was used to load the chamber rather than the breech, with the result that there was always a round ready to be fired with no pause for it to be extracted from the belt and placed before the firing pin. Using this method, the Mauser proved capable of a rate of fire approaching 1200rpm.

The concept of a revolving chamber in aircraft cannon became the foundation of the majority of postwar weapons with examples being produced in France, Britain, the United States, West Germany and Switzerland. In France, the Mauser principle produced the DEFA family of 30mm weapons. The earliest of these, the DEFA 552, has undergone considerable development during its service life culminating in the 552A of 1971. In this latter form the weapon has a weight of 81kg (179lb) and a rate of fire of 1300rpm. Over 10,000 examples of the DEFA 552 and 552A have been produced and the two weapons are or have been used on the Mirage III and V, French versions of the Jaguar, the Etendard IVM and Super Etendard, and the Italian Fiat G91.

Previous page: These French-made DEFA 553 30mm cannon are one of two options available for the Franco-German Alpha Jet; 27mm Mauser cannon can be used instead. Left: The standard armament of the Hawker Hunter is a four-pack of 30mm Aden cannon; the gun was also used in the Swedish Saab Draken (right). Below: A display of the Mirage III's armament, including 30mm DEFA 552 cannon.

The DEFA 553 is a direct development of the earlier model designed to further prolong service life and to ease installation in a wide variety of airframes. The 553 weighs the same as its predecessor and has the same rate of fire. Provision is made for the ammunition to be fed into the gun from either side and the length of burst can be electrically controlled. The 553 is in use on the Mirage F1, French Jaguars, the Alpha-Jet, the Aermacchi MB 399K, the Spanish Casa 101 and the Argentinian Pucará.

To keep the family current, the 553 has been developed into the 554 for use on high-performance aircraft. The new model weighs approximately 80kg (176lb) and has a rate of fire and a muzzle velocity of 1800rpm and 820mps (2691fps). The 554 can be used in a podded twin mounting as well as an internal gun and is to be fitted to the Mirage 2000. Overall, this family of weapons has proved effective in combat and is especially favoured by the Israelis who have re-armed their A-4 Skyhawks with an unspecified variant and use the 553 on both the IAI (Israeli Aircraft Industries) Nesher and Kfir.

In the UK, the Royal Armament Research Development Establishment, in combination with the Royal Small Arms Factory at Enfield Lock, produced the 30mm Aden cannon during the late 1940s. Over the years the basic model has been continuously developed, with the mid-1980s production version being the Mk4 with an off-shoot, the Mk5 Straden, in development. In its Mk4 format, the Aden weighs 87kg (192lb) and has an overall length of 1080mm (42·5in); muzzle velocity is in the region of 790mps (2593fps) with a rate of fire of between 1200 and 1400rpm. The Straden derivative aims to

improve reliability, to increase the rate of fire by 300rpm and to be completely interchangeable with the Mk4. The Aden family as a whole has had a long and successful service life, being fitted to every gun-armed fighter used by the RAF from the Hunter onwards and to many of the Fleet Air Arm's interceptors. Aden guns have been mounted on the Harrier GR3 and AV-8A, plus the Sea Harrier, both of which carry two with 150 rpg (rounds per gun), the Hawk trainer with a single weapon, the RAF Jaguar with two cannon with 150rpg and the Indian HAL-produced version of the Gnat with two weapons, this time with 115rpg. Ammunition used in the Mk4 Aden comprises a practice round, an HE (high-explosive) round, and an AP (armour-piercing) round, and an API (armour-piercing incendiary) round is under development.

US work on aircraft cannon with revolving chambers began with the US Air Force's 20mm M39 and the US Navy's 20mm Mk11 weapons. The M39 was

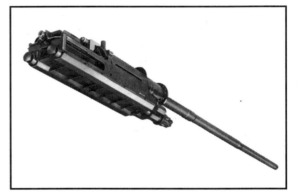

Above: The English Electric (later British Aerospace Corporation) Lightning has a standard armament of two 30mm Aden cannon. The Aden has been in production since the late 1940s and used to equip every gun-armed RAF fighter since the Hunter.

Above right: The Oerlikon 30mm KCA is one of many postwar gun designs to use a revolving chamber. It arms the attack version of the Swedish Viggen. Right: The access hatch to the General Electric M61 20mm six-barrelled cannon on this Luftwaffe F-104 Starfighter is open to allow maintenance work or reloading of ammunition.

developed directly from the MG 213 by the US Army Ordnance Department and had a muzzle velocity of 914mps (3000fps), a rate of fire of 1200rpm and was used in such aircraft types as the F-86H, the F-100 and the F-101C. The navy's Mk11 was an even more interesting weapon; it combined the chamber principle with twin barrels, thereby offering a rate of fire of around 4000rpm. The Mk11 saw most service in its Mod 5 variant mounted in a twin installation designated the Mk 4 Mod O gun pod. The Mk 4 pod was first delivered during August 1965 and remained in production until October 1967, by which time 829 examples had been manufactured. The Mk4 installation saw considerable service in Southeast Asia mounted on US Navy and Marine Corps A-4, F-4 and OV-10 aircraft and was also supplied to Israel for use on its A-4s.

Perhaps not surprisingly, Mauser itself has used the principle in its BK27 27mm cannon, developed specifically for use on the Tornado IDS. Very few specific details have been released about this weapon's performance other than that it weighs 100kg (221lb) and that it has been described as having 'a high muzzle velocity, a high degree of accuracy and ... a high degree of reliability'. Five types of ammunition have been specified for the type, namely AP, APHE, HE, TP (target practice) and TP-F rounds.

In Switzerland, the famous Oerlikon company has used the revolving chamber principle on its 30mm Type KCA cannon which is used on the attack version of the Swedish Viggen aircraft. The KCA weighs 136kg (300lb), and has a muzzle velocity and rate of fire of 1030mps (3379fps) and 1350rpm respectively. The KCA is particularly interesting in that its ammunition uses less propellant than any other current 30mm weapon and has a particularly high round weight.

From the foregoing, it will be seen that the 1945 vintage MG 213 has had a pronounced effect on aircraft cannon design in the postwar world. Within the United States, however, the quest for ever higher rates of fire has continued, resulting in the development of perhaps the most fearsome of all aerial guns, the rotary cannon. As early as 1949, General Electric had produced their first experimental Vulcan weapon using the Gatling principle of multiple barrels revolving to increase rate of fire. By 1965, the concept had been refined into a service weapon and the first example of the 20mm M61 Vulcan cannon was delivered to the US Air Force.

In its current form (the M61A1) the Vulcan weighs 120kg (265lb), has six barrels and offers a muzzle velocity of 1036mps (3399fps) and rate of fire of 6600rpm. The M61 and its self-powered derivative, the GAU-4, have been used in a wide range of aircraft including the A-7, F-4, F-14, F-15, F-16, F-18, F-104, F-105 and the F-111. In addition to its use in fixed installations, the M61 has formed the basis of two gun pods, the SUU-16A and the SUU-23A. Both pods have an overall length of 5·05m (16·5ft), an empty weight of 489kg (1078lb) and differ from one another in using the M61A1 in the SUU-16A and the GAU-4 in the SUU-23A. To date, both pods have been cleared for use on the A-4D, F-4, F-100, F-105 and the F-111, and the SUU-23A is widely used on the RAF's Phantom interceptors.

The success of the rotary cannon concept has led the United States to continue its development and General Electric produced follow-on weapons including the GAU-8A and the GAU-12U. The seven-barrelled GAU-8A is the primary fixed armament of the A-10 'tank buster' and is specific to the type. Weighing some 1723kg (3799lb) fully loaded, the GAU-8A is probably the heaviest aircraft gun in use today. The weapon is capable of rates of fire of between 2100 and 4200rpm at a muzzle velocity of 1066mps (3497fps) and to make it suited to the

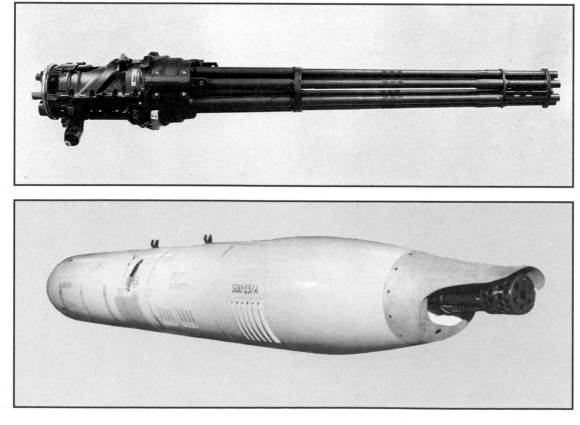

Above: The 20mm M61 cannon of a Dutch F-104 Starfighter is reloaded. Left: The M61 gun first entered service in 1965, with the US Air Force. One of the world's first rotary cannon, the M61A1 can fire 6600 rounds per minute. Below left: The SUU-23A gun pod houses a GAU-4 rotary cannon that can fire 5400 rounds per minute.

Above right: A US Navy F-8 Crusader lands on the USS *Forrestal,* showing the gun ports for its Colt-Browning 20mm cannon. Right: The 20mm cannon of a US Navy Grumman F9F-2 are rearmed before the aeroplane flies a sortie during the Korean War. The 20mm Colt-Browning equipped all gun-armed US Navy fighter planes of the 1950s.

anti-armour role, it is provided with API and HEI (high-explosive incendiary) ammunition. The API round is of particular interest; it uses depleted uranium as a core to enhance both its penetrative and incendiary properties.

The GAU-12U Equaliser uses the technology of the GAU-8A to provide a lightweight, five-barrelled air-to-air or air-to-ground weapon with a calibre of 25mm. Weighing 122kg (269lb), the Equaliser has a muzzle velocity of 1097mps (3599fps) when firing HEI rounds and a rate of fire which is variable up to a maximum value of 4200rpm. The weapon can use a range of ammunition which includes TP, HEI and APDS (armour-piercing discarding sabot) rounds together with a newly developed API type. Currently, the GAU-12U's primary application is on the US Marine Corps' AV-8B aircraft, in which installation it has a rate of fire of 3600rpm and a reduced muzzle velocity.

The original M61 Vulcan cannon has spawned a lightweight derivative known as the M197 for use on helicopter gunships. Weighing 66kg (146lb), the 20mm M197 has three barrels, a rate of fire of between 400 and 3000rpm, and has been used on the AH-1J helicopter and the fixed wing OV-10A. The M197 is also used in the M97 armament system on the AH-1S helicopter. This turret mounting can also carry the 30mm XM188E-1 rotary weapon – with three barrels, weighing 50kg (110lb) and with a rate of fire of up to 2000rpm – the two guns being interchangeable.

Further down the calibre scale, the Vulcan principle was used in the 7·62mm M134 (externally-powered) or GAU-2A (self-powered) Minigun which was used so effectively in Southeast Asia in a variety of mountings ranging from helicopter turrets to fixed-wing gunships such as the AC-47. Illustrative of the Minigun family as a whole is the SUU-11BA pod installation which carries a single

weapon, weighs 147kg (324lb) when loaded with 1500 rounds of ammunition and offers a rate of fire of between 3000 and 6000rpm.

The latest of the American helicopter guns is the M230 30mm Chain Gun which is used on the AH-64 Apache. The weapon gets its name from the chain drive it uses to power a rotating bolt mechanism in the breech. The single-barrelled M230 weighs 55·9kg (123lb) overall and has a rate of fire of around 600rpm. Like the GAU-8A, the Chain Gun is primarily an anti-armour weapon and can fire TP, HEDP (high-explosive dual-purpose) and HE rounds and has been designed to be able to use the ammunition produced for the British Aden and the French DEFA weapons as well as American produced items.

The Soviet Union produces and operates a wide range of sturdy and effective aerial guns. At the lowest end of the calibre scale comes the 12·7mm UBK heavy machine gun. Originally used as a fixed weapon, the UBK is now only seen mounted in turrets on early examples of the Mi-24 helicopter

Above: The Mauser 27mm BK27 cannon of a Panavia Tornado is test-fired. Left: The MiG-19 is armed with three 30mm NR-30 cannon, two in the wing roots and one under the nose of the fuselage, not visible here. Chinese Shenyang F-6s have copies of the NR-30.

gunship. More recently, a 12·7mm four-barrelled rotary weapon has been introduced which, when used in the Mi-24's turret, provides coverage of 70 degrees in azimuth and from plus 15 to minus 60 degrees in elevation.

For fixed and turret installations on aeroplanes, the Soviet Union makes great use of weapons with calibres in the 20-30mm range. The earliest 23mm guns still in service are the single-barrelled NR-23 and NS-23KM weapons. These two heavy-hitting cannons differ primarily in their rates of fire, the NR-23 having a figure of 850rpm while the NS-23 has one of 550rpm. The two weapons are regarded in the West as being interchangeable and NR/NS cannon have been used on the An-12, MiG-17, MiG-19, Tu-16 and the Tu-95. More recently, the twin-barrelled 23mm GSh-23 has been introduced, offering a rate of fire estimated at 3000rpm. Two versions of this weapon are known to exist, tailored to fixed or pod installations; the GSh-23 is used on the MiG-21, MiG-23, Su-11 and some Yak-36 aircraft. In the early 1980s, the Russians produced a 22mm six-barrelled rotary cannon which is used in the MiG-27, probably in the Su-24, and may also arm some of the latest Soviet fighters such as the MiG-29 and the MiG-31.

At a calibre of 30mm and over, the Russians have two weapons, the 30mm NR-30 and the 37mm N-37. The NR-30 is thought to have a rate of fire of about 850rpm using AP, HE and HEI ammunition and has

been installed in the MiG-19, Su-7, Su-20 and the Yak-28. The N-37 has a much lower rate of fire – figures quoted include one of 400rpm – and the weapon should be considered obsolete, carried mainly by elderly aeroplanes such as the MiG-15 and the Yak-25.

Predictions of the demise of the aerial gun as a weapon made in the 1950s were proved false during the aerial combats of the 1960s. This makes the fact that all the basic gun designs in service today are at least 30 years old even more of a surprise; development continues to be dominated by refinements of existing technologies rather than technological breakthroughs.

Above: A MiG-15UTI of the East German Air Force; it is armed with an NS-23 cannon pod under the nose of the fuselage. Soviet cannon tend to have lower rates of fire than those of Western nations, with a preference for larger calibres.

Index